For Joan,
with affection
— Vince Burke

Forgiveness
A Gay Man's Memoir

Vincent Burke

outskirts
press

Outskirts Press, Inc.
http://www.outskirtspress.com

ISBN: 978-1-9772-4405-5

PRINTED IN THE UNITED STATES OF AMERICA

Cover photo: the author, at 17.

*For Frank Grant, Jack Bernard, my mother,
and my sister, Pat, the four loves of my life.*

Table of Contents

Introduction

It is with pleasure, and some pain, that I look back to my teen years of friendship with the basketball boys. Do they suspect? My mind returns to a time long ago...

The six of us are leaving Jimmy's Cafe after our usual brown-bag lunch en route back to school. Huddled together, we walk the long block down Shady Lane, overhung by a canopy of tall elm trees that meet in the middle and turn the street into a dark tunnel. Large frame Victorian houses, some with turrets, some with fancy second-story porches, look on as our little group strides by. We slow our pace as we turn the corner into Jefferson Street.

Ahead we see our goal: tall, ungainly, red-brick St. John's High School. To the group of classmates beside me, the building meant the return to classes and schoolwork drudgery. For me, the awkward structure glistened as a castle of gold, the welcome end to today's noontime misery.

Lunchtime didn't go well. Do they wonder about me? Thomas looked right at me when he talked about queers.

We had gone to Jimmy's with our lunches brought from home, as we did every day. Each ordered a pop, the name in southwest Pennsylvania for a soda. The other boys, all a head taller than me and all basketball team members on the Eagles, had played the pinball machine. I never played the pinball machine. I never played any sport.

How did I merit the company of such popular boys? I had nothing in common with them. They were the jocks of the class, in today's parlance. I was short, much slower to grow than they had been. They were from middle class families; I lived in the Project. They talked about girls; I kept silent. They treated me well, but differently from how they treated each other. It was as though I were a young brother that you give attention to in order to make him feel welcome, but who was not in reality grown-up enough to be part of your world.

I never knew why they took me into their closed group, but I relished the image it gave me in the school. When we'd all arrive outside the school after our lunch together, I'd look around quickly to see how many other classmates observed me with the basketball boys. If the number was at least a half dozen or so, it was a good day.

I felt compelled to contribute to earn my inclusion in the group. I would scan Uniontown's Evening Standard to find local news that might interest them. I would praise their coach, even though he showed no interest in me. I listened to Jack Benny and Red Skelton and remembered the jokes to tell them. I hoped that the basketball boys thought me to be smart and an asset to the group because I was so informed.

Today, Will, curly black hair as usual spilling over onto his forehead, was at the pinball machine. I tried not to look at him standing there, handsome and sturdy. Thomas caught me sneaking a peek. I quickly averted my eyes. That was probably a mistake.

On the walk back to school, Thomas started talking about "queers" and looked back and forth at me. Some of the other boys joined in. Will asked Thomas if he knew any. "Maybe," Thomas replied, and turned his head and stared straight down into my eyes. I felt my face redden. I stumbled. I knew he meant me. He kept staring into my eyes until I had to drop my head and look at the ground.

Ah, we were back at school! No more from Thomas today. I could still feel him staring at me. And just two classmates in front of the school to see us arriving. There was nothing to brighten my drab mood.

Dear Thomas, Leo, Jack, Bobby, and Will:

Back when we'd eat lunch together, I was poor, still short, and didn't play basketball, so different from all of you. Yet you wanted me in your lunch group. How grateful I was.

I had a big worry at our lunches. It was about another way I was different. You would talk about girls, even about making out. I hated it when you talked about girls. It made me realize how odd I was. I wasn't interested in girls, and never would be.

In fact, I thought often about one of you. In the evening when I was lying on my bed reading a book, my mind would sometimes wander and I'd think of Will. I'd picture him standing at the pinball machine, from time to time pushing back a lock of curly black hair from his eyes. I'd see his nice face changed into determination, him biting his lip, as he shook the machine to alter the route of the ball. He was already beginning to get a dark haze on his chin, whiskers at birth. One day going back to school, for no reason at all he tousled my hair, and looked down into my eyes with a broad smile. What did he mean by that? My mind twisted into a jumble of confusion, trying to decipher Will's motive for this familiarity. Although I smiled broadly in return, I felt the blood rush to redden my face. That moment, and that picture of Will, kept popping into my head uninvited for weeks on end. I would try to get It out of my mind by thinking of anything else, but there it would be again. I would dream of the possibilities. It was both pleasant, and awful. I yearned to let Will know that I liked him, really liked him. But I knew I could never dare tell him. Thinking of him was so futile. I also knew better than ever to let any of you know. It was a wonderful, secret, painful infatuation.

Thomas sometimes caught me looking at Will, and suspected. He talked about "queers," and stared at me. You all told jokes about queers, and mocked them. Good thing I was hidden. You would have ridiculed me and thrown me out of the group. I knew that our friendship would end if you knew the real me, and this made me uneasy in the group. I thought about it all of the time, and wondered if anyone at all would ever speak to me if they knew. I felt sneaky, deceptive, not worthy to be with you guys, or anyone. I thought I was almost totally alone on the earth, with perhaps just fifty or a hundred people like me in the whole world.

But we were all young then, and you were just copying whatever you heard from around town. As you get older, your thinking matures. You guys, did you get over your bias? Most people are more accepting now. I hope you are. Are you?

I appreciate, fellas, your wanting me in your lunch group. The image it gave me, and the good times I had with you, was a bright spot in my teenage years. I'd give anything to have one of those lunches with you right now. Thank you for those lunches. In return, let me forgive you for the distress you caused me. You were all really great guys, and I forgive you for the prejudice that a lot of people had then. If we were in school today, would you be tolerant? Most young people are.

Let's go back. I'll be out as being gay. I bet we'll still be friends. I'll get to see Will.

Your lunch buddy,
Vinny

I would guard my secret through life, through a dual life. One life, my surface life, would be led in the straight world with heterosexuals as acquaintances and friends, with relatives, and at family events, in my three careers as a reporter, a Madison Avenue advertising man, a Manhattan landlord. Coexisting with that life would be my hidden, second life, an undercover life, spent with gay friends and with my two long-term partners. This incognito life would be forced upon me by a society that disliked my very existence.

In what is called the twilight of my years, there is acceptance by a large segment of society of those with same-sex orientation, and even of same-sex marriage. Of diversity. In most environments, we're no longer forced undercover. Today even Superman has come out as bisexual. As I write this, a Gallup poll found that 63 percent of Americans favor gay marriage, while 36 percent oppose it. We can even keep our jobs. The Supreme Court said, in a 6-3 decision in June, 2020, that the Civil Rights Act of 1964, banning sexual discrimination in employment, applies to gays and transgendered, too. A remarkable ruling, considering the makeup of the Court. Then, President Joseph R. Biden by executive order extended the interpretation to include most realms of American life. A CBS News poll in 2020 found that 82 percent of Americans say that lesbians and gay people should be protected under federal civil rights laws. That is remarkable. More remarkable yet, is the figure that 14 percent do not favor protection for gay people. We still have a way to go. I hope, and trust, we'll get there.

I won't dwell here on the minority still stuck in the past. I look to the large majority in the present. If I only had been born in this enlightened time, I could have avoided lies and falsehoods and hiding. I could have unashamedly been myself. The society that at an earlier age would not tolerate me if I disclosed my orientation has changed its mind. Or at least about 2/3 of people have.

In turn, I reappraise my opinion of the culture that once held my secret self in disrepute. I have found an emotion that I never applied to that formerly biased society. I have discovered forgiveness.

I will review my years as a newspaperman, and consider a letter of forgiveness to the fellow journalists who told crude jokes directed at my group. I will weigh whether a letter of forgiveness should go to the teenagers about to beat me up. Legislators whose laws made me a felon? Maybe I'll write them a letter. The policemen who chased me as I fled into Great South Bay? Perhaps they'll get a letter. Psychiatrists who called us all mentally ill? They'll be considered for a letter of forgiveness. And my advertising colleagues on Madison Avenue who made me uncomfortable by using a coarse homophobic epithet will get my reappraisal, and maybe a letter.

My letters of forgiveness I hope to spread far and wide to another dozen in my life. I have waited so many years for this new emotion to blossom, and now I am overjoyed to write my letters. It will be gratifying.

Forgiveness is my aim. I researched forgiveness, and found quotes that inspired me. Leo Tolstoy observed: "Let us forgive one another— only then will we live in peace." Mark Twain was poetic: "Forgiveness is the fragrance that the violet sheds on the heel that has crushed it." The mayoclinic.org website suggests, besides the expected better relationships and less stress, some astounding possible benefits of forgiveness: improved mental health, lower blood pressure, stronger immune system, improved heart health. Goodness!

I'm convinced. I'm ready to forgive. But I am thinking of how I got to this point, to be willing to forgive and forget. For many years, for decades in fact, I was constantly, or at least frequently, aware of the diminished feeling or outright rejection of me by my straight friends if they knew my secret self. Those in this non-gay group are the heirs of centuries of social disdain for homosexuals, of indoctrination in contempt from the time they heard the "q" word as children, of peer pressure to conform to society's low opinion of us, and of ignorance due to man's slow acceptance of evidence of a genetic link to sexual orientation. With all that overpowering influence, who can wonder that during most of my life, gay people were held in disrepute? But, as the years and the decades passed, there were subtle changes that I recognize now, but were oblivious to me as they occurred.

I had never announced to any heterosexual friend that I was gay, but during my 40 years with my first long-term partner, we lived together, bought property together, entertained together, had pets together, traveled together. We lived our lives together, as married straight couples do. And people we knew, over time, began treating us as a couple, always asking one of us about the other, never proffering an invitation to one without the other. Although no one ever mentioned the word "gay" to describe us, at least not in our presence, in retrospect I am certain that the secret was not a secret, and thus we were accepted without fanfare for whom we were. Gay couples everywhere received the same treatment. So, although society as a whole was clinging to bigotry, those who knew gay people, and there were many of them, were losing their bias. They knew gay people, they knew they were gay, and they chose to disregard it. This was occurring through decades, so that prejudice was eroding. Then along came the 1969 gay riots during and after a police raid at the Stonewall Inn in Greenwich Village, and people became aware of our numbers and police treatment. In recent years, gay people, many famous, were outing themselves — and society was stunned to realize they were not at all the monsters of folklore, but, rather, people like everyone else. And bias took another hit. My willingness to forgive and forget past prejudice should not be so difficult. I must not hold a grudge. I should treat forgiveness as the culmination of the process that started with the gradual gnawing away of bias years ago, that brought us to the present moment.

Will I succeed to forgive all and everyone, to have no hard feelings? Welcome to my attempt at my letters of forgiveness. Welcome to my life, and my 87 years worth living.

SECTION ONE:
YOUTH AND PRE-NYC

CHAPTER 1

A father has gone missing.

Uniontown, Pennsylvania, August, 1937.

THERE WAS A light rap on the front door of our modest little row house at 68 Lemon Street that afternoon. I should have been apprehensive, but I was too young to be anything but curious. My mother, sitting with my sister and me at the kitchen table with the red checkered tablecloth, looked at us quizzically: Who could be interrupting our Sunday dinner?

I can remember many details of that day, even though it was over eight decades ago. Most anyone can recall specifics of events surrounding a major happening in life. What I didn't recall from that period, my mother filled in while she was alive.

My mother, my sister, Patricia, 6, and I, almost 4, had gone to the 9 o'clock Mass at St. John's that morning. After, my mother took Pat and me with her to the hair salon downtown, where my mother had just gotten a job cleaning up on Sundays. She had let me operate a device, a pole with a magnet on the end, that picked up bobby pins (hairpins) from the floor.

We three had been through a trauma. It was the talk of Lemon Street. A young father had gone off to work one day as usual, kissing his wife on the cheek before going — and had never returned. His clothes were still in his bureau drawers. He left no note, but did call his brother briefly. It was a month now. His wife, Elizabeth, never being other than a housewife, quickly had to find work to bring in a few dollars.

It was my father they were gossiping about, and my mother, too. Teenager Viola Russo was babysitting us when my mother worked, but she would have to return soon to school for her junior year.

I can recall our Sunday dinner that day we heard the light rap on the front door. It was a special treat for my sister and me: hot dogs and sauerkraut, and dumplings that my mother made herself. Affluent families would be having chicken for Sunday dinner, an expensive meal then. But, I wondered, who would want chicken when they could have hot dogs and sauerkraut?

At the faint knock, my mother moved her napkin from her lap to the table, pushed back her spindled white kitchen chair, hurried through the small living room, and opened the windowless door.

There stood a small lady in a dark, flowered, Sunday-best dress, her gray hair pulled back into a bun, her black old-lady shoes with low heels neatly polished. She was a total stranger to my mother, and, after apologizing for the intrusion, introduced herself as "Mrs. Paulo of 79 Lemon, up the street, the house on the corner on the other side." Mrs. Paulo told my mother that she had heard that my mother "may have a difficulty," without mentioning my father's abandonment or my mother's need to work. She complained how quiet her own house was during the day now that her children were grown and at work. "I miss children," she continued. "But you can do me a favor, Mrs. Burke. Your next door neighbor, Mrs. Maruca, and I have been talking, and she would like to care for Patricia during the day, and I would be so grateful if I could have Vincent. It would make me so happy." Mrs.

Maruca had two young sons about my age, so in her case at least, it was not that she missed having children in the house. Mrs. Paulo had had only daughters, and I would be the first boy under her care.

Even though my mother saw through Mrs. Paulo's kind pretext, for the next five years my sister and I spent weekdays at these neighbors' houses while my mother went out to work. The only relief for the two neighbor women was when we were in school, several years away for me. To me, the rap on our front door began my need to adapt to living in a house foreign to me, of years of two homes rather than just one. But on the plus side, there began obsessive attention to my likes and dislikes by a caring Italian senora, of homemade pasta, and a Tootsie Roll now and then, because I said I liked them.

On both their parts, Mrs. Paulo and Mrs. Maruca demonstrated a charity that I believe is rare today.

I would arrive at Mrs. Paulo's house early in the morning, ushered by my mother just before she went to work. I would already have had my breakfast cereal. Mrs. Paulo would devise an entertainment for me. She chose an activity guaranteed to please me, because she duplicated the exact two toys I had at home. One was a set of miniature logs to allow me to build tiny log cabins. The other was a set of little wooden bricks to make whatever structure I wanted. I was into construction in a big way. One day, she surprised me with a paddle ball. It was a piece of light wood about a foot long, shaped like a paddle, with a handle. Attached to it was an elastic cord with a small rubber ball on the end. You would strike the ball with the paddle, it would fly the maximum length of the elastic cord, and bounce back to be struck again. I liked it as a child. I can't imagine why. Sounds frustrating.

After I occupied myself with my buildings or paddle ball, or was out in the side garden area with a playmate or two from nearby, it was lunch time. Mrs. Paulo would knock herself out over her pasta dishes, knowing that was my favorite meal, and still is. She made the pasta herself, hung it on a line on the side porch to dry, and brought it in, fresh for our lunch. Neither her husband or her two grown daughters came home for lunch, so all of that effort was just for Mrs. Paulo and me. We would sit at her small kitchen table to eat, almost in silence. Occasionally, she would smile across the table at me, perhaps content that I was so enthusiastic about her pasta, and I would smile back.

At the end of the day, my mother would call for me, and we would have our supper together, my mother, my sister, and me. There were thorough discussions of each one's activities of the day, although mine were minimal. Often in the evening, my mother sat in the darkened living room and listened to the radio.

One time I came into the room to ask my mother something. "Mother," I started. I stopped speaking abruptly. My mother was unaware that I was standing right next to her. She was in a sort of trance, staring straight ahead at the wall. It did not seem that she was listening to the radio at all, but so deep in thought that she had not heard or seen me. "Mother," I repeated. She jerked as though startled, and gave me her attention. "Are you okay, mother?" I asked, having forgotten my original question. "I'm fine, Vincent. We're all going to be fine, all three of us. I know it for certain. The world is a good place, with good people." I never knew what inspired my mother to have such confidence, but I found her words reassuring. The world is a good place, with good people. My mother said so.

The neighbors helped. For five years, I observed these selfless acts by Mrs. Paulo. What better way to teach a child generosity and kindliness than by constant example? Did I learn these lessons being taught on Lemon Street? I would like to think I did and that I have applied them during my life, but I'm certain that many times I have come up short. Reflecting on the two neighbor ladies' generosity, and comparing it to what I know my own reaction would be if I encountered a neighbor in the situation of my mother, I become ashamed of myself. Much as I would empathize with such a neighbor, I am certain I would never volunteer to take a child into my house. I am not that giving a person. I am too self-centered to consider inconveniencing myself to such an extent. Sad. I yearn to think of myself as charitable, like Mrs. Paulo. I do hope that, at least in little ways throughout my life, her example to me as a child has come through.

As to these women, Mrs. Paulo and Mrs. Maruca, there is no doubt in my mind that, if there is a heaven, they are enjoying the rewards of paradise as we speak. My mother certainly expressed her gratitude to them, but I never did. A failing on my part that I regret decades later, and an effect on the rating of my life. If I could spend just an hour now with these women, I would fill the time with praise.

Today I'm starting a self-assessment by taking Frank, my partner, on a tour of Uniontown, a town 50 miles southeast of Pittsburgh where I spent my first 17 bad and good years, beginning four score and seven years ago. I intend to rate my life on a scale of 1 to 10.

If teen years were all I had to consider, being gay and having to keep it secret would seriously drag down the rating I would give my life. On the other hand, there was the goodness of the neighbors. On a scale of 1 to 10, maybe I'd get a 2 or 3. But, fortunately, things changed.

In the world of the large cities, companionship came easy in the mid-20th century. Then for 40 years, I had an ideal partner, and now I am with Frank, who gives me exciting days, 18 years of them so far. So perhaps the rating of my life needn't be all that low.

Not that there weren't bad times. I've had jobs that many people covet, but that I hated. What young person does not want to be a reporter on a major newspaper, with a byline every other day? Not me, as time would tell. The Madison Avenue advertising industry is thronged with recent graduates trying to get in. I was glad to get out. Who wouldn't want to own buildings on the East Side of Manhattan? First take a course in landlord-tenant law. How many people have three careers in life? With none of these jobs, being undercover, did I experience bias. I did often feel apart, as though I did not belong there, because I frequently saw bigotry against, not my surface me, but my secret self. If my colleagues knew my undercover self, I was convinced that I would be a pariah.

But I labored yet under the glow of my kind treatment in my former hometown, so I could withstand storms. I had been instructed in morality, what was right and what was wrong. I could dismiss the wrong, because I knew it when I saw it.

There are regrets in my life, like Mary, the loss of a friendship, my fault, because I wouldn't—was afraid to—out myself. And I can't count grandchildren, as heterosexual men my age usually do. In fact, I worry that having never married, I deprived some people of life itself. Still, despite such heavy weights, my adult years might end up by giving my life a good rating.

On the right, as Frank and I drive down Lemon Street from Bailey Avenue, will be the house, or rather, the former house, of that Italian woman with the gray bun, Mrs. Paulo. "There it is!" I shout to Frank, who's driving. "Oh, how awful it looks."

And indeed it does. It's obviously been abandoned. I see a window pane is missing. The storm door is fully open and flapping back against the siding of the house, itself missing a few pieces. The once-grand entry door, with a light on either side, is slightly ajar.

"There's her little garden!" I point out, specifying a small patch next to the house at the side street, behind a low picket fence. "How Mrs. Paulo loved that garden." We park, approach on foot, and enter the garden.

A garden left untended will soon be upended. And so it is with this little patch. Frank and I can hardly see the narrow brick walk for weeds growing through it. A tricycle missing a wheel is lying on its side. There's a soiled, collapsed ironing board in the area where once grew tomato plants.

Attached to the walls of the small side porch I can still discern, after so many decades, remnants of the hooks, now just globs of rust, that Mrs. Paulo used to stretch her clothesline to dry her homemade pasta.

I recall the luscious meals that followed.

Uniontown has changed, for the worse in my opinion, seven decades after I lived here, and following the demise of the local coal industry. It went from an ordinary small town to an ordinary even smaller town. Population in the 1940s: 20,000. Now, under 10,000. But efforts at rebirth are underway.

The town is at the foot of the Allegheny Mountains with a spectacular drive to the apex. That will never change. Nor has the Summit Inn, called the Summit Hotel when I lived here, at the pinnacle. Beyond that is Frank Lloyd Wright's "Fallingwater." I remember often staring at those mountains from my bedroom window with a yen to be up there, and every night being transfixed by the light sparkling from the Summit Hotel.

Before leaving Mrs. Paulo's garden, Frank retrieves from the walk a brick embossed, "Uniontown," my keepsake to remind me of the woman and her garden. The next stop after the Paulo house will be the row house at 68 Lemon Street, down the street on the other side, where I spent a dozen years. 68 Lemon is sandwiched among three other row houses, all larger, and all, when I lived there in the 1930s and '40s, occupied by related Italian families named Maruca, the Maruca house on one side being where my sister stayed weekdays while I was at the Paulo house.

The patriarch of these families, "Old Man Maruca," as he was known by everyone, was our landlord. His birth name was Francis, and to his face people called him Frank. As a child, I called him Mr. Maruca. He was probably in his 60s, and at my age today, I wonder how anyone could have called him "old man." But people then did look, and act, the part. We are no longer wrinkled and feeble when we reach retirement age. Perhaps the credit goes to nutrition and medicine.

If I knew any "adult" words in my early youth, they came from Mr. Maruca. He would sit on his front porch in a metal chair, shaded by the green-striped awning, eating red hot pepper after red hot pepper from

In front of 68 Lemon Street, about 1940. My sister, my Aunt Emma, my mother, and me.

68 Lemon Street has been turned into grassy Lemon Street Park.

his garden in the back, and find relief from the burn by unleashing a torrent of uncensored invective against the very food he continued to consume.

Mr. Maruca had the largest house of the four, on the one end; we were next to him with the smallest one, a two-bedroom, and the other two, moderate-sized units, were both occupied by Mr. Maruca's sons and their families.

Behind the four row houses were four back porches, as wide as each house, separated by spindled railings. After the porches came a wide, bricked area about ten feet deep with pansies in pots everywhere, then a raised garden area divided into three equal parts, enclosed by a two-foot wall. The garden continued to the rear of the property where stood an old, derelict and unused barn. The barn in turn fronted on a randomly-paved alley haphazardly lined with wild pink and red hollyhocks, the alley extending behind all of the properties on that side of Lemon Street. The flowers didn't last long. Little girls made dolls out of them, with the pink or red flower serving as the dress.

Julia, the daughter-in-law who lived next to us and the woman who cared for my sister, had one of the garden thirds for her flowers, mostly rose bushes. Another third was in grass. The final third was Mr. Maruca's vegetable plot with tomatoes, green beans, lettuce, carrots and, most certainly, his prized hot red peppers.

It is a mystery to me why we boys in the neighborhood held Mr. Maruca's garden, that single one, as sacrosanct. We had no hesitation about helping ourselves to a peach from a neighbor's tree, a carrot or radish or two from any other garden, especially the rhubarb from the Russo's. But never did we enter Mr. Maruca's plot. I don't recall that he inspired any particular fear in us. Was it respect because he was my landlord? I very much doubt that. We seemed to feel we had a right to all the other gardens. But not Old Man Maruca's. Even thieves have morals. There is an Indian proverb that I'm not particularly fond of: "A thief is a thief, whether he steals a diamond or a cucumber."

A few weeks after my father's disappearance, I was at the kitchen table nibbling on some after-supper jelly bread, when Mr. Maruca appeared at the open door to the back porch and tapped on the screen door. My mother left the sink where she was washing dishes, and went over to him. After a minute or so, she started to cry. Big tears rolled down each cheek. What was he saying to my mother? He's making her cry! Should I go over there? They were speaking in whispers, and I couldn't hear what was being said. Then my mother did something peculiar. She opened the screen door a bit, placed her hand on Mr. Maruca's bare wrist, and sort of stroked it affectionately. What was going on? I'm going over and find out why she's crying! Before I could get up, Mr. Maruca was leaving, and my mother was walking over to me, wiping her cheeks with the back of her hand. She looked at me with still-tearing eyes: "Vincent, he's a good man, our landlord, a good man," she said, sniffling.

Then she lifted me from my chair, set me on the floor, pulled me tightly against her body, and—began sobbing quietly, her body shaking against mine. I was confused, but threw my arms around her lower body and hugged her tightly. In a minute, she stopped crying, stepped back from me, and put her hands on my shoulders. She looked down into my eyes, this time smiling, but with her face still wet from her tears. "You're the man of the house now, Vincent," she said to me. "Every house needs a man of the house." She tousled my hair and returned to the sink to finish the dishes. My mother saying this befuddled me. What must I do since I'm man of the house? Are there things I should do? Am I able to do things? I'm not even four years old yet.

Mr. Maruca, the landlord of the hot red peppers and adult language, when he reached the assumption that my father would not return, had come to our kitchen door and told my mother that he was lowering the rent. He was creative in devising a reason: because there were now fewer people living in our house, he said. His kindness had brought on my mother's tears. Down was going the rent, from $23 to

$16. A good person, indeed, our landlord was, an example for a young boy and a lesson learned on Lemon Street. Old Man Maruca. I hope that in such a circumstance, I would be just like him. I wish I had just five minutes to tell him that today. He may have been overweight from pasta, but he was a beautiful person. Many years later, when my partner and I were struggling to reverse the poor financial condition of two apartment buildings we owned, perhaps it was the spirit of Mr. Maruca of Lemon Street that interceded, so that we exempted widowed tenants from our attempts at rent increases.

The lowered rent on Lemon Street would be a help to my mother starting on her own. My father could not keep money long. Although it was the Depression and no one had spare money whether working or not, the Christmas before my father left, Santa brought me an expensive fire truck that I could ride, with ladders, a light, and a bell. Pat got an elaborate doll house. We had a new floor model Philco radio that my father purchased "on time" at Cohen's Furniture Store. Alone, my mother could not keep the payments current. I stood in the living room next to my mother and sister that Saturday afternoon, watching as two burly men carried the handsome instrument out our front door and loaded it into the back of a truck to be returned to Cohen's. I sensed that something was not quite right about the whole thing, because I could feel that my mother was uncomfortable, but I didn't know what it was. I felt sad, but I didn't know why. I never listened to the radio anyway. The repossession of the console radio was one of the fruits of my father's spendthrift nature.

My father was a truck driver hauling fruit within the area, was six-foot-two, ruddy complexion, and handsome in an Irish way, with auburn hair like Pat inherited. He had terrible vision, far worse than what I inherited from him, but obtaining a driver's license was no problem in the 1930s. My mother, apparently not holding a grudge, in more recent years pitied him for the difficulty he must have encountered in driving for a living.

I don't remember my mother explaining anything to me when my father left. I was only 3, so I likely would have understood little had she said something. I do recall that, in a later year, she said that his leaving was in one way a relief. Money was always in short supply when he was there, principally because he spent so much on his friends. He bought a car, and it was never available because he would loan it to friends.

So, although my mother was worried about finances when he left, as a housewife never before having had a job, she believed that in the long run things would get better financially with my spendthrift father gone. And my mother said they eventually did. Women were paid even less in proportion to men than they are today. However, immediately after my father's departure, with no money and no job yet, my mother was forced to go on "relief," what is today called welfare, or, officially, Temporary Assistance for Needy Families. She received no money, but did get a delivery of food, as I remember, principally fruit and vegetables. Food stamps were almost three decades away, to 1964. My mother has said that she was mortified about being on relief, and as soon as she got her first housecleaning job, she removed herself from it.

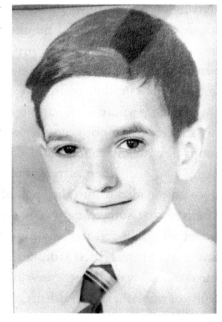

Me, at about 6

When she got work, during the week my mother cleaned houses for two older sisters on the next street, both school teachers. On Sundays she cleaned the hair salon. She had plans to go to Penn State College Extension classes in an elementary school on Beeson Blvd., to learn bookkeeping. She would complete the course and become a bookkeeper.

Her father's absence affected my sister most of all. He, as many fathers, doted on his daughter, his only daughter and first born. He called her his little angel, and in his eyes, she could do no wrong. I was the other child, three years younger, and certainly not the apple of his eye as Patricia was. She was his little girl, he would say. Wherever his little girl was, the father was, too.

Our mother recalled his constant mother-hen attention to Patricia. At dinner, he would make certain she was eating adequately and would replenish her plate himself. I remember when we were out he was the one who would order an ice cream cone for us and would stoop over to hand hers personally to her.

On her sixth birthday, he dressed her in a new dress and took her to a photo studio downtown for her portrait. In the photo, one sees a little girl with large dark eyes and dark auburn shoulder-length hair, in a white frilly dress. She is sitting on a bench with one leg folded under the other. Her father then put the portrait in a gold frame and inscribed it in his own handwriting, "I daddy's girl."

Yet shortly after that portrait and those tender words, my sister's devoted father left the house that morning as usual, and never returned.

He would not be there to see his little girl dressed all in white at her first communion. He would not be there with our proud mother to hear her introduced at Ursuline College's Baccalaureate ceremony. He would not walk her down the aisle at her wedding. He would not be there to console her when the marriage failed after six months.

According to my mother, when he left, Patricia took her father's disappearance personally, blaming herself. She was pessimistic. "He's not coming back. He doesn't like me." That was her simple, often-repeated conclusion. My mother through the years often apologized to me that she had to devote a disproportionately large amount of time to Pat to assure her that she was loved, and my mother felt bad that, comparatively, I was short-changed. I would have to keep convincing my mother that I never felt neglected, and remindIng her that she frequently sat me on her lap and sang a sweet little song to me about her little boy. Every few years, the lyrics return to me, but this isn't the year.

Despite my mother's efforts, my young sister's personality changed immediately. Instead of the smiling, extroverted child she had been, she became sullen, shy and introverted. She would not see a favorite play-mate, would not play the usual out-door games with other children, and instead obsessed over a particular doll that she now refused to leave a room without.

My mother at about 25.

Eventually, as her father's absence extended into months and then years, Patricia's life assumed the trappings of normalcy: elementary and high school, boyfriends and dates, college and career.

Pat grew up to be an attractive woman, large hazel eyes, auburn hair, blemish-free white skin. She had a graceful slim body of medium height, and was always expensively and tastefully dressed. But she brushed off complements, believing herself plain and unremarkable even though I, her brother, saw many a young man become tongue-tied in her presence.

She was poised, cultured, knowledgeable of social graces. But she felt awkward, clumsy, and a misfit in almost any group setting.

She had graduated summa cum laude from her college and was chosen to give the commencement address. She would become a compensation analyst for the Defense Department overseeing three states. She was a whiz at math. But she took no notice of any of this, and considered her success in her career as barely mediocre.

She yearned for praise, and got it. But she never allowed it to alter her limited opinion of herself.

This is what our father's abandonment of the family and my sister Pat did to her, and how it affected her life.

I don't think Pat obsessed for years over what she interpreted as a rejection of her. I hope not. She developed an enthusiasm for just about everything in her path: gardening, travel, her two black cats, her house.

But nonetheless I always wondered about the long-term effect of the disappearance on her. I hope I am mistaken, but I perceived a limit to her joy, as if it were overshadowed by her feelings of inadequacy and unworthiness.

I thought it peculiar that in all her adult years, I don't believe Pat mentioned her father a single time.

We were a close family, just the three of us. My mother and sister relocated to Fort Lauderdale after my sister retired so that we would be close together.

Patricia died at age 78, in 2009. After a while, I went to her house to pack up her things.

In her bedroom dresser, second drawer down, under some white and flowered blouses, lay a gold-framed portrait of a little girl with large dark eyes, in a white frilly dress, one leg folded under the other. Still clearly legible in the upper left-hand corner was the cursive inscription "I daddy's girl." I hadn't seen this photo in over 70 years.

This was the gift from her father that Patricia cherished all of her life and kept close as she moved from place to place. This was her father's last gift before the rejection. This photo, still in its gold frame selected by her father, and with his tender words still clear on it, now sits on the mantel of the fireplace of our den in Virginia to honor my sister who treasured the photo so much, and as a reminder to me of the contrast between my father who vanished and my mother who devoted herself to the happiness of her children.

As for me, being so young when my father parted, the only real memory I have of him is his bringing a huge cluster of bananas home one day. The only intimate tie with my father that I remember, the only personal attention he ever gave me, was my father and I both standing at the toilet of the house on Lemon Street urinating into the bowl, him towering over me, standing to my right on the side. I suppose this was a lesson in male hygiene.

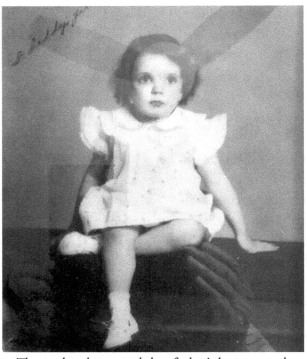

This is the photo, with her father's loving words, that my sister treasured in secret all of her life.

I have just a vague impression of what my father looked like, although in my youth I nurtured an image of someone not unlike Cary Grant. I do have a photo of two men standing in front of a large truck, probably a semi, staring at the camera and posing. I found this photo among many others in a cardboard box of family mementos in a closet of my sister's house. I remember that photo, now in bad condition, from many years ago. My mother had said that the man in front of the left side of the truck's cab was my father. Or at least that is what I think, now over 50 years later, that she told me. However, the man on the right side of the truck looks more like my father's brother, my Uncle Dave, than the man on the left, who doesn't seem to have any family resemblance at all. Am I remembering what my mother said correctly, or have I gotten mixed up? I value having a picture of my father, reprobate though he was, so I have put a closeup of each man on my iPad. One of them is my father. But which one? Incidentally, neither one looks like Cary Grant.

I have always thought that I was too young to be affected by my father's departure. However, I believe what did influence my life was the effect his irresponsibility had on my sister's personality. I observed as a young child the suffering of Pat due to his disappearance and his abdication of his duty toward his family. As an adult, I have a strong sense of obligation, even in insignificant matters. I'm loathe to cancel an appointment no matter the justification. Neither snow nor rain nor heat nor gloom of night stays me from my appointed rounds. I wonder if this is a reaction to a childhood judgment of my father's sin of irresponsibility. I hope that any responsibility I have comes from my father's lack of it, so that there has at least been some benefit from his abandonment.

I noted recently that it wasn't until maybe three years ago that I told anyone but my two partners the story of my father. I kept it secret. Why? I think I know the answer. I was embarrassed about his action because I considered it a despicable thing to do. I was ashamed that I was the son of a father who would do this.

I've wondered what kind of a person I would have turned out to be had my father not abandoned us. Seeing how my Uncle Dave, my father's brother, mingled with his five sons gives me the idea that my father and I would have become very close, going places together. Maybe he would have put a basketball hoop up and we'd play together. I could even have been very good at sports if my father had taught me. My cousins, taught by Uncle Dave, were good. Though these cousins were straight (I assume) and I am gay. Maybe, being gay, I wouldn't have been good at all. However, to accept that idea is to buy into the stereotype that gays are poor at sports, which has been debunked by some famous gay athletes.

Surely, my dad would have come to my school on the one day a year the parents were invited, and I would have introduced him to my classmates. He would tower over them. He had a good build, and a full head of hair. He was good-looking, and my friends would have admired him.

It was a rare thing to have a father disappear back in 1937. Now it's not that uncommon. And with divorce rates what they are now, and with many women being single mothers, children being raised without a father is not unusual. I hope that the effect I suffered from a missing father is not prevalent with the fatherless children today. It recently came to light that Boris Johnson, the British prime minister, in an article in The Spectator in 1995, described the children of single mothers as "ill-raised, ignorant, aggressive, and illegitimate." Good grief! Was that me?

Our family, my father, 29, my mother, also 29, my sister and I were living a pretty happy life back in 1937. even though it was the middle of the Depression. My father had a job. We had moved into a two-bedroom row house on a nice street.

My father was one of seven children of an immigrant father from Cork, Ireland, and a local Irish girl. His father settled in Dunbar, a dot-on-the-map near Uniontown, to work in the coal mines. I suppose my father completed high school. I know that all his siblings did. I have blamed my father for tarnishing my sister's life, for my mother having to clean houses and go to bookkeeping classes, for my failure to play sports or to learn sports, for my latching onto a man I regarded as a father-figure, and possibly sending him the wrong signals that encouraged his advances.

I have allowed my father no excuse for his disappearance. I have not admitted a possibility that his psychological makeup may have made it impossible for him to continue to accept responsibility for a family, and that his departure may have been excruciatingly painful for him. And who knows that he did not come through town during the years, check on us, and find some consolation that we were ok.

Have I been unjust to my father?

Dear Father,

Maybe I should be calling you "Daddy," because that's what I called you the last time I saw you. It would be strange, 84 years later, to call you "Daddy." It seems equally odd to call you "Dad," because I never used that intimate word for you. I didn't use father, either, but father it will be. Unlike daddy or dad, father, a clinical term, to me can convey a feeling of coldness, and that is what I intend.

A "father," in any sense, you were to me just for three years. Off you went to no-one-knows-where, not caring you were leaving us to fend for ourselves. Only memories of you remained. Mine, weak. Patricia had the most painful ones. She missed you, and didn't even want to play with her friends anymore. She even stopped liking me for a while. Mother? It was a nasty thing to leave her all alone with us, with no money, and never even having had a job before. Did you love her? It doesn't seem like you could have. You had been married to her for 13 years! Pat and me. We were your children. Did you love us? It doesn't seem like you could have.

One time mother told me that now I was the man of the house, and she was sobbing when she told me. That scared me. What did she expect of me? I wasn't even 4 years old yet. I was the man because you weren't there as you should have been.

I remember clearly your absences, how I felt ashamed going places with my mother instead of my father. Mother took me to the circus and bought me a cotton candy, not you. Mother took me to school the first, frightening day. I would have felt better with those strange people dressed in black if I was next to you, because you were big. It was not you who played basketball with me; it wasn't anyone. At sports events, where other kids brought their fathers, I sat in the bleachers by myself. I would sneak a peek at a classmate with his father, and imagine how it would be for me and you to be there together. Would you have gotten hot dogs and pop for us? Mother gave me the money, but I had to have my hot dog alone. It would have tasted better if we had hot dogs together.

However, Father, I want to consider forgiving you for leaving, and me having to be all alone. Maybe I've judged you all wrong. If you found it psychologically impossible, untenable, to continue to be responsible for a family— what can I do but forgive you? If I could have an hour with you, you'd make me understand.

If you merely decided that your life would be better without us tagging along? I wouldn't forgive you in a thousand years.

But, do you know what, father? I do have something to thank you for. I owe you my sense of responsibility. Observing the suffering you caused my sister has given me the urge to be the opposite, never to be irresponsible and cause hurt. Your actions gave me that, father, so I owe you a "thank you."

Yours truly,
Your son

My mother was from a nearby town of about 5,000, Masontown. She was a small woman, five feet, not even a hundred pounds, with black black hair and snow-white skin. Her father was named Massimo

Filippi upon leaving Trento, at the time Austria but now Italy. He become Max Philippi upon arriving in America. Her mother, Mary, Hungarian, came to America after the death of her first husband, and brought with her, her only child, Mary, my mother's half sister. I have the family photo from about 1913 showing the large family formally dressed, two of the girls with huge bows atop their heads. People have remarked that it looks like a photo of European royalty. Perhaps in Masontown, they were royalty. After all, my grandfather was the town's only beer distributor. Iron City Beer, from Pittsburgh, was the big seller.

My mother and father were very young when they met and married. My mother has said her decision was influenced by having a strict father and an older sister who, after her mother's death, ran a

The Philippi family in about 1913. Mary, the Hungarian-born daughter of Mary, the mother, is standing in the back. On the far left in front is my mother, born in 1908. On the far right is her younger sister Sabrina, called Bea. Bea and my mother will be close sisters throughout life.

tightly-ruled household.

To marry, my parents were not yet of legal age in Pennsylvania, which was 18, so they traveled to Cumberland, Maryland, where the requirement was two years lower for a civil ceremony. As a civil ceremony was not recognized by the Catholic Church, a few years later, just before the birth of my sister, they corrected their teenage impulsiveness by a second marriage, this time by a priest. Therefore, my sister was born to a married couple.

When my father left, the intervention of Mrs. Paulo and Mrs. Maruca to care for my sister and me allowed my mother to clean houses free of concern about us children. Mrs. Maruca had heard of the two maiden ladies, the schoolteachers, who wanted a woman to clean and prepare some meals. My mother worked a half-day Saturdays, but the three of us were together the rest of Saturday, and Sundays, even though my mother cleaned the hair salon on Sundays. Two mornings a week my mother went to school to learn bookkeeping. Afterwards, she quickly got a job at Fike's Dairy, also working five and a half days, that she kept until we all left for Cleveland 14 years later.

My father did have two sisters and a brother, my Uncle Dave that I mentioned earlier, in Uniontown. None of them was prosperous, although the families had money coming in regularly even though it was the Depression. The husbands of my father's sisters were both miners, and Uncle Dave commuted all the way to Pittsburgh to work in a steel mill. They probably were not in a position to help my mother financially, but assisted her very little psychologically. My mother's siblings lived in Ohio and Michigan. Years later, my mother remembered how she welcomed the comforting letters from her sister, Bea, in Youngstown, Ohio, with sympathy and advice. We didn't have a telephone, less than 40% of families did in 1937, and long distance telephone calls were expensive and would be out of the question.

Incidentally, I refer here to my mother as my "mother," not my mom, mama, mummy, or certainly not "Half Pint," as my father's relatives called her. Pat and I have never called her anything but "mother," in addressing her or speaking about her.

My mother's free time through the years was often spent reading mysteries. When I lived in England years later, I sent her the complete works of Agatha Christie that I picked up at a flea market, a welcome gift. She always refused to read Christie's final work, "Curtains." She could not bear to say goodbye to Inspector Hercule Poirot, a man she had come to love.

So there's now a little park here, where our Lemon Street house once was. Is it right that a government without a thought can destroy your memories? Will a dog-walker using this park reflect on my history there? In our daily lives, do we ever think back to the lives, families and events that have preceded us on the same soil? I must admit here, however, that a park is an acceptable substitute for my little row house — and I thank Uniontown for that.

Then, Frank and I drive down Lemon Street to North Gallatin Avenue to go to St. John's. Past the funeral home, still a funeral home, that as a child I could not go by without walking on the wall, now quite a bit shorter than I remember. Then past Gallatin School where I went to kindergarten and behind which the Ringling Bros. Circus set up once a year.

It was when I was at kindergarten, in 1939, that parents were asked to provide a bed cover for the daily nap. My mother somehow found the time to make a colorful blanket about 2x5 with a large rabbit and a few chicks with a house behind them, that I had framed ten years ago under a glass cover — and that I haven't been able to donate. This bed cover is important to me because it is a symbol of my mother's determination to provide for her children.

Gallatin School is now a county social center, and didn't want the cover. I phoned St. John's Elementary School, that I attended, and was told its walls are full. The blanket is over 80 years old. 80 years! Can you believe it? An antique is an item at least a hundred years old. My mother's bed cover will soon be an antique. My gosh! I'm not far from being an antique myself. Just 13 years to go. Even now, I'm vintage. Vintage is something old, but not as old as a hundred years. To call myself vintage sounds better than antique.

We continue on North Gallatin Avenue. It's gone now, and there's

The bed cover for my naps at kindergarten that my mother made in 1939. That's a long time ago!

an apartment building in about the same place. I'm speaking of the Victorian house where the tall, too-thin elderly lady, sitting on the front porch, would invite me up for tea and cookies as I passed going home from school. The teas were about twice a week during the school year, beginning when I was probably 9 or 10, and lasted regularly for several years until our family moved from Lemon Street, and after that occasionally when I went out of my way to visit there. I thought the woman talked with me as though I were an adult, but the only subject I can recall now is her excitedly speaking to me of World War II. As an adult, I have always followed news events closely, and I wonder whether this habit of mine, that I find pleasantly engaging, doesn't owe its birth to the news stories she relayed to me. I believe that this woman taught me to be interested in the world around me, a valuable lesson.

In serving us tea, that I never got at home, she poured it from a flowered china teapot into small china cups. I was in awe of the thin, delicate cups that were so different from what my mother had. My mother's were common white 5&10 cups. I was careful with my cup, and, in the years I went there, I never broke one, no doubt a record for me. "You!re very mannerly, Vincent, and gentle with your china cup," she once said to me. "Your mother is raising you to be a gentleman." She always called me "Vincent," as my mother did, not "Vinny," the name my schoolmates used. The cookies were plain butter cookies. I preferred cookies with some sort of sweet goo inside, such as jelly or a cream filling. The butter cookies were still cookies, so, of course, I ate them. I tried to make a good impression by limiting myself to two cookies. "Go on, have another, Vincent," she would invariably say. "You're a growing boy." I would then take a third cookie.

I liked this lady and would often knock on her door when the weather was too inclement for her to be on the porch. On those occasions, we would have our tea and cookies on flowered placemats at her big, dark dining room table under the crystal chandelier. I believe now that she may have been lonely, or was particularly fond of children, or both. For me, maybe this woman took the place of a grandmother, as both of mine were dead. I never knew much about her, except that she was kind to me. Her house would have had at least three bedrooms upstairs, perhaps four, but in the years she hosted me, I never saw another person there but her. It seems unlikely she was unmarried, with such a large house. She never mentioned a husband, alive or deceased, nor children, who would, because of the woman's age, certainly have been grown. I relished very much knowing this lady, and bragged to my classmates at school about drinking tea at her big table, under her big chandelier, in her big house. I described the elegant table service, the dainty and fragile teacups. I tried to make them envious by telling them of some of the news events we discussed together, and boasted that she never even once had called me Vinny as they did, but always Vincent. I can no longer recall the woman's name, and that bothers me because she deserves my personal acknowledgement by name. This woman of the 1940s has probably been dead 60 or 70 some years by now. I still remember her, with affection. I very much doubt that anyone will think of me in six or seven decades.

I told my mother about my stops for tea and my lady friend of the Victorian house. She said she'd already received a note from the woman, and replied. My mother seemed inordinately curious. "How did you meet this woman?" she inquired. I told her we had first said hello as I passed her porch; another time she asked my name; finally, she invited me up for tea. My mother wanted to know every detail.

I answered my mother's questions about the woman: her age, the big house and its furnishings, the china used, and the tea. She even wanted to know the kind of cookies served. Soon, the three of us, my mother, sister and I, started having teas together, with butter cookies. Thus began 70 years of our family's teas. Whenever we were together, there was the pot of tea and cookies on the table before us, although the butter cookies were eventually replaced by cookies more to my liking.

It was sometime during my early elementary school years, before my meeting the tea-and-cookies lady, that I ingeniously devised an entertainment for my solo 30-minute walk from school to Lemon Street. Immediately on leaving school, I would spot a rock, or rather a large pebble since it was never big, and kick it all the way home, the resulting condition of my shoes no concern to me at all. Down Jefferson Street we would go, my pebble pal and me, up East Main past the court house with men going in and out in suits, a right turn past the jail which held no end of fascination for me. Then my pebble pal and I would go down the hill with me being careful not to let him run out of control. A right turn into Gallatin Avenue, helping him across the train tracks, then we proceed all the way to Lemon Street and home, with me barely lifting my head to acknowledge my surroundings since leaving school. This companionship no doubt lengthened the time the trip took, but no matter. My pebble became a cherished friend during these intimate moments as we purposefully pursued our way together as a couple. I would be terribly saddened if somehow I lost my chum along

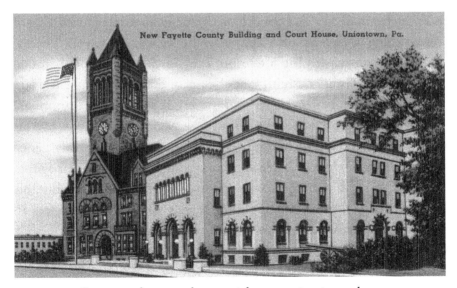

New Fayette County Building and Court House, Uniontown, Pa.

"....past the court house with men going in and out in suits...my pebble pal and I would go..."

29

the way to a busy street or a sidewalk grate. Finally arriving home, today's pebble would join those from past days in a corner of the front porch, the place of honor for high achievers.

Was I mentally challenged? Should I have had a pet?

After getting home, I would sometimes closet myself in my bedroom to engage in another cherished activity: combining chemicals from my Christmas chemistry set to fill the room with a dense smoke. I was not bored by this unproductive activity.

I did have a worthwhile project, at about age 10. I decided I would increase my vocabulary by taking a dictionary and learning one word a day, starting with the As. I imagined myself being admired for knowing every word there is. My intention to expand my knowledge was laudable, but my follow through dismal. So, alas, every word in the dictionary will not be found in this book.

My distraction at an even earlier age was not any more erudite than the pebble amusement. I would walk very quickly around the neighborhood, making a loud humming sound and waving a stick back and forth in front of my face. Some of the neighbors recognized that I was claiming to be a car on a rainy day, the back and forth stick being the windshield wiper. The attention went to my head, and I would wave the stick faster and hum louder. Sort of creative on my part, but Mozart did much better. He was composing at age 5. I was humming.

We now approach St. John's from East Main, a quick pass by the modest, if not slum-like, house I was born in, then down Shady Lane, lined with grand, now very old, houses beginning to show their age.

St. John's Church for some reason was renamed St. John the Evangelist after I left Uniontown, or if that name always existed, it was not used before. There was already a St. John the Baptist Greek Catholic Church in town, so my St. John's had to go with the lesser St. John.

It's an attractive red brick building on top of a hill with a thousand steps (literary hyperbole) up from Jefferson Street. Its architecture has been described as eclectic, with a Romanesque bell tower. The elementary school is behind the church and the high school sits—or, rather, did sit—below the church across Jefferson Street. The high school was three stories with two classrooms and auxiliary rooms on each of the first two floors, and a library and auditorium on the 3rd. The building was old when I was young.

*St. John the Evangelist Church,
with a thousand steps.*

The first time I saw it had disappeared, some years earlier, was a shock. The site is now a church parking lot.

My years through the eight grades at St. John's Elementary School are rather a haze to me now. It was, after all, a long time ago, between 70 and 80 plus years, depending on the grade. I remember butterflies in my stomach the first day of school each year. I recall the "star" reward protocol; you got a small star of a color of particular significance, reflecting your performance, affixed after your name on a large chart hung on the wall. And I remember, as I grew up, secretly adopting a classmate as a girlfriend. I did not have any particular feeling for the girl, but thought she was pretty. First there was Paula. Then, being fickle, I turned to Catherine. It was simple to switch, no breakup scene needed, because neither girl ever knew I was eyeing her. Then puberty set in, and my interest turned exclusively to boys. I found several in my class alluring, and they never knew it, either. I developed the lifelong habit of not noticing a male that I have noticed. I am of the belief that my genes dictated my being gay, but I have no explanation as to why, pre-puberty, I selected girlfriends as though I was headed for heterosexuality. Perhaps it was peer pressure, my interest in girls being because my male classmates were. When I reached high school and then in puberty, there was no question that males were my choice. It was the triumph of genes over peer pressure.

I can't forget the childhood illnesses I had. I've been healthy as an adult. As a child I was always getting a sore throat. My mother would treat it with over-the-counter medicine, and I'd take honey, but nothing worked but time. One year I had the mumps, the upside being that I got ice cream. My sister got measles, and then I got it. A lot of kids got measles, and it didn't seem to be treated as seriously as it is today. The other memory I have is of the dreaded enema. When my father was still with us, he and my mother gave me an enema. Apparently it needed both of them to do it. Bad day that was. In childhood, I remember also waking up many times with so much matter in my eyes that I had to struggle to open them. Today, a child would be taken to the doctor with such occurrences. Back in the 1930s and '40s, people didn't run to the doctor with every complaint. Who could afford it? You just hoped you'd get better, and usually did.

The only photographic record I have of my old high school alma mater is a photo of Sister Hilda Marie, principal and disciplinarian, ascending the front exterior steps. She is looking at the camera and smiling, which makes this a rare photo indeed. I took this photo myself, during my photography phase, when I experimented with filters, time exposure, zoom. I do have a self portrait, as so many famous painters do. I suppose I should call it a self-photo. My egotism was easy to satisfy; I just shot myself in a mirror. Great photographers have started young, but after a year or two, I was on to something else.

I did not realize until recently that St. John's was an Irish parish. There were four other Catholic parishes in Uniontown, all ethnic also. There was an Italian church, a Polish church, and so on. St. Mary's, the Slovenian church, had a grade school but didn't have a high school, and so when the St. John's group entered the high school, names like Maher, Walsh and Riley—and Burke—were joined by those such as Dvorchak, Haky, Harto coming from St. Mary's. The pastor of St. John's was an Irishman named Father Dunn, whose overly dramatic mannerisms were attributed to his being shell-shocked in World War I. He lives on in the Rev. Thomas J. Dunn Knights of Columbus Council.

Even after the influx of these new students, we were a class of just 38. We would graduate as St. John's Class of 1952. Being a small class, of the same religion, in a small town, we became close. There have been about 60 reunions called, and attended. We watched each other age, and learned when one of us died. The 62nd in 2014 will have been the last reunion. Mike, Steve, and Ray, the organizers, have all died now.

I was at the 62nd. There were only eight of us there, but some sent regrets. Mike and Steve organized it, but Steve was in a wheelchair after a fall. Ray had already died. One man had a walker. The wife of another classmate came in and asked if we would come out to the car to say hello to her husband, because he refused to get out, not knowing where he was. A few, with the right genes, were in good health and appearing ten or twenty years younger than they were. My classmates, reunion after reunion, I'm sure did not suspect my sexual orientation, because I camouflaged it under fantastic fabrications. The closet door never opened.

I consider myself as a teenager a little strange. At ages 14. 15, 16, I experienced the first rumblings of lust, always for other boys. The gender of my attention was not acceptable, I realized, and to hide my desires became a daily obsession in Uniontown.

In high school, two of my best friends, my only close friends, were girls in my class. Caroline and Gloria. I knew this was unusual, a boy befriending girls at that age without any hidden intent, and I was embarrassed to be seen with them by my male classmates, but I suffered the shame because I enjoyed their company. At lunchtime, I did hang out with the basketball boys, but I felt under stress with them and could relax only with my two girl friends. They never hinted that they thought a boy hanging around with two girls was odd. The subject of sexual orientation was never brought up with them. And thankfully, they never talked about sports. I could be myself with them.

Grades never were a problem and even though my outside jobs consumed a lot of my time, I still did well. I always took a pugnacious position in class discussions. My radical views would make me the center of attention for at least a short while, a position that, apparently, I desired as a welcome diversion to my usual shyness. For example, I took the view that Lincoln was not the sensational president he is reputed to be. I maintained that, since new states admitted to the Union would not be slave states, and that frequent uprisings were causing fear among slave holders, slavery was likely to end relatively soon of its own accord. Was it worth a war with proportionally more deaths than the US has ever had? I could express this thought without emotional involvement because, as a white boy, my ancestors never were slaves. My fallback was that Lincoln should have just let the South go, rather than engage in such a costly civil war. I was certain I was right, as teenagers always are. I have questions today about my arguments, but I recognize them as a forerunner of more recent unpopular positions that I have taken.

My same quarrelsomeness surfaced at least once with my basketball lunch group. We were walking down Shady Lane en route back to school. When one of the boys in conversation mentioned something about the United States of America, I interrupted him to say that it really should be the United States of North America, as we certainly are not the United States of Central and South America. There was a howl of opposition to my assertion about adding the word "north." Not content to let the issue lie there, I continued on, saying that in the least we should not be called Americans, but instead United Statesians, since North America includes Canada and Mexico. This was greeted with indignation and scoffs. I was lucky I wasn't ejected from the little group then and there. My contrariness did serve to put myself in the limelight, something that didn't happen every day, and that could have been my goal. I should have learned from that experience not to put too fine a point on things, not to take everything literally. But that did not sink in, and I still tend to be annoyingly picayune.

In thinking back to my claims of a lifetime ago, I find through research on the internet that I wasn't being entirely absurd about our being called Americans. It seems that Europeans, from the era when we were an English colony, did in fact refer to us as Americans, as apart from those in French and Spanish colonies. This was true of English-speaking Europeans only, whereas others then and to this day may call anyone from any of the American continents an American, the country made clear by the context.

I had never learned sports, and I've said that I blame this lack at not having a male figure at home. So I merely sat in the bleachers at basketball games and watched my classmates play. I remember my anxiety on Fridays at school in the spring. That was the day the boys were taken by Lash (we called him by his first name), the coach and history teacher, to Bailey's Field to play baseball. Never having played, I sat and watched, feeling out of place, and not daring to humiliate myself by trying. "Mortified" is not too strong a word for my sense of myself on Fridays as I watched the boys in my class play baseball. How heavy the burden is when you yourself wonder if you're a sissy. As an adult, I have questioned why Lash, no doubt knowing of my father's absence, did not take me aside and teach me the basics. There was total misery on these Fridays during high school, and even on the preceding Thursdays, anticipating the Fridays. Mentally I could never join in with my male classmates' unbridled admiration of this man. I resent to this day his disinterest to step in and be to me what he was called: a coach.

When I was still a paperboy, probably aged 14, a fellow paperboy, who lived in the same direction, and I happened to leave the Standard office together. At the point where our paths separated, we were so engaged in conversation that we stood on the sidewalk for perhaps an hour talking, and reluctant to part. This brief union with another boy was so rare to me, and the encounter so important to me, that I have never forgotten the details, the corner where we stood, or the boy's name, Jack. Looking back, I find my longing for male companionship a little pathetic.

I did have a few days with three boys my age. I won a trip to New York City by selling subscriptions to the paper, and my boss drove me and the three other winners along the Pennsylvania Turnpike, through the Lincoln Tunnel, and into Manhattan. How noisy everything seemed! There was a loud background thrum coming from everywhere, or from nowhere. We were checked into the Piccadilly Hotel just off Times Square. As we were all 14 or 15, the boss apparently thought he could let us fend for ourselves most of the time. It didn't go too well.

None of us had ever used a bathtub shower before, so none of us thought to put the shower curtain inside the tub while taking our showers. After the last shower, our bathroom was ankle-deep in water. We hadn't taken the hint earlier that something was amiss when the water on the bathroom floor had been rising. As we were staring aghast at our watery handiwork, there was a sharp rap on the door. The maid immediately entered, quite cross she was, and informed us in an unnecessarily loud voice that we had flooded the bathroom below. We sat, two on each bed, facing each other, chagrined, as she used a mop and pail to clean up the mess. She was muttering something the whole time, but we couldn't decipher a word. Maybe it's a New York accent, I thought.

To take our mind off the scolding, when she left we turned to the bag of red grapes we had purchased from a vendor on the street. We were on the fifth floor, and our window made a perfect firing post to launch grapes at the taxi drivers standing by their cabs at the hotel's entrance on the street below, waiting for fares. We would then quickly duck back into the room so as not to be seen. Evidently our ploy didn't work. There was a sharp rap on the door again and the same maid entered, even more cross than before, muttering something about children. This time I understood her accent.

Then John challenged me to a wrestling match, and we rolled around on a bed for a while. But it was Tommy I wanted to wrestle with, and he wasn't wrestling. I had casually asked him, but I could not be insistent. I was aware that any desire for contact with a male must be concealed. I had to be in hiding. I was undercover.

The next day we ate — again — at Romeo's Italian Restaurant that we all agreed had the best food we had ever eaten, and the cheapest, too. We found it miraculous that there was a Romeo's on practically every other block. New Yorkers sure know how to eat!

Somehow we found our way on the subway to the Staten Island Ferry, which the boss said not to miss. For a nickel, we went to Staten Island, right past the Statue of Liberty, and for a nickel, returned to Manhattan. I was overwhelmed by the skyscrapers towering above us as we came into port. Maybe someday, I thought... Later that year, when I sat in the State Theater in Uniontown on a Saturday afternoon watching "On The Town," about three sailors on a 24-hour leave in Manhattan, I had the same yearning to one day live there.

That night, for our Manhattan farewell dinner, it wasn't Romeo's again. The boss took us to a restaurant named 14 Barrow Street, in Greenwich Village. It had peanut shells all over a black floor, and the tables were made out of dark, crudely-cut wood. There was practically no lighting; you couldn't see anything. I loved it.

Back home, my chief entertainment, usually my only one, was to go to a movie every Saturday afternoon — always alone. Early in the week I would check the paper to see what would be playing at all three movie theaters. I never paid attention to what time a movie started, because I entered the theater at whatever time I happened to get there, whether it was in the middle of the movie or even toward the end. My going down the aisle and into a row while normal, on-time theater goers were engrossed in the film must have made me persona non grata, but I took no notice of it. I would then watch the present showing to the end, and the following showing from beginning to end. I can't explain the logic of this peculiar habit, to see the end of a film before seeing the beginning. I had my favorite section and seats of the theater that I never deviated from. I was always in the side section on the far right, five or so rows from the front, and I always tried for an aisle seat.

During my high school years, I must have seen several hundred films, but because it was so long ago, I remember only a few. The scenes in "The Day The Earth Stood Still" impressed me so much that I picture them now, as though I saw the movie recently. I recall that every energy source was immobilized by the alien to demonstrate his power to enforce his demand of humans to stop wars. Never could I imagine that one day the world would worry that cyber attacks could take control of energy as the alien had done. I can't forget, either, "Samson and Delilah" and the collapse of the temple. I'm certain I saw "Gone With the Wind," because I remember it, and also my guilt afterwards, knowing that the movie was rated "objectionable in part" by the Legion of Decency, the Catholic group that listed films according to moral content. However, that movie was released in 1940, when I was only six years old. I saw that movie alone by myself, so it must have been re-released about ten years later. It was the kind of adult film I liked. I saw very few Westerns; I didn't like them. I knew of Gene Autry and Roy Rogers, so I suppose I saw each of them in a movie or two. I remember laughing my head off watching comedy shorts with super accident-prone Pete Smith. As for favorite actors, it wasn't Betty Grable or Ava Gardner, as future straight boys my age would select. For me, it was June Allyson, the girl next door with the raspy voice. For a male actor, I chose, no surprise, blond Alan Ladd.

I never saw my lunchtime basketball group, nor my two girlfriends, at the movies. I would feel a little awkward when I ran into other classmates in leaving the theater, because they were in pairs or threes and I was alone. "You're here all by yourself?" one would ask. "Today I am," I'd quickly reply, as though my loneness was a rare exception. However, I did not mind at all watching a movie alone, without anyone to make comments to. I only minded being seen alone. My solitude wasn't, I told myself, because I was grotesque, so that no one would sit next to me. A little short, a little thin, sometimes a canker sore on my lip. Despite this, in high school there were a few girls buzzing around me. No boys.

The child's admission to a movie was 10 cents (adults, 25 cents). I added luxury to the event by buying a box of chocolate-covered cherries beforehand at Murphy's 5 &10 for the budget-busting price of 25 cents. The cost seriously cut into my earnings, but I considered it an essential. Usually halfway through the movie, I'd feel a little nauseated from gorging on the candy and swear to eat no more, righteously placing the box on the floor in front of my seat—only to retrieve it some minutes later. I am sure that I never divulged information of my weekly gluttony to my mother. There are things that you do in life that are too shameful to be revealed.

While I would be going to my Saturday movie, Pat would have met my mother after she got off work at noon. They would then see a movie together. It was probably about the same time I would be at my movie, but I don't remember ever running into them.

My only other amusement, introvert as I was, was reading books I found at the library. I became engrossed in a series of books called Banner Boy Scouts. The titles strongly hint at the plot: "Banner Boy Scouts Afloat," "Banner Boy Scouts Snowbound," "Banner Boy Scouts On A Tour, or, the Mystery of Rattlesnake Mountain,"'and so on, written by George A. Warren in the early 20th century. The books are available, free, through Google, where they get four or five stars. These were the stories of the Stanhope Troop of scouts and their fascinating, to me at least, adventures, sort of the Harry Potter series of a century earlier. I would lie on my bed in an evening, fully dressed, with a couple of pillows stuffed under my head to prop it up, and refuse to stop reading no matter how sleepy I got. I remember my mother waking me up to get me to get ready and go to bed, this time with pajamas on.

CHAPTER 2

The Nun. Was she a demon or an angel?

THE NUNS AT St. John's I considered an odd lot. As teachers they were part of the world and took an avid interest in their pupils. But they dressed as though they were in the Middle Ages and they retired to their convent and closed world every evening, not to be seen again. Sister Hilda Marie, the disciplinarian principal, was the most fascinating of these women, and her reaction to events was unique and, to me, questionable.

In one instance, girls in our class had gone to an electric cooking demonstration at West Penn, the local utility. Sister, hearing of the boys' complaints at being left out, arranged for a demo for us. We would go as a group and return to the school as a group, unchaperoned. That was the plan, but instead of returning right away, we went, as a group, to a pool parlor for a few games.

Not a trusting soul, Sister apparently called West Penn and learned the time we left. When we arrived at the school, she was waiting at the front door and briskly ordered us, "Into my office!" There, we were roughly arranged into a line facing her. The assault on our cheeks and pride occurred forthwith.

She stood before the line of us boys in her traditional nun's habit of the 1950s, black with white. Not even five feet tall. It was impossible for me to guess her weight with the flow of silky material around her, but her face was slightly cherubic, so I assumed she was a little overweight. There were crow's feet at her eyes, but they were nearly hidden by her round metal-rimmed glasses. Even the shortest of us boys towered over her.

There was no doubt in my mind that she was angry, very angry. Her dark eyes flashed. She moved slowly, with deliberation, from one of us to the next in line, barely able to reach us in order to slap us one by one across the face. When she came to me, I unwittingly reacted the way I always did when under stress, and smiled a little.

"Don't you smirk at me!" she shrieked, her anger fired up anew. She pushed up the sleeve at her right arm and slapped me so hard across the face that it brought a tear to my eye. To my relief, she then went on to the next in line.

In assessing my opinion of this nun, I weigh her harsh disciplinary actions such as this, odious and even unlawful as they would be in today's world, against her extraordinary kindnesses.

My father's abandonment of the family, a rarity at the time, would have been well-known in the parish and certainly to Sister Hilda Marie as well. It was an era before the term "single mother" was even coined. Her considerations toward me, I believe, took my disadvantages into account.

When I was 16, Sister initiated a driver education program after school, so as not to take us away from academic work. I enthusiastically signed up. However, just at the same time I got the offer of a coveted part-time job as editor of the Junior Reporter Club. The Club had a section in the Evening Standard, the local paper, where stories sent in by teenagers were published. The caveat in the job offer was that the starting time was 2:30 in the afternoon; classes at St. John's didn't end until 3:15. What to do?

Presto! My class schedule was changed overnight so that I now had a study hall at 2:15 that I was assured I could miss. How did the principal even know of this impending job? Then another presto! The driver education classes were switched to the lunch hour, and I could take them.

These things made possible by the nun who had accused me of smirking at her, and slapped my face.

When one day I arrived at school without having had breakfast, Sister Hilda Marie had me pulled out of class and sent to the convent for breakfast. It was uncanny. She knew everything!

My sister complained to my mother that classmates would comment on her clothing. Unable to afford to dress Pat the equal of her more affluent classmates at St. John's, my mother withdrew her from St. John's in favor of South Union High, to the chagrin of Sister Hilda Marie, who no doubt told Father Dunn. The pastor contacted my mother and demanded to know why. The following school term and thereafter, the girls at St. John's were provided uniforms. I absorb a morsel of learning from Father Dunn's example here.

The most serious event affecting my opinion of this nun occurred just before graduation. About eight or 10 of us boys one lunch hour discovered that a school window was left unlocked while the nuns were at the convent for lunch.

We poured through the window, roared up and down hallways, went through costumes behind the stage, even examined the principal's office and desk. Indeed, we turned ourselves into juvenile delinquents that day.

It did not take Sister Hilda Marie 30 seconds to discover the breach, and the guilty, and to devise a severe punishment not just for us boys but for the entire class. She announced the cancellation of the graduation awards ceremony in the school auditorium, a once-in-a-lifetime event. Only the proffering of diplomas in the church by Father Dunn would proceed. It took me years to appreciate the lesson this nun taught us that day: serious wrongdoing earns serious consequences.

At our 25th reunion, I tried to thank my former principal for the consideration she had shown me so often. She claimed not to remember, although she knew me at once and asked about Patricia by name. She was sitting on a sofa with another nun and seemed uncomfortable at my praise. She squirmed in her seat, and looked away from me, her gaze dropping to the floor. It seemed that I had offended her. She gave me no license to continue. I had wanted to explain that her strict discipline made me aware of the fruits of bad behavior better than any other lesson in my life, that her severe punishment at graduation was merited. But I didn't have the chance.

Then I remembered something. I recalled the daily prayer of her order that I had heard the nuns recite in the church: "We commit ourselves to living in the most sincere, true, and profound humility..."

Was this nun a demon or an angel? I have come to a conclusion.

Dear Sister Hilda Marie,

I bring forgiveness, and also thankfulness. I tried to thank you at our 25th class reunion, but your vow of humility got in the way.

My forgiveness? It seems misplaced, given your considerations of me, to question the severity of your discipline. However, I believe that slapping teenaged boys across the face was improper, even in 1952. We were humiliated, and, terrible as it may seem, maybe that was your intention. I hate to think that you got satisfaction from mortifying us.

When a group of us boys entered the empty school, roared down corridors, and even dared to examine your desk, we did earn sharp punishment. You found a doozy. You denied us the awards ceremony at graduation. After

that, it took me a while to think kindly of you. As I matured, I realized we got precisely the punishment that would teach us a lesson. So, of course, I forgive you.

I forgive you for the unpleasantness I felt in just seeing you in a corridor. You were a disciplinarian to the point of always appearing cross. I don't know that was necessary, Sister. A smile now and then would have been nice.

Let's turn the page. I want to thank you for the considerations you gave me, no doubt because of the disappearance of my father. You had unbendable rules, so it must have been painful to tweak them for me. Also, I want to thank you for the girls in future classes who could not afford to compete with the attire of classmates. When you heard about my sister's problem with this, you and Father Dunn began providing uniforms. How understanding of you.

At the class reunion when I wanted to thank you, what I really wanted to do is grab you and give you a big hug. I was grateful and wanted to show it. But what would be your reaction to a hug, when you were always so cold? I would still like to try.

Sister, it seems that the items I recall to thank you far exceed those to forgive you for. So let's call this writing a letter of thankfulness.

Sister Hilda Marie, thank you!
Yours respectfully,
Your student 1948-1952,
Vincent Burke

There was another nun who through my high school years I pitied. Her problem was that she could not control a class. Perhaps I could have helped her by speaking up for her to classmates, but I did not. Sister Rose Marie was short, a little overweight, wore wire-rimmed glasses, attired in the nun's habit of that period. She taught math and frequently oversaw a study hall. The pupils in her classes went wild, shouting across the room to classmates, dropping books on the floor. She could do nothing about our shenanigans, although she tried and tried, by scolding and then by pleading. Occasionally the principal, Sister Hilda Marie, would burst into the classroom to establish calm. The moment she entered, the room went silent. Sister would march quickly to the head of the class, and with her arms folded, face us without uttering a word. Her dark eyes would travel across the rows of pupils, stopping occasionally for a second on a known troublemaker, who would squirm in his seat. Then, still without a word, she would head toward the door. Invariably on her way she would give Sister Rose Marie a piercing dark look. I cannot figure what there was about the demeanor, or appearance, of this pitiful nun that encouraged our crude behavior. I thought she seemed like a particularly kind woman. But I remained silent in my sorrow for this nun, and did nothing to assist her. Since she could not control teenagers, why on earth wasn't she assigned to teach the 1st, 2nd, or 3rd grade? My non-support is not a plus in the rating of my life. And a lesson is here for me: rise above peer pressure when you're in the right, or live with regret forever for not doing so.

Lash, the coach, a large, burly man who, as I said, also taught history, was at the opposite extreme. Any boy — never a girl — who misbehaved in history class was directed to come to the front of the room and told to, "Assume the position!" The position was assumed by leaning with the reluctant boy's hands on Lash's desk, with his derrière accessible. This large man would then, with considerable force, whack you one time on the behind with a wooden paddle he kept next to the desk. The whacked student would then return to his seat smiling, so as not to reveal that the whack was anything but a love tap. I never was told to assume the position. The unlucky recipients of the coach-history teacher's largesse were always the boys he coached on the basketball team. Out of class, they joked about the bruising, and it did not affect the high regard in which they held this man. Can you imagine this kind of punishment in the 21st century?

Next to the high school and now the site of the church parking lot was a large white Victorian house with a wraparound porch, which was the convent before a new one was built. It was rented by my Uncle Dave, my father's brother, for his family. Hordes of people would assemble here after Christmas Eve midnight mass to gorge on my Aunt Ann's buffet while we kids played under the tree with the Lionel train, with its coal loader and electric crossing gates.

My Uncle Dave and Aunt Ann had only boys, five of them. It was a family I envied, with a mother, and a father. The big house was always noisy, even chaotic, with shouts and laughter everywhere. After high school, I never saw my five cousins again, although I did see Uncle Dave and Aunt Ann at a funeral. Bobby, in my class, died in his 30s from cancer. Regis, the oldest, died in his 20s in an auto accident. Pat, a year older than me, I heard, had a career on Wall Street and was living in Connecticut. A banker, stock broker? No idea. Mickey had a car dealership. I'm not sure what happened to Jack, the youngest. I think I heard that Aunt Ann ended up living with him out west someplace. Maybe Arizona.

After my father left, we were not as close with his many siblings. My mother had wondered whether it was because the family did not want to be reminded of their brother's absence, or maybe his abandonment of his family. Theirs was a respectable Irish family, and, I regret to say it, my father was the "Black Sheep."

Before leaving Jefferson Street to continue the tour, I made a quick climb up to the gallery of the church to relive the view I had from there of weddings, of funerals, of First Communions, during the years I was a choir boy. Mrs. Mason, the organist, was ancient, probably about 70, and no doubt is long gone. She used to sing the responses at weekday high masses, a kindness given to Mrs. Mason but not so kind for parishioners. I shouldn't have said that. She seemed like a nice lady.

Now we are driving up Church Street past the Herald Standard. Almost seventy years ago when I worked there after school, it was the Evening Standard and the Morning Herald. First I was a paperboy. I won a maroon Roadmaster bike selling subscriptions, then a trip to Pittsburgh to see the Pirates play baseball, and a banquet after at the William Penn Hotel, and, of course, the trip to New York. The last two years of high school I edited the page called the Junior Reporter Club from the offices there. As I said, high school students would send in news of their schools to be printed in the Standard. When submissions were scarce, I would fill in by writing fictional short stories. I don't recall whether I used my name or made up a name, a nom de plume. In any case, I never achieved fame. My name's not unique enough for celebrity. Mark Twain may never have made it if he had been called John Doe or Samuel Clemens.

This little Junior Reporter Club introduction to journalism would take me to a Cleveland newspaper when I left Uniontown after high school, and then to a job as a reporter. And after, when the paper closed, to New York and advertising copywriting.

Also part of my job was assisting at the Junior Reporter Club teenage dances held in various nearby towns every two weeks. Being a young employee, my responsibility was to run the coat-check room. I still remember my interior panic when a man presented a claim check for which I could find no corresponding garment. A search by me, my boss, and his assistant turned up nothing. We eventually packed up and left as usual. I have no idea of the denouement of the lost garment situation, whether my boss compensated the man for it, because my boss said not one word to me about it, ever.

JUNIOR *The* REPORTER — CLUB —

Registered U. S.
Patent Office

THE JUNIOR REPORTER CLUB

A National Newspaper Feature
Registered U.S. Patent Office

More than 32,000 enrolled members in
Uniontown district

Designed to promote more interest in
Journalism and Reporting among active young Americans everywhere.

Don C. Hayman .... Club Editor
Bernard Andrews .... Associate
Vincent Burke .... Secretary

TIME IS AN IMPORTANT ELEMENT

When writing your column for the Junior Reporter section, time plays an important role. Many times some of the best reporters fail to take this into consideration.

For example, if you're writing about a birthday party that you attended yesterday, never put that you enjoyed the birthday party that you were at yesterday.

When your column is printed, it will no longer be yesterday. A word such as recently would do for anytime within the next couple of weeks.

THERE WILL BE a rather small high school section on Monday. By the way, after next week there will be no more high school sections until schools reopen in September.

JOE FUDALA AND his orchestra will be featured at the Junior Reporter Club dance at the Ivory next Tuesday evening. If you were one of the ones who attended last Tuesday's J. R. C. dance we know you won't want to miss this one.

WE'RE TRYING TO have an

MY TRIP TO THE MOUNTAINS

by JOAN McGALLA
Uniontown

Last Sunday afternoon my father took my mother, sister, and I up to the mountains. While there we stopped at the museum at Fort Necessity.

There we saw many things of interest such as the bullet that General Washington used and the bedroom that Washington slept in.

We even saw the flag that had only 45 stars in it. There were also French and English flags there. We all enjoyed going up in the mountains and visiting the museum at the fort.

THIS WEEK'S NEW MEMBERS

The boys and girls whose names appear in the list below have joined the Junior Reporter Club within the past week. They have already received their Press Cards and Club Pins.

We wish to welcome them to the Junior Reporter Club and we hope they enjoy being members. When they have a total of ten stories sent in, they will be eligible to become star reporters.

NORMAN McCULLOUGH ......
.... Uniontown
ALBERT OHLER ..... Leckrone
SYLVIA GRANGER ....
.... Conellsville
JUDITH GRAY ...... Uniontown
NORMA BRYNER .. Uniontown

SPRING

by GREGORY RICHTER
McClellandtown

The cold winter is now past,

BOY SCOUT NEWS
By ROBERT PIKULSKY
Footedale

There is an organization of B Scouts in New Salem. The sco master is Mr. Rogers. We ha quite a few troops. The boys Footedale have a troop call "The Wolf Troop."

It consists of about nine bo They are: Donald Harshman, Jo Brinza, Charles Froncek, Jan Kovatch, Francis Timpa, Thom Solarsick, Richard Crouse, B Froncek and myself.

Our meetings are held und the New Salem public school. have a lot of fun there. We p games, have hikes and parties.

Not many boys have their B Scout suits. When we get th we will be able to go camping, in parades, go on hikes and ma other things. We are plannin trip to Conastoga, Pa., soon.

Mr. Rogers said that the Scouts of Footedale and New em are going on a hike. Our thers will go with us because for fathers on Father's Day.

We all enjoy all the activ offered us in the Boy Scouts, we think that all boys should

Fuzzy self-portrait. Isn't it the thought that counts?

After the dances, I would look forward to returning to Uniontown, as the boss always took the assistant and me to an Italian restaurant, the Venetian, for—what—a late late dinner, a just-before-midnight dinner? It seems there must have been an arrangement regarding the serving hour. My boss made me the center of attention, even though his young assistant was always with us at those dinners. The conversation dwelled on whatever subject I chose to bring up. I've always managed to eat no matter the hour. The first dinner there was also the first time I had ever been in a restaurant. I liked it! I always ordered ravioli. To this day, that is what I always order in an Italian restaurant.

For a reason that will be clear later on, I am not going to call my boss by his correct name. From now on in this book, I will call him 'Robert." Robert was a single man about 40, I would say ordinary-looking, a little pudgy. Always pleasant; I never saw him angry. He wore a double-breasted suit at all times, which probably made him look a little heavier than being just a few pounds overweight, as he was. He was never seen without a white shirt and tie. He drove a really snappy cream-colored DeSoto with a chocolate stripe down the side. White walls, white leather seats. Robert's assistant, a young man about 20, was permitted to drive it at times. I yearned to, but I didn't even have a license yet. Even given the opportunity, I may have been afraid to; the cream DeSoto was so splendid and so expensive.

After driving by the Herald Standard, Frank and I pass the school-yard where, in April, 1951, I stood with a crowd to hear loudspeakers broadcast General MacArthur's farewell address "Old soldiers never die, they just fade away..."

Around the corner, to West Main, and the building that was Liggett's Drugstore. The Manos Theater was on that now empty lot next door. The whole town would crowd into these one or two blocks on Saturday night, would congregate two, three or four people deep on the sidewalk, to observe and meet friends. It was like an Italian passeggiata!

The crowds are gone now, there is barely a passerby. Kaufman's Department Store, where I rode my first escalator, closed generations ago. Wright-Metzler, where from the sidewalk I watched my first TV in the store window, has gone missing. Stores are empty. A thrift shop has moved in. A pocket park replaced Murphy's 5&!0. Over there is the building where Dr. Kaplan, my dentist, had his office. He can't still be there after 70 years, but really it seems like it was yesterday.

West Main Street in Uniontown. The State Theater, which was my favorite, is in the foreground on the right.

CHAPTER 3

The Assault.
A father figure?

ON THE CORNER of Pittsburgh Street is a tall yellow brick building, the tallest in Uniontown. It is where one of the most confusing episodes of my teenage years happened, that I continued to go over in my mind years after.

One afternoon not long after I got the Junior Reporter Club job, Robert (my boss) asked me to accompany him on foot to his apartment, to carry some items for him. He pointed to a pile of about a dozen file folders. As we set out walking, I noted that he was not carrying anything. I wondered why he needed me to carry such a light load. Certainly a mature man would have no difficulty.

I was surprised when we entered the Fayette Title and Trust building, the yellow brick building. I had no idea where Robert lived, but I would never have guessed this building. I had thought it was exclusively commercial. I was

On the 10th floor of this yellow brick. building occurred the event I would not soon forget.

familiar with it. I had taken an evening class in an office here.

As home delivery manager, one of Robert's responsibilities was to supervise the paperboys, and he also managed certain promotional elements of the Standard, including the Junior Reporter Club. When he needed to fill a vacancy for editor of the Club, he offered the job to me, at the young age of 16. I accepted eagerly. Actually, as it turned out, the masthead of the Club's page in the paper listed Robert as editor, although I was totally in charge and he involved himself little. Nonetheless, my name never replaced Robert's as editor. The masthead also listed his assistant, even though his only job was to manage the paperboys. I was listed as "secretary." I don't remember that it bothered me much, or at all, because I enjoyed being given full authority. Even if it did, I was hardly at an age to challenge an adult.

But there was a stipulation before I took the job: I needed to learn to type. I went to typing classes on the fifth floor of this building. I never had occasion to go to the upper floors, so I was unaware they were residential and surprised that Robert lived there.

We take an elevator to the 10th floor, Robert unlocks a door off the wide corridor, and he ushers me into the living room of an apartment, his, furnished in various shades of grey in a contemporary style that today we would call retro. I place my file folders on an end table and prepare to leave.

Robert will have none of it. "Come look at the view," he tells me. I go to the window where he is standing and look out west over Uniontown. The view was sensational. I had never seen Uniontown like this before. When I was in New York on the paperboy trip, we had gone to the Empire State Building. That was spectacular, but that was New York. Here I am looking at places I know, but in miniature.

Robert asks if I would like a pop. I decline, not ordinary for me. I somehow feel an urge to leave, and I say I should get back to my work.

He tells me to stay a while, and rather guides me to the sofa. We both sit down simultaneously side-by-side, me being lowered by a gentle push. It flashes through my mind that he has something serious about my job to talk to me about.

Then, without a word, he leans over and he kisses me. A passionate kiss.

I am stunned, and I am repelled. The kiss is right on my lips and he holds it for a few seconds. I find it disgusting; I had never been kissed on the lips before. By anyone.

I am also confused. Why did he do that? It was...icky. What to do? I liked this man. I did not much remember my father, and this man was kind to me, asked about my school, about my mother, was interested in things I was doing. He had chosen me out of all the paperboys for the job that anyone would want.

But this is — unpleasant. I leave no time pass. Immediately when he withdraws, I jump up from the sofa, blurt out that I have to go, and head straight to the door. He has barely time to get up from the sofa, but no time to react or say anything before I open the door and am out in the corridor.

I don't remember taking the elevator down, nor do I remember the walk back to the Standard. Robert must have timed how long it would take me to get there. A minute after I got in, I got a phone call from him, announcing a raise. Not at all necessary, I thought. I was over his action already. Or getting over it.

He made no mention in the call of what had just happened. I took the raise, not questioning the reason for it or the timing. It did not occur to me that the raise was to buy my silence. He had tried to take advantage of my youth or my position as an employee — but failed. I had been shocked and disturbed at the moment, but I can't say really offended. I would never have termed the encounter an assault, although that's surely what it would be called today.

Eroticism, sex, was not foreign to me. With a cousin, I had already had certain episodes, not uncommon with teenage boys. However, in my case I wasn't after just release. I sought friendship, or maybe it was intimacy, with another boy. I did not equate this occurrence with Robert at all with the incidents with someone my own age. Robert was old.

It is true that I never told a soul what had happened with Robert, or almost happened. I didn't say a word to my cousin who I was continuing to see. That fact alone, I know today, meant that I probably felt shame or embarrassment. It is certain that I would have become the celebrity of the hour if I had shared the story of that afternoon with my basketball lunch group at school. Although I was always seeking their attention, I resisted.

The next day at work when I saw Robert, I, as a teenager using my vast knowledge of psychology, detected in him an effort to be friendlier than normal, to be all smiles. I made an effort to act as usual but to stick to business, and that was the end of the matter, at least so far as Robert ever again making an approach. However, I was wary of Robert from then on, even though everything seemingly returned to normal at work. I remained at the Standard for two more years, until I graduated high school and went to Cleveland.

I don't use Robert's real name in this book, even after more than 70 years since the event. First, he is certainly dead, and it would be unjust to tarnish his name when he cannot defend himself. Also, I found him amiable, he treated me well, and I liked him. And I was not offended then and can't convince myself to be offended today. So he tried and failed. My attitude is—so what?

I have thought about this would-be sexual assault of a minor through the years, especially in recent times when so much publicity has been given to such actions against both young boys and young girls and women. I had just turned 16 at the time, Robert was at least 40. By treating me well, he had won my favor. A classic example of an older person preying on a younger person. But his attempt was unsuccessful because I was strong and removed myself from the situation. Even though teens seem mature today, was I stronger than most victims because I had no father and was therefore somewhat independent? Was I stronger because, contrary to many of today's teens, my mother was not in a position to give me any luxuries, so I took responsibility and earned everything I needed myself? Did my schooling, which was not light on discipline, have an influence? Was I better prepared to confront an effort at assault?

Is my father, his abandonment, the cause of this advance? Is he to blame? Was I so desperate for a father-figure that I transmitted the wrong signals, signals that were interpreted by Robert as availability?

I realize now that my failure to make a fuss over the encounter with Robert may have encouraged another assault a few months later —by a friend of his. This man, about 30, from Pittsburgh, was visiting Robert, and Robert invited him to accompany us to the bi-weekly Junior Reporter Club dance in a town a dozen miles away. En route to the dance, Robert and his friend sat in the back of the car, and I was in the front passenger seat, with Robert's assistant driving.

I don't know how the change in seating occurred. On the return to Uniontown, I found myself in the back seat with Robert's friend, Robert having taken the front passenger seat. The friend began groping me almost immediately upon us leaving for home and evidently without any fear that I would object noisily or violently. I did not, although I seethed in anger internally at the man's presumptuousness and audacity. I assume that I felt that any loud objection on my part would not be received sympathetically by Robert. In fact he probably had conspired in arranging the seating. I was a gift for Robert's guest. And, even though feeling uncomfortable, my silence made me a consenting gift.

My failure to say anything to anyone in authority regarding this assault and the earlier attempted one by Robert has to go down as a serious fault in my ranking of my life. By my silence, I gave these two men the belief that they could approach a 16-year-old with no repercussions. Did my failure to make a fuss cause them to assault others my age? Were they encouraged by my nascent attraction for other males—that Robert may have perceived in me?

I soon learned that Robert branched out and had acquired a reputation for approaching teenage boys. This information came to me from the conversations of my lunch mates, none of whom volunteered that he himself had been a victim. I said nothing on their mentions of Robert's name and continued to remain silent about my experiences. I have always thought it odd that classmates never questioned me about this now infamous man, even though they were aware he was my employer and that I would be in frequent contact with him. In retrospect, it bears out my sense that I was a part of this group of boys, my lunchtime companions, but nonetheless apart. To ask me whether I had ever been approached, they may have subconsciously considered too intimate a question and beyond my standing with the group. I also wondered if they didn't ask me of any involvement with Robert because they suspected I liked boys.

I wondered, too, whether my mild or no reaction to Robert and his friend encouraged Robert's attempts with other boys. In the present day, you hear of victims of sexual abuse who have been traumatized by it, and whose entire lives are tarnished. I was not affected in such a way, but did my failure to go to authorities—or in the very least make a fuss—result in other teenaged boys being victimized and perhaps traumatized? Robert unwittingly taught me at a young age to speak up for the benefit of others who may follow.

My experience has prejudiced me in favor of empathizing with the women who have come forth in the #Metoo movement. I know precisely how an assault proceeds on vulnerable people and how silence of the victim can follow. I have been there. My compassion for victims I owe to Robert and his attempted assault, and his apparent invitation to his friend to succeed where he had failed. So to Robert: a "thank you" for my understanding of the turmoil and silence of victims. A lesson learned through you, Robert.

I add a comment here, which will annoy, even outrage, some. Much of the harm that victims suffer, I believe, is caused by society's attitude toward the assault of minors. Society expects them to be injured, so they are. Victims are told they are traumatized, so they are. Sexual abuse of minors, no doubt, always existed, but it is only in the last years that we have publicized it and shouted about it warping a person's entire life. So, to accommodate our belief, it does to victims what they and society expect. I suggest that society itself is to blame for much of the harm.

> Dear Robert,
>
> It's peculiar that I'm writing you to forgive you for your — attempted — assault when I had just turned 16. It's odd because, even though you got me to your apartment under a pretext, sat me on the sofa next to you, and kissed me passionately, I was never offended. I was stunned, and jumped up from the sofa and quickly left, but I got over my shock right away. I didn't like what you did, but I didn't consider it was wrong, or that you tried to take advantage. I didn't even think about me being a minor, or you being my boss. You had always treated me well, so I didn't give it much thought.
>
> What I can thank you for, Robert, is the experience. I know, because of your action, what an assault is, how a victim hides it even to himself, or herself. It has instilled in me an empathy for the victims coming out today.
>
> Where I do think you were way off is when you arranged to put your friend alone with me in the back seat in the trip back to Uniontown. Of course, you knew, probably intended, that he would continue the assault that you started in your apartment. That was not right of you. I was angry at your friend, but even more so at you. I was

not yours to give to your friend, and it was humiliating to be treated like that. I resented it. The next few days at work, I had to let you know I wasn't happy, by being all business, no smiles. I'm not sure you noticed. Did you know that many young people who are assaulted are not like me, and are injured for life? You could not know that I would not be one of them. What about other young boys you might have forced yourself on? Robert, you alone might be responsible for ruined lives. It's not up to me to forgive you for those.

In your defense concerning me, maybe you thought of me more as an adult, rather than a minor. Or you considered us friends, rather than you being my boss. Or maybe somehow you had an idea I'd be gay, and you were just advancing things.

Maybe these are excuses, maybe not. In any case, Robert, let's continue as the friends we were. I hold you harmless, and am willing to forgive. Except for turning me over to your friend.

Cordially,
Your former employee,
Vince

Now I take another look around West Main. Where now is the Penn Theater that showed westerns with Gene Autry and Roy Rogers, and where the drinking fountain in the lobby never worked? Ah, I still see the State Theater, my Saturday place, and where the nuns in 1945 took us, class by class, to see "The Bells of St. Mary's."

Now we drive to — The Project.

During World War II it was Pat, probably, who learned that the federal government was constructing a "project" which would be shiny spanking-new row housing. Pat probably waged a campaign to convince my mother to move us there, although my mother said in later years that she wanted to free Mr. Maruca's property so that he might get a better rent.

The Project was a mistake for us.

Initially, it seemed just fine. We were given a 2-bedroom row house at 13 Furlong Court. My mother and sister would share a room, and I would have a bedroom all to myself. Rent, $20 a month. My mother's salary at Fike's was $20 a week, so she figured it was within her means. Choice of four interior paint colors; my mother chose light green. My aunt, my father's sister, Betty, with a husband, two boys, Vincent and Bernard, and a daughter, Kathleen, were given a 3-bedroom on MacArthur Terrace. She chose buff.

It is from my bedroom window here at night that I would see the dazzling lights of the Summit Hotel at the top of the mountains, built in 1907. It was a different world from mine, a place of luxury. It had an indoor and outdoor pool, golf, a spa, four-poster beds, and a wrap-around porch overlooking Uniontown and me, far below. I also made myself aware of the comings and goings of a muscular blond boy about my age in an apartment across the parking lot, and wondered how I could meet him. Where did he go every weekend morning when he walked quickly out of the parking lot and disappeared?

I had a tiny flower garden on our small plot of land, and had beginner's luck with nasturtiums, a splash of orange blooms even when the undersides of their leaves were covered by pests called leafminers. How many teenaged boys are into flower gardens? I was strange. My interest certainly couldn't have been an attempt to impress the boy across the way. I could see from the items he often carried that he was interested in football and baseball, not nasturtiums. I didn't know until recently that the flowers and leaves are edible. Raising plants for food would have been somewhat praiseworthy.

World War II was raging in Europe and the Pacific. The husband of my mother's sister, my Aunt Bea, went into the Navy and my aunt and little cousin Maureen arrived from Youngstown. Ohio to live with us for the duration of the war. My cousin and I got along famously even though, as I pointed out when I was 12, I was double Maureen's age. We're much closer in age now. We were good on long walks, passing time in the nearby cemetery, and hiking to the extensive and magnificent grounds of Mt. St. Macrina, the location of the motherhouse of the Sisters of St. Basil, where the nuns seemed to make an effort to ignore us. In later years, I would take my cousin Vincent Cummings there. It was my place and I was eager to show it off.

Maureen would become an Ursuline nun, leave the convent in the mass exodus of the 1960s and '70s, marry, and is having a happy life with her husband, Milt. They form a couple that seems totally simpatico.

Maureen is one of two relatives I remain in touch with. Years before this tour, she knew that I am gay, and it hasn't made an iota of difference.

The other relative that I remain in contact with is Clara in Masontown, a woman half a dozen years older than I am. Her grandmother was the sister of my mother's father, my grandfather, Max Philippi. That makes her my second cousin, if I understand Google correctly. I will never tell Clara that I'm gay; I'll always keep that secret from some. Clara has told me that she is a lifelong Democrat, and that's a good sign. However, I know she is active in her (Protestant) church, and that rings warning bells. Early on, I knew that Maureen was a liberal, so I felt there would be no problem letting my secret of being gay out. No one has ever guessed that I am gay, but at my age, never having had a wife, and instead having a good "friend," maybe everyone reaches that conclusion. Maybe my secret is no longer a secret. Other relatives have appeared. I'm in contact with Michele in Italy, from the Philippi line, and Bruce, Aunt Mary's grandson, who lives outside Cleveland.

There must be quite a number of others out there somewhere. I'm not going to worry about finding them or about my lack of family ties. What's their attitude toward gay people? When you're gay, that's something you wonder about all of the time.

Frank and I continue our tour of the Project. I switch to the present tense. "The war is over," I say to Frank. "I am already on my second job." I am 13 years old as I struggle along Berkeley Street with my heavy newspapers in a canvas bag over my left shoulder, causing me to stumble from time to time and my body to droop on one side. I cup my hand under the bag to lift it a little to try to relieve the ache of the weight on my shoulder. It is Thursday afternoon, the day the Evening Standard has the most advertising and therefore weighs the most. Despite Thursdays and the heavy papers, I think back: this is so much better than my first job, delivering the Sunday Pittsburgh Press. I go over in my mind those terrible mornings, especially the bitter cold winter ones. My mother would wake me when it was still dark outside and I would have to get out of my warm bed into the chilly room. I hear her now: "Vincent, Vincent, time to get up. It'll be getting light out." While she made me hot cereal, I would bring in the bundles of papers that had been left on the stoop, and put the sections together on the living room floor. After the cereal, my mother would peck me on the cheek and I'd be off. It is just barely getting light. I'm pushing my two-wheeled cart that looks something like a big wooden box, with me holding the handles. When it had snowed, my cart and my footsteps would emit a crunching sound as they made the first tracks. I hated the snow, I hated the cold, and I hated my cart, but I had to have a cart, with so many papers and each one huge on a Sunday. It happened that I would be pushing my cart along, in the middle of my route, far from home in the Project, when a cotter pin would snap and a wheel would fall off. Then what to do? I'd take maybe five papers at a time, deliver them, and then have to keep returning to the cart for more. Someone could take some papers while I was gone, I worried. It took much longer to finish my route, going back and forth. After I was done, I would have to get the cart home, pushing it while balancing it on just the remaining wheel, and that wasn't easy. Then I'd have to go back sometime later and collect.

One cold morning I had arrived home after delivering my Sunday papers. My mother was already dressed for us to go to church, and sitting at the kitchen table with her coffee, reading the paper. I went to the closet under the stairs to put away my jacket, scarf, and gloves. "When you're finished, Vincent,' she said, "come over here. I want to talk to you."

I went over and sat down at the table opposite my mother, curious about why she wanted me. She looked at me intently, and began: "Vincent, I've been thinking. I would like you to quit your job. It's too early in the morning, it's always too cold, and your cart keeps breaking down. When Chester comes to collect the money, I want you to tell him you can do it one or two more Sundays, until he finds someone else, but then you have to quit."

I was dumbfounded. "But don't we need the money?" I interrupted. "Aren't I a help?"

"Of course you're a help, Vincent. You're a big help," she said quickly. "But we can manage. It's more important that you quit this job. Eventually, you'll get another job. There are better jobs, ones that you don't have to go out in the cold when it's barely getting light. And I think you should be able to sleep late if you want."

In less than a month, I had gotten this new job. I deliver afternoon papers, six days instead of one, but I earn more and don't have to get up when it's still dark and cold out. And I don't have to have a cart.

I am 4 feet 8, almost 6 inches less than the boys in my class, and I weigh just 85 pounds, 10 or 15 pounds lighter. Ahead, on her front porch, stands matronly Mrs. Tatum, there to offer me a peanut butter and banana sandwich. "It's a good sandwich, Vincent. Sit at the kitchen table and eat. Do you want a glass of milk?" I gladly accept the sandwich, but I can't stay, saying customers are waiting for their paper. I'm too thin, and customers are always urging me to stop to eat

*My mother, returning to the Project
from work. She's stopped for groceries.*

something. Maybe they think I'm so poor I don't get enough to eat. Maybe they know I live in the Project. A girl in my class called me skinny. I think it's supposed to be good to feed the hungry. Maybe it's in the Bible. I get plenty of food at home, but I love my customers for caring about me. If I could see any of them today, I'd tell them how much their concern warmed the heart of a skinny, 13-year-old boy.

On my route, I continue on, munching on Mrs. Tatum's sandwich. With my free hand, I smooth down the cowlick in my black hair, but it bounces right back up.

Because of my size, I suppose, people always think I'm younger than I am. Some people guess 10. No doubt because I'm small, my big paper route, and it being a Thursday, the papers are almost too heavy for me. But I whistle along the way and greet my customers by name. They all know my name, too, and call me Vincent. I'm feeling on top of the world today. I have this good job and good customers. I'm earning money. I'm helping my mother out.

Even though I'm happy with my job, I never mention a word about it at school, not even that I have a job. I don't feel that delivering papers is something to brag about, and except for Mike, who works after school for his uncle who has a bottling company, I think I am the only boy in my class with a job. At lunch with the basketball group, the boys often talk about what they had done after school. I keep quiet, reticent to say anything about my job to kids who have nothing to do after school but have fun.

My mother now has been working as a bookkeeper for nine years. But in this age, a woman earns far less than a man would. She is earning $25 a week, $450 in the equivalent of today's money, a sum that puts our family squarely in the poverty class. Luxuries do not exist. To help, Patricia, now 16, is working at a grocery store after school, and I have this paper route. I clear about $3.50 per week, or about $40 today, a big help to my mother. I am doing my duty.

I am of the opinion that, although I met many unpleasant moments as a paperboy while still young, I learned an invaluable lesson. A sense of responsibility was further reenforced in me, and a determination to see a project through to completion no matter the difficulties—to reap an eventual reward. If only all teenagers could be taught such a lesson.

In Uniontown, moving to the Project was a mistake for our family because it became so badly regarded. It achieved an atrocious reputation. Maybe it was because there were poor people there, and I think people always like to think the worst of them. If they were upstanding, they wouldn't be poor and society wouldn't have to take care of them with tax money. Maybe it was true that some of the young ladies, a small minority, were not quite ladies. So it became embarrassing to live there, and I became ashamed. My sister, tainted because of her gender, probably more than me.

I began, because of the sordid reputation the Project was getting, to tell customers on my paper route, when asked, that I lived "near the hospital." That was true, but I'm sure they guessed the precise location despite my vague response. From then on, through my entire life, location, the area, would be paramount in my thinking. I never wanted to be ashamed of where I lived again.

The Project was not at all conveniently located, except if one of us would be a patient in Uniontown Hospital, right next door. My mother had to walk nearly two miles to work, winter and summer, as there was no public transportation. Midway in her route was a patch of "company houses," owned by H.C. Frick Coal & Coke Company, a subsidiary of US Steel. These were rented just to Frick coal miners. Close by these houses, my mother would pass a large store, called the Union Supply Company store, also owned by Frick and selling groceries, clothing and everything else, chiefly to miners. Even though my mother passed right by it, my mother avoided shopping there because the prices were extremely high, much higher than in stores downtown.

Coal miners, all working for Frick in its mines nearby, charged their purchases. The company was certain to be paid, as the rent for the company house and the bill for the company store was deducted from a miner's paycheck. The life of such miners was immortalized in the song 'Sixteen Tons," by Johnny Cash: miners indebted for life to the company store.

While we lived in the Project, a model house, a small modular 3-bedroom house which was called a Gunnison Home, opened on a hill street off North Mount Vernon Avenue. We all three went to see it at a Sunday afternoon open house and loved it. We would each have our own bedroom. It was on a tree-lined street. It had doors on its closets, that the Project did not. We talked about it for days.

There was no way my mother could afford this house. It cost

almost $10,000! We were poor. But a few years later my sister and I, after I graduated high school, gathered together the down payment on a comfortable house in a Cleveland suburb where my mother lived for 50 years.

In our tour, Frank and I now go to retrace my paper route along South Mount Vernon. Not one of my customers would still be here of course, or perhaps not even be alive. Maybe an heir or two. Gone are all those people who called me The Whistler, because, as the name says, I always whistled while delivering papers. Their houses are here, but the people are not.

For a moment I am overwhelmed by a wave of loneliness. Nostalgia? A desire to return to the past that can never be?

Then, "See that yellow house on the corner over there?" I say to Frank. "That's where the guy lives—lived—who always had an excuse when I came to collect. He still owes me 50 cents, worth maybe $5 now." I'm never going to get that 50 cents. Maybe it's time to take the loss on my 1040 form.

That man's gone like everybody else. And come to think of it, what ever happened to my Roadmaster bike? To my fire truck? What about my collection of buckeyes from under the trees at Berkeley School, polished and kept in a cigar box? Where could those things have ended up? Could some kid here have them right now?

Everything in Uniontown is gone or changed.
The coal mines are exhausted.
The radiator plant went belly-up.
The stores have all moved out to the Uniontown Mall.
The movies are there too.
The Venetian restaurant is a law office.
The woods at Mount Macrina is a nursing home.
Mr. Andrews' corner grocery is empty and forlorn.
My boss's cream DeSoto is no more.

The cemetery where I roamed is all filled up.
The Junior Reporter Club was dropped years ago.
Why, even the trees in town are mostly gone.

In my tour, there was so much left only to my memory, of the place, of the events, of the people. It's as if a giant fog from space descended on Uniontown and snuffed out my places: my house, my school, Jimmy's, my Main Street. And snuffed out my relatives, my friends, my classmates, my customers...

Then the fog put down new: new stores, new parks, new roads, new library... And new people with new relatives, new friends, new classmates...

To these new people, the new people of the new Uniontown, please take care of my old Uniontown.
The memories of my youth are there.

Before we leave Uniontown, I want to go back and have Frank

The house on East Main Street where I was born. That's me in front, 87 years after.

take my photo in front of the house where I was born. First floor, second floor, I don't know. Fortunately I don't remember ever living there. Unfortunately no one ever put a plaque on the house saying I was born there: "In this house was born Vincent Burke on October 10, 1934." I suppose you have to be famous. The house is on East Main Street right next to what was once Jimmy's, our hanging-out and lunch spot. The house was ramshackle in 1934, my mother once told me, and I hate to say it but there's been no improvement. The move to Lemon Street was certainly an upgrade. Frank takes my picture in front of my birth place.

Redstone Creek still meanders behind the house and, if you're lucky, you can glimpse a rat or two sauntering along its sunny shore. (I love animals!)

My sister was born in a real hospital, St. Elizabeth's in Youngstown, Ohio. It was the Depression and jobs were scarce, so that might explain why my parents returned to Uniontown and rented this house. My father did work when they were in this house, as a local truck driver. Not bad in the Depression. Money was scarce with just about everyone so I never dared ask if my birth and another mouth to feed was greeted with unfettered joy.

CHAPTER 4

My Mother's House. Recalling the Pandemic of 1918

WE PASS THE abandoned Hatfield Ferry Power Station, approaching Masontown, the tiny town 40 miles from Pittsburgh, where my mother grew up. A few minutes later, Frank and I are standing across the street staring at the yellow two-story frame house with the double up-and-down porches, at the corner of East Church Avenue and Water Street. Inside myself, I am somewhat heartened. It still seems kept-up, and the yard is manicured, just like my mother told me it was a hundred years ago. From the size, I can see that this house would have been suitable for the large and prosperous Philippi family.

I take a photo with my phone. A young man runs across from the bottom porch and demands to know why I took that photo. I tell him my mother lived there many years ago. He shrugs and returns to his house. His house it is, not having belonged to my mother's family for 100 years.

Being on the corner, the backyard is exposed to the street. The

My mother's house, a century later.

small rustic barn is no longer there. No evidence at all that it once existed, and housed two horses and a carriage that my mother's father Max used in his little beer distributing business.

My eyes survey the backyard, a little overgrown now and no longer as my mother told me. The large elm is gone and an oak, I think, has taken its place. I can see my mother as a young girl and her young siblings, two boys and two girls, running along the well-marked paths past their mother's precious flower beds, zinnias in a bed in the sun, impatiens in the shade. I can hear the children's shrieks of merriment.

The kitchen door opens. Mary Philippi, their mother, comes out on the stoop. She had come to America from Hungary as a widow with her young daughter, my mother's older half-sister, Mary. She calls the children in for dinner, for the second time. Reluctantly, they acquiesce.

I recall the detailed words of my mother about holiday dinners in the dining room of this house. Being immigrants, her mother and father treasured American holidays, above all Thanksgiving. My mother's half-sister Mary assisted her mother in food preparation. All nearby relatives were invited, including, of course, Max's brother, Nicole, who had emigrated at about the same time. Before departing from Trento, the two brothers had stood on the steps of the cathedral joyously bestowing a hat from Nicole's haberdashery to any passerby.

As I stand here, I can see my mother, Elizabeth, as a teenager now, arriving home from the nearby library with Sabrina, her sister two years younger, both carrying books in their arms against their bodies, like girls always did before backpacks. They step onto the front porch, lost to themselves in conversation. Their parents, Max and Mary, sitting together and gently swaying back and forth on the glider, greet them. Mary, the older half-sister, sitting in a green metal chair, nods. Elizabeth is distracted and locks across the street to the elegant Roch house. She is being called by Camilla, her best friend.

Those were the good years for the parents and their children. Then there was World War I and its victorious end simultaneous with the flu pandemic that was ravaging the world. My mother's older sister and younger brother came down with it, and after a week of worry were out of the woods. The Connors two doors down were not so fortunate: Mrs. Connor had died and the many children were being distributed among relatives. The two boys were already in Pittsburgh. 1918 ended with sorrow and relief in the Philippi house. Neighbors had died; the Philippi family had gotten through the resurgence in the fall. All had survived.

But fate had yet an evil design for this presumptuous family. Hardly had 1919 dawned that Mary the mother developed a fever and a weakness. It could only be one thing. The doctor could do nothing. In a short two days, Mary Philippi was gone.

"Mary now lies in All Saints Cemetery just down the street, next to Max, who joined her 18 years later."

I see from our position on the corner the bay windows of the front parlor where she was laid out, the front door where the funeral wreath was mounted, and I imagine the relatives and friends in black speaking in hushed tones on the front porch. Mary now lies in All Saints Cemetery just down the street, next to Max, who joined her 18 years later.

Her daughter, Mary, would take care of the young children and the family. Max would continue the beer distributing business, in time living alone. Again in my mind, I see my future father nervously ringing the front doorbell to meet with him to ask to marry his daughter.

Based on my mother's recollection, I see the house after the mother's death. The house has begun to deteriorate. There is peeling paint. It's summer, yet the porch furniture has not been put out. The flowerbeds in the backyard are now nothing but weeds. A mother has been missing for five years, and with her has gone the heart of the family.

Eventually all of the children will marry, have their own children, and lead good lives. They have all passed away now, as have most of their children.

Their house on the corner that has seen so much is now with new people, who have never heard of the family of a century ago.

In talking with Frank, I now revert to the Junior Reporter Club and the period after the assault. Robert and I treated each other as friends for the rest of my time with the Junior Reporter Club, without a mention of the afternoon he took me to his apartment. I tried to act as though nothing had happened. I perceived that he tried to be extra nice to me. He was all smiles. But maybe that's my imagination. In any case, when I graduated from high school, I was off to Cleveland where we had relatives, determining that Uniontown was not the place to start a future. I never saw Robert again.

CHAPTER 5

Aunt Mary.
The purple liquid.

CLEVELAND WAS A dynamic city when I got off the bus at the Greyhound station on Payne Avenue in June, 1952. It was a shock and fascination to me after my town of 20,000. Its population then was 915,000, making it the country's 7th largest city. Now it's 390,000, the 45th city. As many Rust Belt cities, Cleveland lost manufacturing to foreign competition, the steel industry in particular.

My cousin Eddie was waiting for me and stood on the side while I collected my hard suitcase with my two pairs of trousers, a few shirts, briefs, t-shirts, socks. I had packed my interview-for-a-job pants, a dark green ribbed fabric, and chinos for scuffing around, light tan of a thin fabric with about a six-inch-long belt of the same fabric attached on the back, just above the buttocks, serving no purpose at all but to assure me I was cool and in on the latest fad.

I hardly knew Eddie. I had met him once when for a summer

vacation my mother saw me off in Uniontown on a bus to Medina, Ohio, near Cleveland, where my mother's sister, my Aunt Emma, and Uncle Tom had a farm. Jimmy, an older cousin, taught me the art of milking, but only after I suffered the indignity of being squirted in the face by an udder aimed at me. I returned home with a practical gift for my mother, a clothes basket, but not practical to carry onto a bus. It was worth the effort. My mother was overwhelmed, and said it was the best clothes basket she had ever seen.

When Eddie met me at the bus station, he was 24, married, a father, a fireman, and city-wise. He was tall with a handsome face, voluminous sandy hair and sharp blue eyes, and, in my estimation, sophisticated. I was impressed by my cousin Eddie. I was still 17, from a small town, small and still developing physically.

Seventeen years old, but probably looking a little younger because I was a slow grower. I had felt intimidated by the big lads in my high school class who were already a head taller than I was. This feeling of size inferiority followed me to Ohio. I remember a few months later being in Taylor's Department Store and hearing a young man order pants with a 32-inch waist. How I envied him! I was just 28 inches. But in time I would have my sweet revenge: I would be ordering pants with a 36-inch waist. Onward to 38 inches? I hope not.

I was eager to leave the bus station with Eddie and get a glimpse of The City on the way to his mother's apartment, where I was to stay a while. We drove past the Terminal Tower on Public Square, then the tallest building in the world outside of New York. I knew all of the statistics before Eddie could inform me, having read about the city voraciously while still in Uniontown. I could find only a small map in an encyclopedia at the library, but used a magnifying glass to study every detail and memorize the layout of the major streets. So, I was familiar with the Shoreway when we entered it and knew we were headed to the West Side. Eddie stopped briefly at Edgewater Park to show me a view across the water to downtown.

My Aunt Mary, a widow whose married name was Bluell, occupied one of perhaps 500 apartments in a two-story building arranged in a large square that enclosed a park-like area in the center for residents. I told Eddie that there weren't this many apartments in all of Uniontown, maybe not in all of Fayette County.

Aunt Mary realized I must be hungry after my long trip. It took eight or nine hours with the connection in Pittsburgh. She assured me that dinner would be ready in just a few minutes, and that I should seat myself at the table. I waited patiently, sitting at the dark walnut Duncan Phyfe table in the corner of the bright living room. I assumed that Eddie would be eating with us rather than returning to his own family right away, because the table was set with three rose-colored placemats and three white cloth napkins. The only silverware was a single silver spoon on each placemat. There were no glasses or dishes. Eddie then sat down, too. I heard the buzz of a small motor from the kitchen, which I learned later was from a food processor. "Ah, it's coming," Eddie said.

Aunt Mary

Aunt Mary, smiling, exited the kitchen and came toward us carrying on a silver tray three tall glasses containing a purple liquid. One she placed in front of me, one in front of Eddie, and the last one at her place at the table. She then sat down and began to educate me on nutrition and the benefit of getting all your recommended vegetables in a single glass that takes just minutes to prepare and minutes to consume. "You don't have to waste your precious time at a dinner table," she exalted. "We'll be up from the table in a few minutes." I didn't think of labels at the time, but I suppose Aunt Mary was a vegetarian. Actually, I was a vegetarian, too, during the time I lived in her apartment. My memory is that every meal came in a glass, with variety being the different colors of the contents. My recollection is that it all tasted pretty much the same, no matter the color. But on Friday nights, when Aunt Mary was paid, there was the blue and white box with pastries from Hough Bakery!

On the other hand, I recall that, in the years to come, Aunt Mary ate absolutely everything offered when my mother would have her in for Sunday dinner: meat, potatoes, vegetable, dessert. And nothing was in a glass but wine. So if she was a vegetarian, she was polite enough not to insult her hostess by refusing offered fare.

There were little problems for me at Aunt Mary's, which I deemed at that age a crisis, but now realize they were practically nothing. As my mother learned when she was a child and Aunt Mary took over the household, she was an exacting woman. "Vincent, don't put your damp jacket on the chair. Hang it up, dear!" "No, Vincent, not in the living room closet. On a doorknob." "No, Vincent, dear, maybe it'd be better in the bedroom closet. There's room." "No, Vincent, don't you see there's an empty space on the left? Where's your mind, dear? You'll get everything wet!" I became sensitive to Aunt Mary's close scrutiny of me, and thought of renting a room someplace—but this was a strange, big city, and I was fearful of going off on my own. In any case, time, and my mother, sister and I moving into our own place, took care of my "crisis."

I would become fond of Aunt Mary for the affection she showed my mother, Pat, and me, but especially for the interesting idiosyncrasies that governed her life. What I learned about myself was that I appreciated people who were different and unique, even a little weird.

As I mentioned earlier, Aunt Mary was my mother's half-sister, born in Hungary, and was roughly ten years older than the other children in the family. She came to this country with her mother, my grandmother, when her father died. Here in the US, my grandmother and grandfather met and had five children together, with Mary being a sixth child, the half-sister to her siblings.

When my grandmother, Mary Philippi, died in 1919 during the

flu pandemic, Aunt Mary, being considerably older than the other children, assumed the role of housemistress—with a vengeance. She turned into a despot, desperate to fulfill a responsibility thrust upon her. The house must be perfect, everything cleaned and polished every week. Floors, furniture, silver, Saturdays and weekdays after school. No one was exempted. Entertainment, "fun," was unnecessary. It was this unpleasant home environment, my mother said, that made her want to get out of the house, and brought her to an early marriage at age 17.

But all this had been long-forgotten when I arrived at Aunt Mary's. I saw an elegant woman in her mid-50s, thin, and tall for that period. At my young age, I considered her old. She already had a few grey hairs visible in the waves of her coiffure. She often, but not all of the time, wore metal-rimmed glasses, usually resting on the end of her nose. I would call them "granny glasses," and to me she looked the part. When I arrived at her apartment, she was long past the responsibility of organizing a household and overseeing five young children. To me, she was a sweet, elderly lady who spent all of her time making certain guests were comfortable and had whatever we could possibly want, except solid food, of course.

As many women during World War II, Aunt Mary took a job on an assembly line. Hers was at Thompson Products, where war products were manufactured. She would never disclose precisely what her job was. When asked, she flipped her hand in the air and mumbled, "Oh, it's just nothing." But she admitted the money was good, and she kept this job far beyond the war years. She lived on the West Side of Cleveland, and her work was deep into the East Side. So she had to take two buses, with a change downtown where she would wait in a partially-open bus shelter, in a city known for winter cold and wind. The journey would consume an hour in each direction.

Aunt Mary had a solution for her exposure to zero weather and piercing winds. She bought an expensive ankle-length lamb fur coat. She made a fine picture: black fur from her neck to her feet, black boots, a long black fake-fur scarf wrapped around her head and ears. When my mother joked with her about her extravagance of a fur coat, she became serious: "A woman has to think of her health, doesn't she?"

She saved her "good money" from her factory job and fulfilled her dream of owning her own little house in Florida where she could tend a garden. She died there just a few years later in her house in Port St. Lucie. Much too early, I thought. Eddie was her heir. She was buried in Masontown next to her Hungarian mother, Mary, and her Italian stepfather, Max.

Aunt Mary died too young.

I had a lot on my plate when I arrived at Aunt Mary's, goals that I wanted to accomplish before the arrival of my mother and sister in Cleveland. The whole family was taking up lock, stock and barrel and moving to another state, getting new jobs, and changing lifestyle. The plan was for my mother and Pat to come here on their vacations and get jobs. My mother would then return to Uniontown for a week or so and have us moved. I felt it was my responsibility to be employed before they got here. I had also investigated evening classes at Cleveland College downtown, but the next term wouldn't begin until September, almost three months away.

My first days searching for work were disheartening and, really, a little humiliating. At the Evening Standard in Uniontown, I had earned a modicum of respect during my almost two years as editor of the Junior Reporter Club. I felt important in Uniontown. So I started applying at nothing less than the major newspapers—

My high school graduation picture. I was just short of 18.

there were three of them—for a job doing what? I had no idea. A star reporter, a columnist, an editor?

At the Cleveland Press, the muck-raking paper that had the largest daily circulation, I applied to the assistant city editor who minced no words. "You start out at the Press as a copy boy, and for that you must have a college degree. Come back when you get out of college!" I was roughly advised. (Newspapermen can be hard people.)

At the Plain Dealer, a more refined paper, with a large morning circulation and the only Sunday issue, I was received more gently but told that there, too, one begins as a copy boy, and that the paper used students from area colleges. My interviewer suggested I try the News, the Plain Dealer's sister paper with afternoon editions.

I got the job at the News and I was happy to become a copy boy.

Quite content, was I, to respond to a shout of "Boy!" from an editor, a writer, or a reporter who wanted a piece of copy delivered, an old news article on file in the morgue, or most any other service desired. I must say that a copy boy essentially is a servant to all the editorial employees with a higher status—and that's everyone. The job gets its name from delivering copy, the typewritten sheets of paper containing stories that will appear in the paper. Generally a reporter will shout "Boy!," you go to him, and deliver his copy to City Desk where it may be edited. It has several stops after that until you are inserting it into a pneumatic tube to shoot it to the composing room to be set in type. Besides delivering copy, a copy boy will bring the latest editions of the paper from the press room where it is printed to the City Desk, and will exit the building to go to the rival paper's press room, in a two-way courteous arrangement, for copies of its latest edition. Sometimes you will even, grudgingly, go for a coffee for someone. Name the task, and I suppose it would fall under the job description of a copy boy. Surprisingly, the copy boys at the News could not claim "I don't get any respect," as comedian Rodney Dangerfield did. Even though we would hurry over when hearing a shout, without a single exception I can say that when I was a copy boy, I was treated politely, often warmly. At the News, some reporters were hired as journalists directly out of college, some came from smaller newspapers, but a good number started out as copy boys themselves. That gave reporters an empathy for the beginning job and brought on courtesy. Worth knowing, a copy "boy" is often a girl.

I remember precisely my weekly salary: $32.50. The base salary for a cub reporter was $125. $32.50 provided everything I needed. I could give my mother board, have a dollar or two for a restaurant once a week, 50 cents for a movie if I wanted, save some...

I don't know whether I came close to being fired after a few months at the newspaper. In my new job, I was replacing a copy boy who was being promoted to be a police reporter. When I started, he came to me and suggested I take over a little task he had been doing. He was the copy boy who would go to City Hall twice weekly and collect the list of vital statistics prepared for the press: births, marriages, deaths. This list would be published in the next day's afternoon run. But on the way back to the News, he would stop at a small advertising company downtown, where someone would copy the list, and once a week give him $20. $20 was good pay when you were earning just $32.50.

I eagerly accepted the assignment and did this for a few months. One day the city editor called me to his desk by my first name. (I was surprised he used anything but "Boy.") He asked me point blank whether I was selling the "vitals" to an advertising company. I readily admitted my role, and squealed its history: that I had inherited the job. He ordered me to stop, and explained that there were complaints that one company was getting the jump on others by getting the vital statistics before their official release. I, of course, ceased, and nothing more was ever said about it.

I always suspected that the copy boy-now police reporter who bequeathed the $20 job to me was getting probably another $20 a week for finding me as his replacement. He was not the type to relinquish such a plum. I got a glimpse into his ethical standards later when, as a fellow police reporter, I loaned him $1.00. One dollar had a value of $10 or $15 today. Upon taking the $1 bill, he immediately said that would be the last time I would see that dollar. He was true to his word.

Cleveland College on Public Square in about 1952, when I attended my first classes.

CHAPTER 6

Am I, or Am I Not?

THE PLAN TO move the family to Cleveland went into operation. My mother and sister arrived on their vacations. My mother, still a bookkeeper at a dairy in Uniontown, got the same job at Miller's Dairy in Cleveland. She then had our household furniture moved. Pat was hired as a teller at National City Bank. Our family was reunited, and soon was awash in funds.

With the help of my Aunt Emma, who with Uncle Tom left the farm since my vacation there and moved into town, my mother found a nice lower duplex in a

My mother at about 44, just after our move to Cleveland.

good neighborhood near my aunt. Several upgrades from the Project in Uniontown. But it was in the southeastern corner of the city, almost in the suburbs, and, with no car, it was a 45-minute trolley-bus ride for each of us to get to work.

My sister in about 1953, when she would have been 22.

I enjoyed that ride because it was through the big city. I especially liked the long section passing the Sohio oil refinery. At dusk, the lights on the huge vats and intricate ironwork would seem to twinkle as we rode by. The vastness of the installation imbued me with a feeling of witnessing power, in the city and the country, and pride, even though I understood little of what I was looking at. The refinery gave off a pungent, almost sickening odor throughout the area that anyone who's ever been close to such a plant would recognize. I even liked that overpowering repugnant odor!

Things went swimmingly for a couple of months. But, evidently, my mother knew little about having a lease on the apartment you occupy. With a landlord like Mr. Maruca on Lemon Street, and then living in a government project, one would hardly be necessary. Apparently, we had no lease on our pleasant apartment, because one day, after living there just three months, the landlady rang our doorbell and gave my mother some very bad news. The landlady was separating from her husband and would be moving into our apartment; therefore, we must find another place and move at once.

Additional pressure was put on my mother when the landlady had furniture moved into the basement, and began living there.

In a frenzy, the three of us would search ads and together take buses all over the city, frequently getting lost, in search of an accommodation. We did quickly find a two-bedroom apartment on the near West

Side — but not nearly as attractive as our present one.

In our haste to leave for an appointment one day, my mother left a heated iron on the kitchen counter. It, of course, burned a mark in the Formica. On the morning of the move, when the landlady came up from the basement to inspect the apartment, we had laid a newspaper over the burned area and the three of us grouped ourselves at that spot. The landlady did not approach.

A person in the wrong can always find a justification for his wrong-doing. Ours, for concealing the damage, was that it was caused by the landlady's pressure for us to find an apartment and move out quickly — and not negligence on our part. Did we believe that? Another minus in the rating of my life.

I wonder where my rating stands thus far, at this still young age. Was I that miserable when I was in high school, in trying to hide being gay, that by now I should be rated really low? I'm not sure. There were good times in high school, such as every Saturday at the movies. The day of the week I certainly dreaded was Friday when I just sat there and watched the other boys play baseball. But I should get a few points hike in the rating of my life for my Junior Reporter Club job. Inside me, I might have been worried a lot about how I was thinking about other boys, but on the outside a lot of people were admiring me in Uniontown. I'm going to give myself a break despite my troubles in school. I'm beyond school now. I say that thus far my rating is a 6. But what will happen to my rating in Cleveland, with a new job, with a new life?

My birthday was coming up in October. Every male was required to register with Selective Service and the draft by his 18th birthday. So one early fall day found me in the vast area on the second floor of the Standard Building in a long line of young men being called one by one into a medical office. Apparently I was passing the physical exam with flying colors until the vision test: 20/80 and 20/100. It didn't take the ophthalmologist but a few minutes to trace the cause to optic nerve atrophy, a genetic condition affecting many in my father's family. My sister suffered less than I did, but I have cousins who are nearly blind. Optic nerve atrophy is the existence of a weakness or pallor in the optic nerve, the pathway for visual images from the eye to the brain, making it impossible to send accurate data. There is no treatment or cure. The diagnosis at Selective Service was no surprise.

The nuns when I was yet in elementary school at St. John's had told my mother about my poor vision. A local doctor, not being able to determine the cause, recommended an ophthalmologist in Pittsburgh. So my mother and I boarded a Greyhound bus for the 50-mile trip, got the diagnosis, and the word that nothing could be done to correct the condition. Glasses would correct only that deficiency caused by near-sightedness and not that resulting from optic nerve atrophy.

Because of my vision, I was classified 4F by Selective Service. For several days, I was despondent. It was not that I was eager to go into the Army. It was that the Army was telling me that it did not want me in the Army.

No doubt I would have been exempt for being "homosexual." But, although I had passed some questioning years in high school trying to quash the appeal males had for me, that my only sexual relationship thus far had been with a male cousin, and that I was not the least interested romantically in girls, I would never have admitted, let alone volunteered, that I was gay. I would need a little more time—but just months. And I wondered: even if a young man did admit to being homosexual in order to be exempt, what proof would be demanded?

Although the apartment at our family's new location was closer to our jobs, our family collectively decided that the city was so large, it was time for our first family car. My sister had a Pennsylvania license, so she converted to an Ohio license merely by passing a vision test. My mother had never driven a car, and didn't want to. I also had a Pennsylvania license, having passed the driver's test after driver's education in high school.

However, I failed the Ohio vision test flat out, and was advised to get corrective lenses and return with a form filled out by an ophthalmologist. I, of course, knew that I had optic nerve atrophy, so glasses would not correct most of my deficiency. My ophthalmologist did the best he could and corrected one eye to 20/60, and the other to 20/80. From what I understand, if you have 20/60 vision, it means that you must be as close as 20 feet to see what a person with 20/20 vision can see at 60 feet.

The ophthalmologist, although telling me that he considered my vision satisfactory for driving, had no choice but to write down my visual measurements — that were not sufficient for Ohio law. The doctor scrawled on the form "Does not have night blindness." very prominently. With the form, I presented myself a second time at the licensing bureau.

I was in crisis when I entered the office. Knowing that my vision did not qualify me for a license, I felt that my life was in tatters. Gone would be the career I planned for. And how would I have any kind of social life if I couldn't drive?

The policeman who greeted me told me that night blindness was not at all the issue, that the issue was inadequate vision. I hope that I did not have tears in my eyes, but I was very upset as I told the policeman that I was a copy boy at the News, that I was hoping to be a reporter — which would not be possible without a driver's license.

He issued me a license.

I was able to keep that license for many years by renewing it from out of state, where I actually was, and in which the procedure does not require a vision test. There's no doubt that I was making a determined effort to avoid the requirement of law. There certainly is a penalty in the law for my subterfuge over so many years, so the fact that my action would lower the rating of my life is the least of it. During that long time, aware of my deficiency, I practiced cautionary driving and never had an accident except once when struck from behind, and another time when hit by a car driving on the wrong side of the road. Not being involved in a serious calamity due to my vision was a matter of good luck. Vision standards are there for society's protection.

After so much of my life struggling to keep a license (and my independence), I was overwhelmed with emotion when my deviousness came to an end, and I could no longer renew. I quite broke down. In my mind, I saw that the house I lived in would now be inaccessible, the life I was leading would be impossible, and in an instant I had joined the group called "disabled." Actually, as it turned out, I was exaggerating my situation, as most of my life I have had a partner and, therefore, an in-house chauffeur. Now that time has passed without driving, I look back at my flaunting of the law and recognize that I may have been a danger. I would not admit it during those years, and still find it difficult. I must confess to it now, and that's no easy thing. I see the rating of my life tumbling.

About the same time I was issued my first Ohio license, I began admitting to myself that being attracted to males as I was in high school was not going to pass. I saw the photo of an attractive — sexy — basketball player in the paper, and I, reluctantly, realized what road my future would take.

Autumn of 1952 was here, and it was the time to think about enrolling at Cleveland College. Not having any funds whatsoever to attend college full-time, I planned on going part-time, and I had no regret about this limitation. It was just the way things were. I don't know whether scholarships existed then. In any case, I didn't investigate. It was frequent that students worked their way through college. At that time, Cleveland College offered courses just in the evening. It was the downtown division of Western Reserve University, and in later years would move to the main campus on the East Side. I never even thought about the fact it would take me eight years to graduate.

Throughout my high school years, it was assumed that I would take college courses, but I don't think it was ever discussed that I should graduate. My mother, who was kept from completing high school by the domestic demands of her suddenly-burdened half-sister, my Aunt Mary, valued education and brought up the subject frequently. Although she herself had limited formal education, she was a voracious reader and became knowledgeable in a variety of subjects. English literature was her forte, but she had a wide knowledge in many areas.

It was never even considered or mentioned that I should attend school full-time. As a woman in the 1950s, my mother's earnings were not adequate to support me and my college tuition. But the News did fund one course per semester for employees, and since I registered for just two courses each term, that paid for 50%.

There was no such thing as a SAT test then, but as I prepared to register, I did take a similar test designed by the University. There was an aptitude test, too, in which it was decreed that I should be an architect. No way was I going to follow that: I was going to be a reporter!

By now, my sister had gotten a car, a new Chevrolet. Several years later, I got a 1956 Pontiac, two shades of blue with chrome everywhere. I felt that going up one make on the General Motors brands, it would give me a certain panache. If my memory is correct, there was a $200 difference in price. ($1800 in today's money.) After that, it would be a white 1957 Pontiac convertible with a red stripe down the side. Then a navy blue1960 Thunderbird convertible that cost as much as a Cadillac and really was beyond my means. Showoff!

At the News as a copy boy, I was stationed in the City Room, also called the Newsroom, a very large room with perhaps 100 individual desks, including City Desk, the heart of any newspaper's local news operation.

City Desk, despite its name in the singular, was actually a number of desks set together, forming a neat rectangle. The News' City Desk seated nine people, all men at the time: the city editor, John Rees, at the head facing the others. On his left was the assistant city editor,

City Desk at the News in about 1958. At the head is the City Editor, and the man with the phone is the Assistant City Editor. The other two men seated are on rewrite. The woman and man standing are reporters.
—Courtesy of the Michael Schwartz Library, Cleveland State University.

Russell Faist, and then followed seven rewrite men, whose job was to write the news articles from the information being phoned in by reporters in the field. The pneumatic tube device, where I and other copy boys whisked copy directly to the composing room, was between City Desk and the copy editors.

The six copy editors sat at a large U-shaped marble table. Their job was to check the conformity of articles to the News' style guide and to write headlines for them. It was also their responsibility to cut news articles to conform to the space allotted by the news editor when the space was reduced in a later edition. The rule was to cut from the end of the article, so reporters knew to put all of the important facts near the top.

There was an editor in charge of national and international news, reports of which arrived in an adjacent room via teletype machines. All editorial operations were overseen by the managing editor, who, with associates, determined the news worthiness of an event and the prominence it merited. Besides the editor, only three people had private offices in addition to their Newsroom desks: the managing editor, the political editor, and one of the columnists.

Three desks off in a cozy corner of the Newsroom were occupied by the women of the Society Department, who always had flowers on their desks. Nearby, a desk belonged to Nina Donovan who wrote nothing but obituaries, and who archived obituaries of prominent people years before their deaths, to be updated and rushed into print at a moment's notice someday in the future. When a new mayor would come in, for example, Nina would sit right down and begin working on his obituary.

There was a desk in the Newsroom for Mary, the education editor, for several years my best friend until our sad breakup. There was a desk for the political editor, several for columnists, a section for the financial editor Jack Cleary and his financial writers, and so on. The Sports Department was on one end of the room with about eight desks.

I enjoyed the hubbub of the Newsroom, but it couldn't be my whole life, and I resolved to get out more. At this time, it happened that our parish church announced a hayride for young people, and I signed up. By a stroke of luck, in the wagon I was seated next to the prettiest girl there. She was truly a knockout, with lily-white skin, silky dark hair to her shoulders, and a body that was attracting the thorough examination of the other young men. She introduced herself to me as Marie, and we became so engrossed in conversation during the ride that we hardly saw the countryside. When we returned to our starting point at the church, she exclaimed, "Oh, we're back? How awful!"

I figured this was my cue to offer to walk her home, which, in any case, was on a route I could take to my own house. On the way, Marie gave me her phone number, that I said I'd memorize. While she talked, my mind wandered to the worrisome problem about to present itself. What is the protocol here? Should I kiss her goodnight, or not? We just met tonight, but we're already very friendly. Is that an argument to kiss her, or not? Maybe she'll be insulted if I don't. At her house, I walked her up the driveway, and stood next to her on the porch as she opened the storm door. She paused there before opening the main door. I figured this was another cue. I looked into her eyes, she looked into my eyes, and I moved my face forward to kiss her.

Marie was quick, and moved her face out of my path, so that my head stopped above her shoulder, and I had to rebalance myself to avoid falling forward. I was stunned by her manoeuvre. It was a shock. I was as humiliated as though she had slapped me across the face. I stammered something almost incoherent about calling her, turned, and hastened down the driveway. Later, I wasn't sure whether she said I should call, or that she said I shouldn't call. It was my first rejection, out of zero prior tries, and it was painful and crushing. I would never put myself in a circumstance to be rejected again, because I would never make the first move again, not with a woman, nor a man. I would, in the future, appear to be receptive, but never would I make an approach. It's frightening how, in one minute, your personality can be warped for life.

Maybe she avoided my kiss because this was our first date. After all, it was 1953. Well, actually, it wasn't even our first date, since we just happened to both be on a hayride and sat next to each other. But, from Marie's standpoint, any liaison with me would have been a waste of her time, as it would have eventually ended.

Dear Marie,

At the time I met you on the hayride, I was in the throes of agonizing over whether I was gay. You were so beautiful, so easy to talk to, so vivacious, so informed.

After an hour, it was as though we knew each other all of our lives. You captivated me.

Two things went through my mind as I walked you home. One was whether It was proper to kiss you. The other was wondering, after meeting someone like you, whether I might be straight after all. You could really be the one, I mused.

Then I tried to kiss you. I was naive; it was too soon. Naturally, you refused me. I was overly sensitive, and felt humiliated. No other young man would have been as crushed by rejection as I was. I had questions about myself, and the gender that I was concerned about was turning me away.

Marie, I forgive you for rebuffing me. I was out of bounds. You were not responsible for the exaggerated hurt I felt. It was also wrong for me to put you in the middle of my inner turmoil on whether I was gay. It could be that when I attempted to kiss you so soon after we met, that I was trying to prove something to myself. Did I really want to kiss you, or did I think that I should want to kiss you?

I want to thank you, Marie, for your sweet companionship on the hayride. I wish I could do it in person. In the weeks that followed the hayride, I thought deeply on whether I could actually have a romance with any girl. I concluded that, since I couldn't overcome my sensitivity to pursue you, Marie, as fantastic and lovely as you were, there must not be a girl in the world that would appeal to me. So I finally knew for sure.

It was just as well, for your sake, that we never saw each other again. Marie, I hope you found a young man who deserved you. A fortunate young man he would

have been.

Yours truly,
Your hayride friend,
Vince

By now I was near to, or maybe just turned 19, and had become convinced of my inclinations. Not that I hadn't had repeated hints. Even now, I thought longingly back to the sexual liaison with my cousin that lasted several years from the age of 14 or 15. I was interested in him, and when he went away to what was called reform school for six months, I was eager, let me say desperate, for his return. Apparently, he wasn't all that enthusiastic, because he delayed several weeks before seeing me. Now at 19, I was getting mighty restless.

Strange. Although every mention at the newspaper of "those men" was blatantly antagonistic, and even though I knew I must never reveal in certain environments my own feelings, I did not feel guilty about my desire for males. I was uneasy that the people at work might guess my undercover life, but I had none of the self-loathing—and suicidal thoughts—that one hears that young gay men often have because of societal norms and pressure. I finally accepted myself as I was, although it had taken a while. The worst of my reactions to the homophobic banter in the Newsroom was discomfort and worry that my secret life would be exposed.

Perhaps my mother instilled in me a feeling of satisfaction with myself. It was being borne out in my life so far. I had gotten good grades in high school without even trying. When I was a paperboy, I was the best one of perhaps a hundred, winning trips and prizes for getting new customers. I was the teenaged boy chosen as editor of the Junior Reporter Club, a job anyone would want. Everything I did was right, and if I was attracted to men, that must be right, too, and the people talking against homosexuals were wrong and could be ignored.

Nothing I would overhear in the Newsroom would lessen my opinion of myself. Apparently, I had a colossal ego. I was totally self-satisfied. That was a fault. Come to think of it, I haven't entirely gotten over it.

Today I think about my colleagues at the newspaper and their hostile attitude toward gay people. Why did they develop their viewpoint that we, gay people, were disgusting? Did it come from their parents, and their parents? The bigotry was certainly society-wide. I examine the polling now, that says that two-thirds of Americans favor same-sex marriage. Why did society change its stance? How did that happen? And when? It didn't happen overnight, as the polling favorable to acceptance of gays began with low figures that improved over years. Would the newspaper people I worked with, if it were today, be in the two-thirds favorable to gay marriage, or the one-third opposed? I want to think well of these people, who were good people in many regards, so I want to place them in the two-thirds group. Their bias I forgive, because it was nurtured by society. And I'm going to forget their smirks and laughter. It harmed me not an iota at the time, so it need not disturb me now.

Why is it that some heterosexual men conjure up so much bigotry against gays, and devote so much of their time to it? Perhaps psychiatry should search for an answer.

Was it a failing for me not to admit and defend who I was? It would have taken courage to do so, but that is what we honor in those who show it. We call them heroes. I was not a hero, did not come out early on, in fact never with many people. In rating my life, that's a consideration. It would have been so difficult in the 1950s to announce that I was in that group that was so despised. "Now hear this, everyone. I have a confession to make…" What would I have said? It was before the word "gay" was being used. Would I have called myself the then pejorative word "queer"? That was the most common word I heard. I shudder to think what turn my life would have taken had I been such a hero. At the News, with the climate I observed in the Newsroom, I'm certain I would never have gone beyond being a copy boy. And the crude jokes likely would have been directed at me.

Dear Fellow Reporters of the News:

You told homophobic jokes that everyone in the Newsroom laughed at. That included gay me. Even though I hated the jokes, I had to laugh, or you'd know about me.

I was very careful about my laughter. It couldn't be too loud or prolonged, or it would seem insincere, and attract attention to me. Yet it had to be sufficient to seem that I really was amused by the joke. Eventually, I zeroed in on following the lead of one of the rewrite men. When he laughed uproariously, I laughed uproariously. When he snickered or just smiled, I did, too. I was on edge, careful never to reveal myself.

I forgive you, fellow journalists, for your jokes, and for putting me in the terrible position where I was laughing at ridicule of myself.

Back in the far reaches of history, men with same-sex orientation have been vilified by all of society. This was passed down through generations, and to you.

It was like an inherited gene. You were the victims yourselves of society's pass-along bias. I can hardly hold you responsible for the past. But when does a person apply logic to his bias, and conclude that it doesn't pass?

How it hurt me to see your prejudice each day while we cooperated on stories and were friends—and to realize your opinion of me would change in a flash if you knew my sexual orientation. I listened as you told me of your wives, your children, your personal life. I told you nothing of mine. Did you notice? If I could talk to you now, I would find pleasure in telling you of my life, as much detail as you'd want to know.

Society today has nearly broken its chain of bigotry and hostility. I believe that you would be the first to tolerate and to accept.

So, I forgive you. Today, we would be straight and gay working together.

Sincerely,
The gay reporter,
Vince

I learned from the Newsroom talk that there were three "queer bars" downtown: one frequented by older men, one a bar with dancing to rock and roll, and the third, a piano bar. Thanks to the data from my biased coworkers, I was all set.

Gay bars, and much of gay cruising, become most active after midnight when the city has quieted down and most of the straight world is at home cozy and snug in their beds, and unaware of the secret night city. When I first discovered these entertainments, at home I would announce that I was going on a date and leave at about 7:30. But then the problem was to fill in my time until close to midnight. I saw a lot of bad movies. Then I would need to rush home at 1:00 or 2:00 so that I would be getting in at what was considered a respectable hour.

I came up with a brilliant idea: Priscilla. This was the story: I had met a nurse. This nurse was on duty in the emergency room at St. John's Hospital. She worked the 4:00 to midnight shift. I would meet her when she quit work. It was all believable, but a total fabrication. As you see, lying did not seem to bother my conscience. The story allowed me to leave the house just before midnight, and to get in at any wee hour of the morning that I wanted.

No matter what time I got home on an early Saturday morning, a few hours later I would be out in the driveway washing my white with red trim Pontiac convertible, armed with car wash, white-wall cleaner, chrome cleaner and leather protector, with my basset hound, Monroe, looking on. It was a work of love that I'm sure was duplicated by young men all over the country. Detroit held us captive with its dazzling chrome-covered beauties of the 1950s.

Even though lying apparently did not faze me when I created the story about a Priscilla, it bothers me terribly now, 20 years after my mother's death. How could I have lived a lie? It makes my skin crawl to think of such deceit. I wonder if my mother suspected it was a lie, because she asked no details about this Priscilla or how the relationship was progressing. Or maybe she was just respecting my privacy. I consider that, with this falsehood, I betrayed my mother and descended to a low level indeed. As an excuse, I'm trying to consider whether I can blame society's antiquated attitude toward homosexuality in that era, in essence that society made me lie. A gay friend I discussed this with seemed to accept my blaming society. "Back then, we all had to lie," he asserted, explaining that families would not understand or accept our being gay. Friends would drop us, employers would fire us, he added.

I would feel a little better about my big lie if I learned that such duplicity is common with all young people. I surmise that the parents of a young man whose girlfriend becomes pregnant are usually stunned because they were not aware of the intensity of the relationship. But did their son actually lie? Do young people normally lie to their parents about their lives? If they do, it would put me, with my Priscilla lie, in the company of many. On second thought, knowing that young people are lying shouldn't make me feel wonderful, either.

My own experience with my Priscilla tale has made me wonder how many people that I encounter are leading double lives. They may be one thing to one set of people, as I was with my family and straight friends, but something totally different with another group, as I was with fellow gay men. It can make you suspicious of everyone. Questioning others' sincerity is the penalty I pay for my own untruthfulness.

Back then, I must have eventually sought parental blessing, or someone to talk to. I told my mother that I was concerned that I thought I was attracted to men. Her first reaction was probably how many mothers react to that news from a son. She wondered if she was to blame. Then she theorized that the fault, perhaps, was because I had no father figure to emulate. She asked herself if she could have involved my father's brother, my Uncle Dave, in assisting in raising me — but dismissed this idea saying he already had five sons, and acted distant to us since my father left. Finally, she suggested to me that I see a psychiatrist. There was no consideration that my genes may have dictated my proclivities. The notion of the influence of heredity was still far in the future.

I did see a psychiatrist, just once. After the advice he gave me, it didn't seem necessary to see him a second time. I reported the result to my mother. He told me my orientation could not be changed, but with therapy, I could be made happy with it. My mother asked me if I was happy, and I assured her that I already was. "Well, that's that," she said, and we never approached the idea of a cure again.

I didn't like the loud music at the dance bar downtown, the Zanzibar, and I certainly would not dance with a man. I, too, was the product of society, and I considered that two men dancing together would be unnatural and unacceptable. I was frequenting gay haunts, but I considered dancing with another man out of the question. Too gay. The Cadillac bar was for older men, and I was young. So when I went out, I chose the Orchid Room, the piano bar, and it was there, sitting at the U-shaped bar, that I met Terry, a young man my age, blond hair, blue eyes. At the bar, we exchanged phone numbers, and soon began seeing each other regularly. Terry involved himself in local politics: Republican politics. He attended GOP events, and he participated in chores such as distributing leaflets promoting a candidate. I myself at that time had little interest in politics. It would be many years before I settled on my current, liberal beliefs. While Terry spent hours with politics, I tagged along, but was quite bored. However, I very much liked Terry. We considered ourselves a couple, and saw each other, except for time out during a spat or two, my remaining eight years in Cleveland. My mother welcomed Terry, and she, my sister, Terry, and I frequently took weekend trips together. One time we went to Uniontown.

There was a six-month hiatus from Terry after an argument, during which I met a really nice fellow, a physical therapist a few years older than I was. His name was Dick, and he drove a huge silver Olds 98 convertible that would make any car today look downright puny. Those months with Dick were super-active, much busier than time with Terry. We went to Cape Cod, to a resort on Lake Erie called Cedar Point, had picnics in a park, tried new restaurants. But, even with Terry, there was more than just politics. Terry and I spent occasional weekends at a friend's lake cottage, where our group would parade around, our outstretched hands grasping the shoulders of the marcher in front of us, singing, or shouting, "When the saints come marching in..." There was our trip to Washington, when we slept in the car to save money, our every Friday evening dinner at a tiny Polish restaurant where we had pierogi stuffed with sauerkraut, cheese or potato, smothered in sour cream. Sex with Terry occurred only after I stomped my feet and pleaded. I consider my time seeing Dick as the best sexual period of my life, so I continued meetings from time to time with Dick for years. Terry eventually knew about my extracurricular activity, and did not object, perhaps because it freed him, somewhat, from my pitiful entreaties. Terry, not as exciting as Dick, nonetheless was comfortable and relaxing. I do believe that the sex drive in humans is a wee bit exaggerated. What problems it can create! Decades later, I would contact Dick, when I lived in Fort Lauderdale and he lived in Sarasota, Florida. We spent a nostalgic and glorious weekend together.

There's an industrial area in Cleveland called the Flats, which is a valley separating the East and West Sides, with bridges overhead, and, running through the valley, the Cuyahoga River, made famous in 1969 when it caught on fire. The Flats at the time was crammed full with steel mills such as Republic Steel and Jones and Laughlin, and other heavy industry, with their tall smoke stacks belching fire and smoke. Especially at night, the pulsating valley as seen from the hills was something to behold. Terry and I dreamed of building an all-glass house on one of those hills and spending our evenings gazing on the beautiful fire, smoke, and light extravaganza below us. There were signs on plots for sale all over. We dismissed the pollution problem, saying that we'd merely seal the windows. The sealed glass house, with two men at the windows enjoying the show, would never come to pass, but it was fun to anticipate it. Good luck on ever trying to sell a house in that location.

Time was rolling by. My mother had gotten a job in the same suburb to be close to work. Pat had finished high school by attending class in the evenings, and was now enrolled part time at Ursuline College. The three of us in our family were living in my mother's house in Euclid, a suburb, that Pat and I had saved the down payment to buy. We paid $26,000 for it, a sum that bought a substantial property in 1953. It was brick, a two-family, on a corner lot. We planted evergreen hedges along the side street, climbing roses on the garage, and tulip bulbs for the spring. We planted a pin oak in the front yard that now, 60 years later, is huge and mostly hides the house from the street. For most of the rest of her life, my mother lived in that house.

My mother's house was directly east of Cleveland. By this time, her sister, Emma, and husband, Tom, had relocated to a suburb southeast of the city. At that time there was no freeway in that direction, so it was a good 30-minute drive between houses. The result was that we drifted apart—even though we three in our family remained on intimate terms with my Aunt Bea and her husband, Joe, in Youngstown, 60 miles away, and visited frequently. But with Aunt Emma and her family,

A proud day for my sister, but especially for my mother.

there seemed to be a lack of warmth, and both families rarely made the effort to visit the other.

The explanation may lie in a warning found in Shakespeare's Hamlet: "Neither a borrower or lender be." Before we bought my mother's house, Aunt Emma's son, a long-haul truck driver, asked to borrow $1800 to buy a new car, realizing, no doubt, that all three in our family were working. $1800 was a goodly sum in 1952. He paid the loan back in advance of the date agreed. A few months later, however, there was a request to borrow a larger amount. By that time, we three had accumulated sufficient savings to be the down payment on a house. We regretfully declined the new loan, giving the reason, which we thought to be a reasonable one. Our refusal was not accepted enthusiastically, giving me reason to believe there is merit to Shakespeare's quote. It was about that time that a chill developed between us and

Aunt Emma and her family.

Or maybe there was another cause. A biological relative of Aunt Emma's husband, my Uncle Tom, had surgery, and Aunt Emma's two sons gave blood. Afterwards, Aunt Emma suggested to us that everyone donate blood at a specific hospital where an account would be established with a credit for the donations. Anyone in the families could call on the credit when needed. We in our family were lukewarm on the idea and did not participate. We thought we were in good health and would not need blood in the foreseeable future. Not a response to win friends and influence relatives.

Just after that time, Cleveland College moved out to the East Side to the campus of its parent, Western Reserve University, next to the park at the Cleveland Art Museum. It was a park where gay men gathered. I spent too much time driving my car around the park, and my grades suffered.

One evening after class, the professor told me that the Dean's office would like to see me. Right now, that evening. I was curious rather than concerned. At the suite of offices, I was directed to a small windowed office. There an academic advisor sitting at her desk introduced herself and invited me to sit in the chair in front of her desk, addressing me as Mr. Burke. I observed that she fit my idea of a schoolmarm rather than a university advisor: about 35, slim, short brown hair coiffured in a practical rather than fashionable way, tailored brown suit, no jewelry except a simple watch, beige-framed plastic glasses sitting on her nose, so that when she spoke to me, she looked at me over her glasses, instead of through them.

Her first words, spoken without any preamble, shocked me. "Mr. Burke, you're being suspended, you know. Your grades are very poor." Her words were like a glass of ice water thrown in my face. I was aware that my grades were low, but I couldn't believe what she had just said. They were throwing me out! I would never be a college graduate! I felt tears welling up in my eyes. I didn't dare speak because I would be unable to control my voice. For long minutes, we both just sat there staring into each other's eyes. She did not blink. She did not say anything more. The silence seemed deafening.

Finally she spoke. "Or, you could assure me that you will get an "A" in every course from this term forward until graduation. I have studied your record, and you can do it." I began to breathe again, and immediately assured her, stuttering a little, that I would try. "Then it's a deal?" she asked. I shook my head yes and repeated that I would do my best. As I was opening her door to leave, she said to me "Good luck, Vincent. You can do it," this time calling me by my given name. I thanked her and was out in the hallway, determined to turn myself into a conscientious student. No one ever used the words "on probation," but later on I realized that was now my status.

I got an "A" in every course until graduation. The next term, I withdrew from an astronomy course when, at the first class, the professor announced that to get an A, the student would need to know as much as he does. I wondered whether the professors of classes in which I registered were notified that I must get an A, and the penalty if I did not. Was he warning me that I should withdraw? I was disabused of this idea when another professor spoke to me after a few weeks, saying that she was curious. She had looked up my record from a prior class of hers, and found that I was just a mediocre student. She was confused by the startling improvement.

It was in a letter, dated June 16, 1960, that the University notified me officially of my removal from probation. Amazingly, I still have that wonderful letter of six decades ago. It arrived two weeks before graduation, cutting it a little close, I thought, even though by then I had gotten all As in a total of half of my college subjects.

Just after the list of 1960's coming graduates appeared in the college paper, I received a note from the advisor, who I had not seen for two years, with just these words: "I told you, Vincent, that you could do it." Again, I felt tears well up in my eyes. I realized that, unknown to

CLEVELAND COLLEGE
~~NON-RESIDENT HOME~~
~~10950 Euclid Ave.~~
~~EDUCATIONAL COUNSELING~~

June 16, 1960

Mr. Vincent P. Burke
698 East 222nd Street
Euclid 23, Ohio

Dear Mr. Burke:

    In a review of your academic record we note that your grade average has improved to the level where we can remove your name from the academic probation list. The Dean has requested that I inform you of this action and that any restrictions imposed by academic probation are now removed.

    It is a pleasure for us to be able to send you this letter. We hope, and are confident, that you will be able to complete your educational requirements without further difficulty. We also hope that you will remember to call on us for any assistance that we may be able to render.

Sincerely,

Frank J. Heard
Educational Counselor

FJH/nr

This letter to me arrived just before graduation.

me, she had been following my progress from term to term. I'm sorry that I no longer can locate her note, but I cannot forget her words.

I wish I had thought about how rewarding this lady's job was compared to a reporter's job. How fruitful it would be to put a student such as me in the right direction. She may advise students on a path to take, and follow their careers. She would find satisfaction when they succeeded. It is too bad that I did not reflect on how she helped me, and revise my opinion accordingly of the career I should pursue.

It was back in 1954 that I was promoted to the police beat as a new reporter. There were three or four for the News during the day, and one who worked midnight to 8 or 9AM. The Plain Dealer and Press had similar numbers. Each newspaper had a small office down a narrow hallway on the first floor of the police station, where we worked.

Our job was to monitor the police radio for a dispatch that may indicate a news event. We then called City Desk to see if there was an interest in one of us going to the scene. We also regularly checked the record room, where a summary of every police action was recorded. If an entry appeared to be newsworthy, we followed up on it by contacting the police officers or detectives making the report, and often the citizens involved. The chief police reporter, an older man who had held that position for many years, was on a first-name basis with many of the top police officials, and found it productive to pass much of his time conversing with them. The News office in the police station was the building card-playing center, with "Hearts," the usual game. There, a few choice police officers and a few reporters would gather around a desk for several hours each day. The smoke became thick; I am thankful today for my health's sake that I spent only three years on the police beat.

The celebrated Sam Sheppard murder case, where the handsome neurosurgeon was accused of bludgeoning to death his wife Marilyn in their home on Lake Erie, was the lead story for several months in 1954, soon after I was promoted to the police beat. But the cub reporters were not involved; the chief police reporter covered it, as did several veteran reporters from General Assignment. Even the frequent card games in the News office in the police station were suspended in favor of covering Sam Sheppard. The Cleveland Press was famous, or infamous, for its coverage. "Quit Stalling and Bring Him In!" was the talked-about headline of a Press editorial just before prosecutors charged Sheppard with murder. He was convicted and appealed all the way to the US Supreme Court. The Court ordered a new trial based on prejudicial publicity. In 1966 he was acquitted. He is said to have become an alcoholic, and died in 1970 of liver failure at the age of 46.

I became friends with one of the other police reporters for the News, a straight man with a wife, who was exceedingly proud of his newly-born daughter. We often lunched together. One year, I went on vacation to New York City with a straight reporter for the Plain Dealer. He came from a wealthy family and had graduated from Princeton, and seemed to know everything about the New York theater, and about which fancy, and expensive, restaurants to visit. We saw "Pipe Dream," a Rodgers and Hammerstein musical, my first-ever play, based on a short novel, "Sweet Thursday," by John Steinbeck. I spent a lot on the trip, but had no qualms about it. It had not occurred to me so far in life that I should be saving a portion of my earnings for a rainy day. New cars every couple of years prevented that. The next year I was in New York, again spending a lot, with a reporter from the Press, straight also. This was my surface life showing itself, while my undercover gay life continued unabated. I am assuming these men were all straight, and cannot speculate on how they would have considered me had they known I was gay. But I know the bias of society in its entirety in that period. One thing I know for certain. My straight friends on our trips would never have shared a double room with me.

I say that I assume these friends were straight, because most of the population is. I have heard it said that gay people have "gaydar," a sort of sixth sense that gives us the ability to recognize other gay people. I certainly did not have it when I was young. Maybe I have a touch of it now, but it is far from infallible. The weak gaydar that I do have, I believe, takes into account a person's reaction to me as a man. My subconscious probably also considers the way a person is dressed, speaks, acts, is employed, his interests, and a host of other factors.

But I can be certain of nothing with just a cursory glance. Walking down a crowded street I would not know who is, and who isn't. When you're young and attractive, a gay man may hold his eyes on you a short moment longer than normal, and that can be a clue. But later? When you see two men in their 30s or 40s together, they could be life partners, or business associates, or buddies going hunting. An older man and a younger man? It could be a gay couple, or father and son. Two older gentlemen could be—two older gentlemen. Even a man and woman together may be a gay man with a woman friend who finds gay companionship unthreatening, or it could be a married couple with five children at home.

Context sometimes helps. If you're in Wilton Manors, a heavily gay city outside Fort Lauderdale, two men together or two women together are likely gay. If you happen to be redoing your house and go into an interior design studio, your suspicion may be correct. There's a large population of gay men in gyms, but there are straight men, too. So, in my experience, conclude nothing about anyone.

In my job on the police beat, for a year or two I was on the midnight to 8 or 9 AM shift, the quitting time depending on whether you had wrapped up your stories collected during the night. Passing by 5 AM without nodding off to sleep, as my body begged to do, was a particular burden. It was at that hour that the "rounds" were made, the rounds being our name for a series of phone calls to suburban police stations and the emergency rooms of all the hospitals to learn if there were any serious accidents, crimes, fires, and so on. It was during making these rounds that my will would give in and I would nod off to sleep, only to jerk awake a minute later.

I was the only News editorial employee working at night, and it was my call whether to investigate and cover a story. I remember the difficulty my substandard vision presented when I drove out to an address in the darkness, only to have a problem reading street names and house numbers. Oh, for today's GPS! Even a cell phone would have been a boon. When I was out on a story during the day, I was often working against a deadline of the next edition, and searching for a pay phone was an added woe.

While I was on the midnight shift, there would also be a Press reporter in a nearby office. We would try to keep careful tabs on each other, because if one of us disappeared, it may mean that he is out on a story that the other is missing. The first editions of both the Press and the News came off the press at 10 AM. One morning just past 10 AM, when I was fast asleep after my night of work, I was awakened by the phone ringing, with the City Editor demanding to know why I had missed a story that was in the Press. Similar calls from his city editor had come to the night reporter for the Press. The stress became so intense as we spied on each other, and the nights so unpleasant, that the two of us finally reached an unspoken agreement that we would not "scoop" the other on any major story. Unspoken, but mysteriously understood and kept. Our city editors would not have approved.

I did report on celebrated murders, on accidents, on a rare tornado on Cleveland's West Side one year, of fires, of children dying in fires. Perhaps because of my penchant for architecture, I often submitted to the City Desk a drawing of the scene; for example, precisely locating where in a house a body or bodies were found. The City Editor seemed to appreciate these drawings of mine, because, after they were cleaned up a little by the Art Department, they were always published. However, I never really enjoyed being on the police beat. I can't see how anyone would find pleasure in interviewing parents who have just lost a child.

Most of the editorial employees were unionized with the American Newspaper Guild, now called simply The NewsGuild. None of us, so far as I could see, were gung-ho about the union, but all of us, except the top editors, belonged. We even had a short strike of three days, or maybe it was three hours.

"Reporter," was a job that does not better the rating I give my life.

One thing I learned quickly is that my city editor regarded stories about black people — no matter how sensational — as totally worthless, or rather, with a value so minimal that they merited only a paragraph on a back page. It didn't matter that a family had their lives upended, or that a crime was spectacular with tragic results. If it concerned only black people, it was not news. The same event with white people would have warranted front page treatment with a slew of photos. Often when calling into the City Desk about a news event, the first question posed would be, "black or white?" From speaking with reporters from the other papers, I learned that their city editors were the same. And I accepted this situation as being just the way it was. No further thoughts on my part. Could I not have at least muttered a tiny protest?

My daytime life after work when I was on nights, on days I did not have morning classes, was not without notable social engagements. The young lady across the street, alone during the day as I was, soon invited me to her house, and to her bedroom. On her bed, I lay on top of her, both of us fully clothed. My desperate pleas to advance to the next step were met with refusals. Apparently, she was not that kind of girl.

I did spend the night with her, however. One night toward midnight, I left the house as usual to go to work, and at the stop sign a block away, she was waiting, and got into my car. She had had a fight with her mother, and insisted on going to work with me. She spent the night in the car in the parking lot. Her mother never stormed over to my house, as I feared, so she never knew her daughter passed a night with me.

The other distraction when I was working nights was with the attractive boy upstairs, the son of my mother's tenant. It was the summer before his senior year, and he, too, was alone during the day. To occupy himself, he regularly appeared at my door to challenge me to a wrestling match. We rolled around on my living room floor.

Before all of this, I had no idea that night workers were so busy during the day.

CHAPTER 7

The Letter. I regret Mary.

MARY WAS THE rare kind of woman that I could relax with, without worrying whether I was handsome enough, macho enough, sophisticated enough. Maybe it all came down to her being a little plain, so that I couldn't feel inferior to her. What importance we all put on physical attractiveness! Mary was a little overweight, not a lot, just a few pounds. But those couple of pounds made her face too round. I could see that she worked hard to overcome this. And she succeeded, mainly. She always wore a fine tailored suit, a frilly white or flowered feminine blouse, and a simple strand of pearls, or a gold chain. My favorite outfit for Mary was when her ensemble was particularly understated. She wore an expensive navy suit with a single strand of pearls that you wouldn't notice at first, because it hung against her white blouse.

Her refined outfits outshone the other female reporters at the Cleveland News. Although those women were generally more attractive physically, they looked a little dull in the vast Newsroom, with Mary taking the limelight. I imagine that the other women must have resented the competition she won everyday.

I met Mary in her first week at the newspaper. After working from midnight in our office at the police station, at about 7 AM I had gone to the Newsroom to write up my stories. I sat at one of the desks and began typing.

"Hello. I'm Mary." She had startled me. I looked toward the sound of the voice to see a young woman, perhaps two or three years older than my age of 21, clad smartly in a russet suit. I observed the round face, and the short, ash brown hair. But what I fixated on was the welcoming, broad smile and the clear blue eyes, appearing to be full of eagerness to meet me.

I stood up and was about to introduce myself, when Mary spoke again. "You're Vincent, and you're on the police beat. I saw you the other day and asked about you."

Mary continued on to say that she just graduated from Notre Dame College in Cleveland, that she's here at the office so early in the morning because she wants to make a good impression, and that she has time to go to breakfast with me as soon as I finish typing my stories.

We went to breakfast that morning, Mary and me, and to many long lunches on the days I wasn't working that night. We got along famously, and I hated lunch to end because I so much enjoyed our conversations. However, I was aware of a growing problem. I was considering our friendship as totally platonic, but Mary was frequently hinting at a romance. I was trying to limit our meetings to the daytime, but she kept coming up with ideas where we would meet at night for a movie, or a play, an event at her college. My job as a police reporter starting work at midnight provided some cover, but there were two pesky nights a week when I was off where I had to create excuses. They had to be excuses that seemed legitimate. I was recognizing that Mary was a wonderful, caring person. In my eyes, even her appearance was improving as I became fascinated by her vivacious personality. I would have to be careful that I didn't hurt her.

She shouldn't waste her time trying to romance me. There were loads of young men out there who would appreciate her,

With only two exceptions, at least that I recall, we never saw each other outside the workday. I do remember being at Mary's house once, because I met her mother, and once we went to an Ohio State game with another couple. (Correction: Mary and I were not a couple.)

Then one day a malevolent missile appeared in my mother's mailbox. I was still working the midnight shift and was living at home. Since my mother and sister were at work during the day, I was alone and collected the mail. A small white envelope arrived, addressed to my mother in rather a child-like printed handwriting. For some reason, I felt compelled to open that envelope, something I had never done before to mail not addressed to me.

I was stunned by the contents. Inside was a single piece of white lined notebook paper with handwritten printed letters on it in ink. I remember the exact wording today: "Stop turning your son into a mama's boy."

My heart sank. I felt humiliation that someone would call me a mama's boy. But I was relieved that no one would see the note but me. I examined the address on the envelope, written as 222d Street. I noted the peculiar way the number was expressed, as the address is customarily written as 222nd Street, with an "n."

When I went to work on the midnight shift, at about 7 AM I would go to the Newsroom with whatever stories I had. I did this as usual the following morning. As the News was published later in the day, there were only a few people in the Newsroom when I went there. I casually sauntered over to Mary's desk and observed her calendar on the wall next to it. 32d Street, 119h Street, 142d Street. All missing the same letter after the number as 222d Street on the envelope.

I never spoke to Mary again. I gave no explanation, and she asked for none. That alone spoke to her guilt. There was never another lunch, never another animated conversation. It was the end of one of the best relationships of my life, and I regret it. It ended because I did not have the courage to tell Mary at the start that I was gay, in an era when it did take courage, to inform her upfront so that she would not assume that the relationship would progress to romance.

Through the years when I visited Cleveland, I always thought about calling Mary, but never did. I regret that, too. I was afraid of her reaction. Maybe she would hang up on me, maybe she would be cold, maybe she would not want to see me. A good part of the reason I didn't call, however, was that I would finally have to tell her why our relationship never advanced – and I still did not have the courage.

A minus on my life's rating.

Dear Mary,

How I wish that you had never sent that letter to my mother, calling me a mama's boy. What did you hope to accomplish? Even though she never saw it, it really bothered me, mainly because I was afraid it could be true. Then, after I determined you sent it, I regretted it because I had to do something about it. I couldn't just pretend it didn't happen. We had become such good friends, and we could have had years of enjoying each other's company. But I felt sending such a note directly to my mother was a serious thing, and I couldn't continue with you.

Was I partly to blame? Did I drive you to that letter because I never told you that our relationship could not go beyond platonic? At our ages then, you naturally expected more, and I didn't have the courage to tell you that I was gay.

I dropped you immediately after the letter, and that was my mistake. I punished myself as much as you. We had too rewarding times together to let a misstep end everything. How I missed you in the months after. Did you miss me? Every time I entered the Newsroom, my eyes went first to your desk to see if you were there. I felt bad if you were out. I could have finally been brave and told you then of my sexual orientation. I'll bet you would have accepted it, because you were an understanding person, and we could have gone on as we had been. I do thank you for all the happy times we had together. Remembering them is why I regret so much what happened.

Unfortunately, we would never have future years. From afar, I followed your moves through life, your career at your new newspaper, your growing celebrity. I never congratulated you, but I felt proud of you. I never spoke to you again, but I thought of you often. My silence was a misfortune I brought upon myself.

I was in Cleveland around Easter one year, and I saw your picture in the paper. Was it 20 years since I had last seen you, 30 years? You were leading the Easter Parade around Public Square. I would have recognized you anywhere. You were still fighting against weight, but you were yet as smart-looking as ever. Fond memories rushed back to me. They were happy memories, yet they made me feel sad. At that moment, I should have phoned you.

I forgive you for your letter to my mother, Mary, but I cannot forgive myself for my reaction to it.

Forever your friend,
Vince

I followed Mary's life closely. Mary never married, but she became a celebrated journalist. One day when I happened to be visiting Cleveland, I got the morning paper from my mother's front porch, and opened it to the front page. There, with the prominence it merited, was a large article with photo: Mary's obituary. She had died suddenly.

I did not go to the funeral. I was too late now. I regret everything about Mary.

CHAPTER 8

The Crucial Fib.
Benefits of a lie.

DURING A BRIEF breakup with Terry, I was driving around The Mall at a wee hour of the morning. Driving around the park and seeing other young men in their cars there for the same reason was intriguing, very much like the lyrics in Frank Sinatra's, "Strangers In The Night."

A car followed me to a side street, the customary procedure to arrange a liaison. It was Jimmy. We had talked for a long while a couple of weeks before, with Jimmy standing outside my driver's window. He had given me his surname, and I surmised, from his name and looks, that he was Italian. Tonight I stopped my car, and he pulled over next to the curb in front of me and walked back. As we began talking, a police car drove by very slowly on the other side of the street, with both policemen staring over at us.

Having been noticed by the police, I determined it would be wise to leave, and asked Jimmy to get in my car. For several minutes, I drove around in circles while we talked, and then I decided to drive us to the parking lot of nearby Captain Frank's Seafood Restaurant on a pier on the lake. The restaurant would be closed at this hour. I pulled past the restaurant to the end of the pier, and stopped with my hood facing the water and before a short fence. The parking lot was empty and black.

The moment I extinguished my lights, a car approached from behind and stopped directly behind my car, blocking me in. It extinguished its lights. My heart sank. Was it the police? I could see enough through my rearview mirror to determine that it was a dark car, and not the police, and that alarmed me even more. Suddenly, all doors of the car were opening and a number of men were getting out into the parking lot.

One approached my side of the car and one approached the passenger side where Jimmy sat. In the pleasant weather, I hadn't put the window up while Jimmy and I were driving. I didn't have electric windows, as most cars did not at that time. Not even on seeing what was happening, apparently stunned, did I think to roll a window up and lock the door. I saw that the one who came to my side of the car was a teenager, but a big teenager, perhaps 17, tall and husky, with a crew cut.

"Get out of the car!" he ordered roughly, as he opened my door. I did not argue. As I got out, I saw from the corner of my eye that Jimmy also was getting out. In the semi-blackness, I could see that there were perhaps six young men, or teenagers, who outnumbered Jimmy and me. One was strutting around in a small circle like a rooster in a hen house. Another boy stood a few feet away, staring at me and jabbing his fists into the air in front of him, as though previewing for me what was to come. One, seemingly uninterested in what was going on, was examining my car, the spiffy white and red Pontiac convertible with the spinner hubcaps and twin rear radio antennae. Two boys were with Jimmy, and in the dim light I could not see what was happening there.

What would come next? Will all six jump on Jimmy and me and beat us to a pulp? Black eyes, a broken nose, perhaps fractured ribs? Does one of them have a knife? How will I explain this to anyone? To my mother, to the people at work? Is this also going to be a robbery?

Fortunately, I always carried extra money, so that a would-be robber would not be unhappy with his loot and take it out on me.

I had to think of something quickly — and the idea struck me. It would be worth a try. It was the only thing I had.

"I work at the police station," I blurted to the boy who had ordered me out of my car. "I have a lot of policemen friends."

"Oh yeah, sure," he replied, skeptically.

"If you don't believe me," I said, "look at my license plate."

Attached to the license plate, by the same screw that held the license plate, was a green metal disk about the size of a silver dollar. On it was etched in a semicircle the word "Headquarters," and a number toward the bottom. It was my permit to park in the police parking lot while at work, but I did not explain its significance.

The boy with me walked around to the rear of my car, stooped, and looked closely at the disk on my license plate in the dim light. Several boys gathered next to him while he examined it. One of them lit a cigarette lighter next to the license plate. I heard the word "headquarters" from someone. There was a momentary chat among a few of them, a shout to the others, "Let's go!" and the six would-have-been assailants piled into their car, slammed the doors, gunned the motor as they made a screeching semicircle, yelled "Faggots!" out the windows at us, and sped away. I caught my breath and sighed with relief. The idea had worked, implying that I would have pull with policemen-friends to avenge an assault. It was a ruse, actually a bald-faced lie: I had no policemen-friends, and even if I did, I could never have revealed these circumstances.

Jimmy, outside the passenger side of the car, did not hear my talk with the "lead thug." He had been preparing himself to be beaten up, and was stunned when the group drove off. There's no question that I made points with Jimmy that night.

But this experience reminded me that I was a member of a hated group. I realized that these teenagers were no different from thousands of others in the city. Given the chance, they would assault me, because they consider me, due to my sexual orientation, worth nothing. They would boast to their friends about what they did to me. This was the 1950s. It hit me that I better watch my step. My city is enemy territory. That was the lesson I learned well that night.

I drove Jimmy directly back to his car, we exchanged phone numbers, and I went straight home. Jimmy and I saw each other a few times after, but never mentioned the events of that night. It would be too painful to revisit. I occasionally thought of what could have happened. Is it possible they would have thrown us in the lake? Jimmy and I drifted apart, and I was back with Terry.

To the boys about to beat Jimmy and me up:
I didn't forget about you and that night easily. I was scared. You ordered me out of my own car, and made me a captive. There was no way I could escape.

You were all going to beat us up. Out of the car, I looked around. It was close to pitch black, but I could see that there were a lot of you, all eager to pounce on Jimmy and me. I could hear the lapping of the water against the pier, and in the distance traffic on the Shoreway. No one would see us, and there was no hope of escape. Then I thought about the police parking token. I had to try it, but it almost certainly wouldn't work.

You'd brag about this night to your friends, how you followed these two queers and gave them black eyes and bloody noses. You'd probably take my watch and show it to your friends. Maybe you'd go after my car with a tire iron. I tried not to think of knives you might have. In other circumstances, you would have just been normal teenagers, working on your cars, playing football, talking about girls. But that night, you frightened me. You were a gang.

Members of a gang do things that they would not do individually. It's called gang mentality. A few years later, you may have looked back and regretted the whole thing.

Nowadays, a group like yours, that finds amusement by beating up gays, is less common. Nowadays, one of you might even be in the Gay-Straight Alliance in your high school. Out of six of you, one of you may have turned out gay. I'm betting on the leader, who ordered me out of the car. Fighting his inner demons.

Odd as it sounds, I suppose I should actually thank all of you for what almost but didn't happen that night. Our encounter taught me to monitor myself carefully. I became cautious about where I went and the environment around me. You guys may have saved me from something worse than a frightening quarter hour.

With you, fellas, my lie worked, and Jimmy and I weren't beaten up. Except for a bad memory, no lasting harm was done. I'd like to talk to each one of you now, and see how you turned out. You probably became good citizens.

I forgive you.

Sincerely,
The guy in the white Pontiac convertible

By 1958, I had moved from the police beat to the most desirable of the suburban beats: Shaker Heights, Cleveland Heights, University Heights. This was a relaxing assignment after the police beat. Instead of people involved in a police matter trying to avoid you, suburban officials welcomed you, so long as there was a chance their name would be in print.

One of the most interesting potential stories out of Shaker Heights was one that I never reported — that no one ever reported, and that no one in the 1950s would ever report.

Shaker Heights abuts an area of Cleveland off Kinsman Road where blacks (not yet called African Americans) were buying homes and moving in. They now lived on residential streets that were part in Cleveland, and part over the line in Shaker Heights, but they lived on the Cleveland side. Some Shaker Heights leaders were worried that blacks would soon cross the line on these streets, and be living in Shaker Heights. "Heaven help us!" was the attitude. So there was talk that, to make this calamity less likely, the city must purchase homes on the Shaker Heights side of the line on each street, and lease them to white tenants, so that no Shaker homeowner would live next to a black family and be inclined to sell his home to blacks.

Society has certainly changed in the last 60 years. Today, Shaker Heights, still a prime place to live, is a model of an integrated community.

One day in January, 1960, I drove from my suburbs into the city and the Newsroom to type up my stories and submit them. I entered the Newsroom about 3 PM, the time of the day when the shouts and the scurrying would be at its crescendo, just before the final edition.

Instead, there was a hush over the vast room. No shouts, no copy boys running. Not a typewriter was in operation. The only sound was the click click click of the teletype machines in an adjoining room, spewing out their reams of yellow paper. At various parts of the Newsroom stood clusters of my fellow workers, groups of four, five or six, all people I knew well, speaking together softly.

The Cleveland News was ceasing publication, or more correctly, was being bought by our Scripps Howard rival, the Cleveland Press. The latest certified figures showed the News' circulation at 134,550; at the same time, the Press had a circulation of 314,000. The Press also would eventually close. The News that traced its roots to 1868 would no longer exist. It would be announced in the next day's News and

Press, although the Plain Dealer jumped the gun and scooped us in its morning paper. The Plain Dealer, owned by the same company as the News, would move into the News plant.

The News had always suffered the misfortune of being Cleveland's third newspaper, with half the circulation, and advertising, of the Press and the Plain Dealer. Unfortunately, with top management names such as Vale, Bellamy and Howard, the News had the aura of a WASP newspaper in a city with large concentrations of Slovenians, Poles, Czechs, Italians and other ethnic groups. The Press determinedly appealed to these large populations, and became an influential powerhouse. Its longtime editor, Louis B. Seltzer, was often called Mr. Cleveland, and the paper's endorsement of a politician's candidacy often became a prerequisite to election. Seltzer retired in 1966, and the Press began a slow decline, along with many other American newspapers, until its demise in 1982.

Studies have shown that a sudden loss of employment can be as traumatic as the death of a loved one. I can't say that I did not feel a little depressed at my lack of work, but I had mixed feelings about being thrown into unemployment. I, of course, did not welcome the sudden cessation of income. But I did not feel I fit well into some facets of journalism. I was introverted. When I was on the police beat, I often found it difficult, even shameful, to question victims of a crime in order to have them relive their terrible experience. I could see that the most successful reporters were those who regarded victims as opportunities for a byline. They were extroverts who made friends easily with policemen and politicians who would be news sources. They were slap-on-the-back, let's-go-for-a-drink people. I was not. And I don't know that there are many gay men of that type. I never met any, and if I did, I would avoid them like the plague.

As time had passed, I had become interested in what I thought to be the quieter, more dignified field of advertising, and believed that my writing ability and what I hoped was my creativity would enable me to be successful as a copywriter.

So the contribution of my job as a reporter to my life rating is a definite minus. Let's hope for better with advertising.

I still had 12 hours of college to complete and used the opportunity provided by unemployment to attend university full-time. Graduation ended my eight years of college, where I had majored in psychology with a minor in business. Why psychology? I thought that, as a reporter, it would be useful to understand people. It wouldn't hurt in advertising, either.

Soon I found myself as advertising director of a six-office, family-owned savings and loan association. Not copywriting, but advertising nonetheless. I was given a plush, private office in the Terminal Tower branch. The actual advertising was created freelance by a friend of the president who worked at one of the two large advertising agencies in town.

With such a small company, and the advertising provided by an outsider, I had almost nothing to do except sit at my big desk and try to look occupied. I made phone calls to friends. I took morning and afternoon coffee breaks with a friend of Terry who worked in the building. I designed make-believe towns on scrap paper, placing streets and public buildings. I drew cars on scrap paper. I drew buildings. Anything to occupy myself. In short, I was going crazy from boredom. I had to get a new job where I would have work to do.

I submitted my resume to both of the large advertising agencies in Cleveland, with a portfolio of mock-ups of ways I thought my present company's advertising could be improved. I can hardly believe I was that dumb at age 27, to be criticizing the advertising when I was the advertising director.

If that were not bad enough, one of the two agencies I submitted my "improvements" to was the one who employed the president's friend who prepared the advertising. My thinking was that, with 200 employees, my submission would certainly not find its way to him.

I was wrong. In a flash, I was summarily dismissed from my job.

New York City, here I come!

SECTION TWO:
NYC AND POST-NYC

CHAPTER 9

YMCA. It's not the Waldorf.

IT WAS A steaming, hot July afternoon in Manhattan. I descended the steps of the bus from LaGuardia carefully, struggling to lift my big brown suitcase as I stepped down. Around me appeared my first visions of what I hoped would be my brilliant life in New York: the drab Port Authority bus terminal, a large version of the unremarkable design of bus stations all over America; the noisy crowds swarming by on Eighth Avenue; the honking hubbub of densely-packed cars and trucks vying for space in the street. How exciting this was!

As I stepped onto the sidewalk on Eighth Avenue, I was already huffing and sweating with my heavy bag. I had stuffed clothes in, not thinking about weight. It held everything I'd need for job interviews plus two pairs of pants, t-shirts, jockey shorts, socks and running shoes, so that in my free time, I could be "On the Town," as in my favorite movie. Fact is, my suitcase contained most all of my worldly possessions. When you're young, you can get everything you own in a single bag. In a few years, my things wouldn't fit in a single house.

My first plane trip was over, and the plane hadn't crashed. So far so good. I'm on my way! My final destination was the YMCA on West

63rd Street off Central Park West, which, my map told me, is a continuation of Eighth Avenue as you go by the park. So I had over 20 blocks to walk in this dang scorching sun, lugging my big suitcase. No one had thought of putting wheels on luggage yet, so the weight of my bag would nearly do me in. Wheels on bags wouldn't come until the idea in 1970 of Bernard Sadow at a Massachusetts luggage maker.

I knew the walk, or struggle, was going to be difficult with my load and the heat, but it never occurred to me to take a taxi. I had never been in a taxi. When I first went to Cleveland, I took buses and streetcars, and then I had gotten my own car. Besides, taxis cost money, walking was cheap.

En route to the airport in Cleveland, I had driven my car, a navy 1960 Pontiac convertible with a white top, to Terry's house, and turned it over to him for good. He drove me the rest of the way to the airport. On the way to his house, I had made a left turn banned in rush hour, and got a ticket — which I ignored. I was surprised when my mother reported that the police came to the house when I didn't appear in court. But I had told the policeman I was leaving town for good! I suppose I am still listed as a scofflaw in Cleveland, 60 years later. I hope I wasn't fined, with interest accruing.

The liaison with Terry after eight years had run its course. We both knew it, but did not mention it. We parted as good friends, but we would lose touch with each other. A few years ago, checking Google, I found that he had been in an assisted living facility and had died there. How many people who were important in my life are no longer here. I have the macabre habit of searching for obituaries of people I knew, and frequently I find them, thrusting myself into a depression. Finding Terry there, my first close friend and partner in gay life, was painful. I recalled in exquisite detail the night we met, my spotting him across the U-shaped bar of the Orchid Room, and then my joy in having a partner. Terry had called me in New York ten years ago, and we talked for an hour like in old times. I asked for his phone number so that when I visited my mother and sister in Cleveland, we could get together, but when I called the number, I found that he had given me a non-existent number. I felt the sadness of reading his obituary deep in the pit of my stomach. We would never get together again.

Dear Terry,

That telephone talk we had when you phoned took me back to our eight years. When I arrived at the airport to visit my mother, I was eager to see you. I went right to a pay phone to call and tell you I was in Cleveland. How disappointed I was that the number you gave me wasn't a working number.

I forgive you for that, although I try to convince myself that it was my mistake. Maybe I transposed two numbers. Seeing you was going to be my chance to relive my youth and be with the first close friend in my life. I could hardly wait for us to be together.

You remember our idea of a glass house overlooking steel mills? We were young and had dreams. On the plane, I was thinking back to our weekends at Ralph's cottage on Chippewa Lake and our chance to finally be sharing a bedroom.

Together, I thought we could go back to the little Polish restaurant where the owner was so proud of the food from his native country. He knew our names and greeted us with a smile on the many Friday evenings we dropped in. As I write this, right now, I'd love to go back and spend an hour or two with you at our little Polish restaurant.

But it wasn't to be. I left the airport feeling alone and depressed.

In any case, Terry, I have my memories. I'm thank-

ful to you for giving them to me. We met about three times a week for the eight years. That's over 1,200 times together, almost all of them really good. A million years from now, we still will have had those days, and no one can ever take them away.

Still more than a friend,
Vince

Back to my departure for New York. Before leaving Cleveland, I had to find a home for Monroe, my brown basset hound with the big sad eyes, the long flopping ears, the mournful face, and the affection he showed me. He had been my companion for five years, often in the front passenger seat with the convertible top down when I went to Terry's, sitting on the sidewalk and watching me wash my car Saturday mornings, even occasionally coming to work with me when I was on the midnight police beat shift. I couldn't take him to New York, but I did find a good home for him. A reporter on the police beat at the Press, who I remained friendly with after the News closed, jumped at the chance to take him.

It was a terribly sad parting, nonetheless. Monroe would live in Rocky River, a suburb to the west, where, from his reception, I was certain he would not lack love and affection. This helped lighten my turmoil at giving him up, but just a bit. On a trip to Cleveland a year later, and a visit to Monroe (and my friend), Monroe came over and greeted me semi-enthusiastically, then went over and lay at his

Monroe

(new) master's feet. Both disappointing, and reassuring.

Planning my move to New York, I concluded that after bouts of unemployment I would have to find an economical room. The YMCA would fill this need. I found that there were several, and the one near Central Park, the big 600-room Westside Y, seemed ideal. Central location, and this big beautiful park. So I phoned for a reservation.

The man on the phone seemed aghast. "We don't take no reservations at the Y. You crazy? You think this is the Waldorf? You just come!"

But, I explained, I was coming all the way from Ohio. "What if there's no room available?"

"Then you go someplace else," he ended. Then he added: "But there's always a room." (Update: you can now book a room online or by phone. Also, rooms now have air conditioners.)

But first I had to cross 42nd Street. I obeyed the Walk sign and stayed carefully in the crosswalk. I was just halfway across when "Walk"

The Y on West 63rd Street

began flashing. Cars started edging forward. Was the suitcase causing me to go slowly? Either that, or New Yorkers walk mighty fast. I made it to the curb just in time.

I hadn't gone ten steps when a young lady approached me. She was certainly a singular young woman. Long, silky, blonde hair and very dark eyes. I couldn't help but stare at her breasts, because they were so...ample, and protruding here and there from an electric blue halter that definitely was a size or two too small for her. She wore very short white shorts and between them and the halter was firm, bronzed skin. She was certainly dressed for the hot weather. Strangely, she wore high heels.

"You got the time?' she asked me, smiling slightly.

I looked at my watch and gave her the time.

"No, no. I mean, have you got any time," she corrected herself.

"I think my watch is about right," I replied.

She got a disgusted look on her face, said nothing, and turned back to stand in the shade of a building. I looked down the block. There were other women similarly dressed standing in the shadows along the buildings. It took me way too long to realize the employment of these ladies. There was a street just like this in Cleveland, but since I was always in my car, I had never been approached. Being in a car didn't seem to stop the women here. One had just walked out to a car waiting for a red light. The ladies weren't so bold in Cleveland, nor were there nearly as many of them. But this was New York, New York, the most exciting city in the world!

By the time I trudged up Eighth Avenue and reached Columbus Circle, I was panting. The suitcase was heavier with each block. I had been going to the gym two or three times a week. Where was that endurance I built up?

Over there I can see the park and Central Park West. Just three blocks left. But how many lanes to get across Columbus Circle? I learned later that there's a subway that runs through the bus terminal, with a stop just the other side of the Y where I was going. It would have saved all the sweating on arrival.

The man on the phone was right. There was a room.

I never stayed at a Y before, or since. My room, on the sixth floor, was narrow, maybe eight feet wide and about twelve feet long. It was a bright room because it had a full-size double-hung window in such a small room. It faced east but with no view except of an apartment building several hundred feet distant. That building would have views of Central Park. To the right inside the door was a single-width bed. The night table was at the foot of the bed; there was no room for it next to the bed. There was a straight-back wooden chair by the window. On a wall were several hooks to hang clothing. A clean white towel hung from one hook; a small, unused bar of Ivory soap was on the night table. There was a plain wooden cross on the wall. The only light was a bare bulb in the ceiling.

As the man had said, this was not the Waldorf, but I was perfectly happy with the room. What I did not like was that there were no rooms with a private bath. There was a large communal lavatory with about eight sinks under a wide mirror, a number of urinals in a row, several toilets in compartments, but without any doors, and a large shower room, perhaps 10 by 10, with shower heads lining two walls. You could not be an aficionado of privacy. And, I assume, this one was typical of most Ys. For $20 a week, my rent, you could not do better.

There were benefits. There was a large cafeteria where some really awful food was really reasonably priced. There was a gym where I could keep up my workouts. And there was a slew of young men my age, here with the same goal I had: to start a brilliant life in New York. So there was camaraderie, because we had so much in common — especially those belonging to the large gay population at the Y. As the song "Y.M.C.A." by the Village People says, there's no need to feel unhappy, young man, because you're in a new town.

Cruising was conveniently just around the corner on Central Park

West. In the other direction, Lincoln Center was nearing completion. Avery Fisher Hall, now called David Geffen Hall, opened while I was at the Y.

I had to start earning money almost immediately. Someone suggested to me going to a particular temp company that sent you out by the day, and paid $1.00 an hour. Could I type? Yes! That's what they wanted. My first job was at the Foreign Policy Association near the UN, where I spent an entire week — $40! I was having a hard time with my poor vision in typing excerpts from a brochure, but I suppose I did ok. A kind lady at the end of the job went out of her way to tell me that I was a good worker. It made me feel wonderful. I grasped at any praise.

During the Cuban missile crisis in October, 1962, when President Kennedy was demanding the removal of Soviet missiles and was blockading Cuba, I was a copy boy for a week or so, but this time at the New York Times. A copy boy again, but at the New York Times! Now I recalled the magic of working for a newspaper. It was the excitement every hour, and being the first to know everything about everything.

Another $40 for the week. However, the real pay for me was to be back in a Newsroom again, no matter the job. And especially during such a time, in the building at the heart of the constantly breaking news. I remember hearing discussions among editors and reporters that we could be at war at any minute, but that we may never know it if it begins with an atom bomb on New York City. I was not worried at all about being pulverized at any moment. This was exciting! Besides, that couldn't possibly happen. I hadn't made my brilliant life in New York yet.

Things were looking up on the social scene. I always worked at temporary jobs 40 hours, so I had $40 a week. No taxes were deducted and, of course, I would be expected to report earnings. I don't remember doing this that year, but in fact with such low earnings, it probably wasn't required. After the rent, I had $20 left. Dinner at the Y was less than a dollar. Subway rides to work assignments were ten cents each way. Lunch? Fifty cents if I didn't just pick up a piece of fruit. Central Park was free. I spent about $12 of the $20. Enough left for a movie each week, and a scrumptious dinner on Friday nights with a group of fellow gay men from the Y at Aldo's Italian Restaurant on Bleeker Street in the Village. What more could I want? I was having a fantastic time in my new city. Not yet a brilliant life, but getting lustrous.

And here I am, calling it the "Village" like real New Yorkers do, not "Greenwich Village," like tourists. I'm almost a real New Yorker!

After a few months, I was hired by Sarah, the name I use for the woman who would become a valued friend, as a copywriter at Gimbels Department Store, a block from Macy's, its competitor that lives on after Gimbels' long-ago demise. I haven't heard the refrain "Does Gimbels tell Macys?" in years. The job wasn't in an agency, but it was at a famous store that I had heard of long before coming to New York. I would write to my mother, and she would have heard of Gimbels also.

In department store advertising, I learned that there is a style you must follow. I was told the headline must name the product and the copy must be short and pithy. No chance for literature here. When items were offered on a sale, it was the duty of the advertising department to go to the buyer and make certain he could substantiate sales at the pre-sale price. If not, it could not be offered as a sale, which would be risking a citation from a city inspector.

But the Gimbels job I considered a temporary one. Sarah realized this and encouraged me in my quest to go to an agency. She herself had formerly been a copywriter at a large agency, and assembled a list of creative directors at prime agencies that she thought I should contact.

Tragically, Sarah's life came to a premature end. Sarah's husband had recently died from throat cancer, and she had tended him in his last, difficult months. An awful coincidence occurred. After I left Gimbels, Sarah also developed inoperable throat cancer. Not wanting to be in the same condition as her late husband, nor to be a burden to others, she ended her life at the couple's weekend house in one of those towns along the Hudson River north of the city. I was saddened to hear the news, but understood its logic.

When I had first arrived in New York, I registered with an employment agency that specialized in jobs in advertising. There were a couple of such agencies at the time, and I imagine they had several thousand registrants each, young people from elsewhere hoping to break into advertising on their looks, on their university grades, or their charisma... It's not as impossible as getting into Hollywood, but it's not easy. Advertising agencies want a track record.

After a dozen or so interviews with advertising agencies where creative directors gave me no encouragement, the employment agency gave me one piece of sound advice. Since you have no print ads and no commercials to show, create some. Outline a marketing problem and do some mock-ups of print ads that address that problem. Do a TV storyboard or two. Put everything into a black portfolio and show its contents proudly. That is how to stand out from the crowd.

I had had several dollars left for a number of weeks from my earnings, chiefly because I got a raise at my temp job to $1.25 an hour. I was an experienced typist from my reporting days, so maybe I was a good employee. One thing, I was dependable. I had to be; I needed every dollar. So, with my savings from the raise, I bought an impressive big black expensive portfolio.

Outline a problem and create advertising to solve it. That was the advice I was given. This was almost too easy, because I did not have the real-life constraints that I would have later on. In fact, I think I did things backwards. I would come up with an idea for an ad that I considered unique, then would decide what problem it was solving. That's not how it works in real life.

But realistic or not, after a short time at Gimbels, spurred on by Sarah, my portfolio got me a copywriter job at a big Madison Avenue advertising agency, Norman, Craig & Kümmel. I had finally succeeded in getting into Madison Avenue, and I was overjoyed and proud of my accomplishment. I could hardly keep from bragging about it to the guys at the Y. To let my mother know, this time I didn't write a letter, but went to a pay phone armed with quarters so I could tell her directly and hear her reaction.

It turned out to be the worst job I ever had, but still gave me the opening into the advertising agency world that I needed. In the 1960s, Norman, Craig had a reputation of hiring mostly writers and art directors just getting into the agency business, as was the case with me. These neophytes were supervised by a few veteran advertising men. The young people were pumped for every idea they had — and when an individual's fresh ideas seemed to be on the wane, he was unceremoniously let go. I was on the Ajax account and lasted five or six months, about the same as all the others. The firings came about every other Friday, and were so regular that everyone kept his personal belongings consolidated in one place so that he could leave at a moment's notice.

Aside from the certainty of eventually being fired, working there was in itself unpleasant. Each writer would be paired with an art director, and on a given account there may be a half dozen such duos. Each pair was given the same problem to solve, and all teams would report together to the creative director at a conference room meeting with a proposed solution, so that we were all in competition with each other. No idea would be accepted at that first meeting, and maybe never.

To make matters worse, these meetings began about 9 PM. You never went home at 5 o'clock. Each writer and art director would continue working together after normal hours. At about 7 PM, the creative director would take everyone to a fancy restaurant for a two-hour dinner. To me, these dinners were a complete waste of time. I would have preferred to be eating with companions of my own choosing. After presenting your ideas after dinner, you'd get home about 11 PM. The agency did pay for a taxi. Big deal. In 1983, this agency name ceased to exist when the agency was merged with Foote Cone & Belding.

It was about that time in my life that I stopped believing in God. With my mother and sister in Cleveland, I went to Mass every Sunday and did so until I moved to New York. I don't think I stopped to think about heaven or hell or God or faith when I was still living at home. I went through the motions of religion without reflecting on them, like brushing your teeth or having coffee the first thing when you get up. Occasionally during the day in New York as I went about my business, an element of religion taught me as a child would flash into my mind. Like the Virgin birth. Well, I thought about that, and decided, no, I could no longer believe in a virgin birth. So one tenet of my religion was gone. Then came to me a thought about the Eucharist. I had been told in religion class that the bread and wine became, in reality, the body and blood of Christ, transubstantiation. Another impossible thing for me to accept. And life everlasting? If it were only so, but it didn't seem credible. I woke up one morning, assembled in my mind all the elements that I had rejected, and realized that I just no longer believed. I thought about an all-powerful being who created the limitless universe — and this also seemed preposterous to me. I denied that, too.

First, I told myself that I was an agnostic, searching. It didn't take me but a few weeks to admit to myself that I wasn't searching; I was no longer a believer, period. It wasn't easy to accept this appraisal. I thought with nostalgia of my days as a Catholic: as a choir boy singing lovely hymns in the candlelit procession around the church to the manger on Christmas Eve; as an altar boy ringing the bell when the priest held up the sacred Eucharist. I admired the caring nuns who devoted their lives to religion; the majesty and beauty of Church rites that stirred the emotions. The hymn "Ave Maria" would remain a favorite of mine.

My mind went over tiny episodes of my early years. As an altar boy, before Mass I was to light the tall candles on the altar with a long candle lighter. This was no easy task, because they were about four feet above the altar, and sometimes I would fumble. What didn't make it any easier was that early arrivals for Mass were in the pews watching my performance. How annoying it was when a prior altar boy, in snuffing out the candles, had pushed a wick down into the wet wax. How embarrassing it was when I heard a snicker from a classmate in a pew.

Now I was leaving all of this, the culture imbued in me since my earliest childhood. I was joining a minority that stays hidden, just as I had when becoming gay. Being an atheist is not something you're going to boast about. Just as my sexual orientation, I would mention my loss of faith to only a select few. And I would regret the forfeiture. From now on, I would gaze upon churches and cathedrals and be reminded of a life lost. Problems in life I would face alone, without hope of an intervention by a supreme being. No longer could I anticipate a paradise to come, life everlasting. When I get old, I thought, I will die and be dead a million years and forever. Nothingness awaits me. Oh, how I envied those who can believe!

I suppose, since I was baptized, I will always be counted as a Catholic, atheist though I am. And gay, too! Two reasons the Catholic Church should delete me. Somehow, though, for a reason I can't define, I'm glad to still be included.

Since the day I became a non-believer, I have often thought about all the millions and millions of people who do have faith, millions of intelligent people. I ask myself how they can really believe that there is a being, somewhere, who created the planets, the stars, everything, including us. I can't explain how all of everything came about, but, to me, no explanation is better than what religion offers. However, I was not downhearted to forgo the idea of hell, fiery damnation for eternity.

Why so many embrace religion, I think, is that they cannot face death and nothingness, the same future I'm having trouble coping with. A beautiful thought that I was told as a child is that on death, you'll be united for eternity with your loved ones who pre-deceased you. That would be beyond wonderful, so that you'd anticipate death with joy, but I can't believe it. Nor did the Rev. Billy Graham. In 2010, he was asked to comment on that idea, and said he would love to be with his wife, who was deceased, but could find no support for the belief of reunion in the Bible. Various clergymen, however, do cite passages in both the Old and New Testaments that they claim prove the truth of the assertion. I'm certainly a Doubting Thomas on this and every tenet of religion. Is this same loving, all powerful being responsible for earthquakes, the floods in the Midwest, the fires in California, the coronavirus? I wouldn't want to know that being. Science talks about attributing the start of everything to a "Big Bang." Lacking anything better, I'll accept that.

Shortly after my loss to heaven, I would meet someone with the same thoughts on religion as I now had, a fellow atheist. This person was Jack Bernard, who would become my partner for a long, long time.

I had taken a studio apartment in a building that had just opened at Sixth Avenue and 12th Street in the Village. I was making $125 a week, so at $140 a month, it was a little expensive but doable. However, New York apartments were overbuilt at the time, and I did get a three-month concession — free rent — as an inducement. Everything was spanking new, new parquet floors, freshly-painted walls, new refrigerator and stove. This was the life! So it was a studio; I didn't need more. I was on the 12th floor, with an open view through a window as wide as the room to a similar building a full block away. My life was really looking good. I could hardly wait to invite someone in to show them the apartment, or, rather, room.

Since I lived in the Village, I would occasionally walk down to the foot of Christopher Street at the Hudson River, where after dark gay men roamed about among the semis and other large trucks parked there overnight. This particular night when I went there, there were few people. There was no moon, and it was especially dark. I came out from between two trucks to the clearing along West Street, and turned right.

"Watch! There's a police car right behind you!" I was startled by the voice from the darkness. I could see that the source of the warning was another young man, a little taller than me, but whose features I could not make out other than that he was trim and had dark hair. I muttered, "Thanks," and decided to leave the area and head back up Christopher to the center of the Village. On Christopher, almost to Greenwich Avenue, I stopped and sat on the cement stoop of one of the small brick historic houses there.

In just a few minutes, a young man approached me. "Hi. I just saw you down at the trucks," he explained, and introduced himself as Jack. I surmised that he was the same man who had warned me of the presence of the police. I gave him my name; he sat down next to me, and we began talking. He was taller than me, maybe 5'10, slim as most everyone in their 20s and early 30s, dark hair and eyes, very French-appearing, looking something like Louis Jourdan. When I was young I had a type: I liked only fair-haired people, blue eyes. This young man, though handsome, did not fill the bill. But I was enjoying the conversation.

CHAPTER 10

Year One, 40 to go.

IN FACT WE were discovering that our thinking, our personalities, were totally harmonious. After a while, Jack invited me to his apartment. Without hesitation, I accepted. I wanted the evening to continue. Jack's apartment, a few blocks away, was a startling contrast to mine in a new doorman building. It turned out to be a "cold-water" railroad flat on the ground floor of an old tenement in need of a lot of TLC, or preferably a bulldozing. The apartments in tenement buildings are called cold-water flats, but, in fact, for the last decades, they have had hot water available. This was a railroad flat because the rooms were arranged in a line like railroad cars, one after the next. You entered from the public hallway into a sizable kitchen; directly off that was a tiny bedroom consumed almost entirely by a bed, but with a tall chest crowded in. Continuing in a straight line and fronting on Charles Street was an ample living room. The flat did not have the luxury of an interior hallway, so to get from the kitchen to the living room, you passed through the bedroom. Nor, I was surprised to learn, did it have its own bathroom. The toilet was in a closet off the building's main hallway, no sink, and was for the use of the two apartments on the first floor. I was shocked by this. I would have thought that such an arrangement would exist only in a third world country. Then I was taken aback further when I spotted the bathtub in the corner of Jack's kitchen.

My impression of gay cruising is that, as the hours pass, and then as midnight goes, there are less and less social amenities required with an encounter, that is, a pickup. That's an observation I've made, but I can't swear that's a rule. Courtesies for situations like this are never written down. By the time Jack and I finished our conversation on the cement stoop on Christopher Street, and I had gone with him to his apartment, it was past 2 AM. It was a Friday and neither of us had to get up to go to work, However, it was still very late, or early, and we were both tired from our respective exhausting evening of walking around. So, without further fuss, the light was turned off. It would have to be put off to another day earlier in the evening for one to be offered beer, soda, coffee, spaghetti...

Already having gotten a very poor opinion of Jack's environment, I was wakened in the dark of the night by a creature, an animal, walking across Jack's bed. "There's a rat in the bed!" I shouted, sitting up. "No, it's just my cat," Jack assured me, laughing softly.

In the morning, we went to a nearby cafe for breakfast and resumed our non-stop chatter from the night before.

Jack Bernard, who will become my partner for 40 years.

We recognized at once that we were two kindred souls and arranged to meet for dinner. In that summer of 1963 began our conversations that would continue for four decades.

The following days I would be wondering why Jack had selected such living quarters. He appeared to have adequate funds for something better. He at the time was doing freelance editorial work for McGraw Hill, and was under contract to translate Jacques Cousteau's books from French into English. He had PhDs in French history and in languages, and had attended the Sorbonne in Paris and taught at the University of Montreal. Eventually, he would author several well-regarded books: among them, a biography of Talleyrand, a crafty French politician who survived many regimes including that of Louis XVI and Napoleon, and "Up From Caesar," a history of Rome. I had merely a simple BA.

Despite our educational differences, we found common ground in many likes and dislikes, and hit it off from the first day. I found that conversations with Jack about any subject under the sun were stimulating. His knowledge made him a walking encyclopedia. We would see just about every non-kiddie movie that came along. I would accompany Jack to the Strand Book Store on Lower Broadway, and while he studied serious tomes, I'd browse.

For me, who has never advanced beyond a hard-boiled egg, there was the advantage that Jack was a cook. When alone, I confined my consumption to prepared foods. I had two friends, Bob and Don, that I was not ready yet to introduce to Jack, for no particular reason that I can recall. However, I was eager for them to see my apartment, although yet barely furnished. Jack had the idea to go to a fabric store on 14th Street to get a material to make draperies, as my big window was entirely bare. So, we got a green-checked fabric, and Jack stapled hems into it to get the proper length. The place was beginning to look downright homey.

I mentioned my two good friends a lot to Jack, and he suggested that I invite Don and Bob to dinner, not with him present, just the three of us, and he would prepare a meal in advance for me to serve. He made a sauce for a shrimp dish, shrimp creole, and all I had to do was boil the shrimp a few minutes and combine it with Jack's sauce. He also supplied a bag of rice that would be ready to serve if you put it in boiling water a minute or two, Simple enough, even for me. I bought a Sara Lee strawberry cheesecake for dessert, but I upset it in the refrigerator in removing it, and ended up by serving strawberry cheesecake pudding. Incidentally, Bob and Don are still my friends 59 years after that dinner. Actually, Bob, who met my key essentials of being small and fair, had been a trick before I met Jack. A "trick," in gay language, is a one-night affair, and it is not uncommon to make a lasting friend from a brief encounter.

After gestures by Jack like this, such as making my draperies and preparing dinner for my guests, I expressed an enthusiasm for the idea when Jack proposed that we move together. We considered that my apartment, a studio, was too small for two people, and his tenement flat — well, we didn't speak of it.

Actually, Jack was thinking of the opposite extreme from a railroad flat. We began looking for a duplex with two bedrooms and two baths. This, he believed, would give us sufficient space so we both would have our privacy. He could make his bedroom into a bedroom-study with a desk and books. I was working in midtown, and Jack had just been hired as an editor at Doubleday, also in midtown. We found a duplex on East 54th off Lexington, from which we could walk to work. It was the second and third floors of a small townhouse, and had a large 40-foot by 12-foot terrace jutting out in the rear with high-rise buildings soaring up around it. This, indeed, would be fulfilling my dream of a brilliant life in Manhattan.

First, we agreed on a stipulation. I found young men with blond hair and blue eyes attractive, the Nordic or German look. I thought Jack was handsome in his French way, with dark hair. dark eyes. What

I found appealing in him was his intelligence, his knowledge, his conversation. But I didn't want to give up entirely little blond people. Jack also had his preferences.

So the bargain we struck was that we could—with limits—go off on occasion without the other. No overnights, no little notes saying we've gone to Paris for a while. The general restriction was that any wandering could not interfere with our domestic life together. This kind of arrangement is not unusual in gay life. You are generally dealing with two men in their prime with all the testosterone that goes with youth. In my opinion, it is more honest and less threatening to a relationship than the practice, sometimes existing in heterosexual unions, where one or both partners roam about without prior approval. In the case of Jack, however, his intense interest in books and music left him little time to benefit from our contract.

At the new apartment, at mild times of the year, we spent so much time on the terrace that we hardly needed the rest of the apartment. Saturday mornings would be spent scrubbing the week's New York grime off of it, then spreading liquid floor wax over the 40 feet of maroon ceramic tiles so that they would glisten. Sunday morning we retired to the terrace for our breakfast and to read the voluminous New York Times. The chimes from St. Peter's Episcopal Church, along the terrace's west side, were sweet music.

After work we would meet to walk home together, sometimes stop for dinner; other times Jack would cook and we'd eat in. Whenever we were home, we never missed Walter Cronkite's CBS News.

Saturday nights were always busy. We would often go to dinner and then walk to the LOOM, Light Opera of Manhattan, in the East 70s. LOOM always did a first-class production of operettas such as The Merry Widow. We both liked its repertoire of Gilbert & Sullivan. After, we would stop at Mary's Fancy at Third and 57th, quite a lively and chic place, for a hamburger with accessories. (After all, it had been several hours since we ate!)

We read in the Times on a Sunday after our attending the LOOM the evening before that the lead bass, a man about 30, in walking to his apartment on the West Side after the show, took the short cut through Central Park and was stabbed to death. New York, New York.

There were also weekend nights at the Amato Opera House on the Bowery, a small company in a little theater rescued from teardown. Amato Opera was the beloved child of an Italian opera buff couple named Anthony and Sally Amato. Here, a company did very passable opera classics. Our intermissions were filled by cannoli.

The landlord of our 54th Street apartment was a wizened, elderly dentist whose office was on the ground floor. His family had occupied our apartment just before we moved in, and left an old Knabe grand piano in the apartment when they relocated to Long Island. The piano was old but beautiful: ebony, with massive carved legs. We gladly accepted the apartment with the piano in the large living room. We were short on furniture anyway, and it helped to fill the empty space. Then, two years later, when we had taken a duplex in a new building at 1 Charlton Street at the southern edge of the Village, the landlord suggested a trade. We could have the piano if we left the awning we had installed over part of the terrace. Done!

We thought the barter well worth it, even though neither of us played. We were well aware that the piano would not fit into an elevator at the new building, and would have to be hoisted up on the outside of the building to our living room on the 16th floor. But the piano was beautiful! So, on a cool but clear November morning, lifted by a pulley installed on the roof, we stood on the sidewalk and watched our musical instrument make its slow ascent up the side of the building, through the chasm where a pair of double-hung windows had been removed, and into our new duplex apartment.

It was a large apartment, and we had to purchase many household items for it. It was probably no larger than our prior apartment on East 54th, but, in that apartment, we had been content to have mostly empty rooms. Now, we decided, we wanted to live in a furnished apartment. We often shopped after work and loaded ourselves, with our packages, into the subway. We were always exhausted by the time we got home. That mere fact, being fatigued in my early 30s, is reassuring to me now at my late years. When I get tired, it's not, not necessarily, that I'm declining. I always got tired.

By this time in life, I was at my third advertising agency. After being let go (I avoid the pejorative word, fired) at Norman Craig & Kümmel, it was easy enough, now having experience and a real portfolio to show, to change to another agency. The second agency, Cunningham & Walsh, I left because the account I was working on, United Aircraft, was chiefly an industrial account, and I sought a more prestigious and interesting consumer account. As Norman, Craig & Kümmel, C&W was a place where I experienced no anti-gay bias or hint of bigotry whatsoever. Advertising is a liberal profession, and New York, a progressive city. I was at home at this latest agency, and I credit that to the fact that my creative supervisor himself was gay and quickly marked me as a kindred spirit. Here I met Phil, another writer and gay also, who became a good friend. Owing to my years in Europe, we lost touch with each other and, try as I can, I cannot locate him. There are a lot of people with his name who come up when I Google. I would like to see Phil Anderson again.

I will eventually work at four large agencies: Norman Craig & Kümmel, C & W, Tatham Laird & Kudner, and Foote Cone & Belding. It is common for copywriters, and art directors, too, to change agencies frequently. Maybe this is because you get bored working on the same account or accounts. Perhaps the grass looks greener elsewhere. More money could play a part. Or maybe it was simply that we are a restless group.

At about this time, Jack and I were invited for a weekend to Fire Island Pines by a long-time friend of his. We were quite taken with Fire Island: no cars, people pulling little red wagons with their groceries in them along boardwalks, the ocean on one side and on the other side, just hundreds of feet away, Great South Bay. Across the bay, five miles distant, was the dock where you board a large ferry to either the Pines or Cherry Grove.

Cherry Grove is the original gay community that made Fire Island famous, or infamous, as a gay resort, and the butt of homophobic jokes. It has several hundred houses, or cottages, mostly showing their age, but generally given elaborate makeup by their owners to disguise it. Fire Island Pines, called simply The Pines, is a newer community with many sizable contemporary houses along the ocean and bay. On the oceanfront, there are still remnants of private boardwalks extending to nowhere. They once led from the public walk to houses that are no longer there, having disappeared in a hurricane.

We learn during our weekend that Cherry Grove is still almost 100% gay, whereas The Pines is, at that time, about 50-50. A stretch of National Seashore about a half mile long separates the two settlements. There is no road connecting the two, and Seashore and utility vehicles drive on the ocean beach. Further on in both directions are other straight, heterosexual, towns: small Point of Woods with its large Victorian cottages; Ocean Beach, said to be mainly for blue collar, and Davis Park, reputedly a haven for swinging singles. When you include all the communities, straight people are the majority on Fire Island even though the island owes its national fame to its gays. What a cross those straight people must bear when telling people they have a house on Fire Island.

We had arrived for the weekend on Saturday morning, had taken the Long Island Railroad train to Sayville, and then the ferry. We joined the guys in the house — three of them, one being our host, had gone together on a seasonal rental — and accompanied them to the beach. Saturday night there was a cookout on the deck, then everyone went to the Boatel, a motel-type establishment with one of the two bars, and a name that takes notice of its harbor-edge site. The house had three small bedrooms. Jack and I had been given one, and our host slept on the living room sofa. The inconvenience didn't bother him; very little does when you're that young.

Sunday afternoon, before we left to go back to the City, the fellow who assumed the role of head of the house sat down at the kitchen table and added up the food expenses for the weekend, plus, applying only to us, a pro-rated portion of the month's rent. Getting a bill was a surprise to us as we were not told we were to be paying guests. But the weekend was worth it, and we knew already that we liked Fire Island.

We liked it so much that when we got back to the City, Jack suggested that we buy a boat, a small boat without a cabin, and go to Fire Island weekends by boat. At the Pines, we could pull out of the harbor into the bay and sleep under the stars. The idea became reality a few weeks later when our 18-foot Aristocraft, an open boat with seats that folded down in order to lie on them, was delivered to the West 79th Street marina, where we had rented a slip. The boat was red-and-white fiberglass, with an inboard motor in the back (I meant to say stern), and a bullet shape. We thought it was beautiful! Our plan was nearing fruition.

Our first voyage to Fire Island, which would be about 50 miles, began at 7 AM on a glorious Saturday in June with the sun still weak in the eastern sky. We headed down the Hudson River toward the ocean. My job was to be a lookout, alerting Jack, who was steering, whenever the boat might collide with one of the many floating logs, apparently having broken off from old piers. Then out into the open sea we went, with an inspiring view of the Statue of Liberty in the distance to our right, and the soaring Manhattan skyline behind us. We were basking in the joy of boating! This was the brilliant life I sought!

It didn't last. The ocean currents were slamming our little boat, and at times the bow would dip deeply into the water, pushing the stern with the motor above the waterline. It seemed we were barely moving. Cars on the Brooklyn shore to our left were leaving us in their...wake.

At this rate, we would never reach our destination. This called for a conference.

We had a solution. We had studied maps and had seen that there was a boat channel that veered off the ocean at Jones Beach, continued for 30-some miles to Great South Bay, which laps against Fire Island. We would leave the open sea reluctantly, and we would be protected from the strong current by a strip of land all the way to Fire Island Pines. And we were. What the map did not specify, or we did not notice, is that the boat channel has a speed limit of 5mph within 100 feet of the shore. Since in most cases the channel is narrow, the speed limit is de facto 5mph.

We recalculated that it would take us hours. We did not arrive until after 1 PM, when we had left Manhattan just after 7. It was only 50 miles, but at 5mph a good part of the way we didn't do badly. However, we wouldn't want to do six hours all the time, so our plan to do this every week was in tatters.

We were overjoyed when we entered the Pines harbor, and we were all smiles. As we happily putted in, no one on the docked boats seemed pleased to see us. No one was smiling but us.

The Pines harbor is a man-made cove, approximately circular, with a small grocery store, two bar-restaurants, and the three-story "Boatel" with motel-like rooms on the west side, or right, as you enter. On the east side are a few houses and many large yachts docked. Straight ahead, the south side, is the ferry dock and slips for small boats such as ours. Beyond the harbor to the south, near the water's edge, is a 300-foot-long horizontal pipe anchored in the ground to which residents attach their little red wagons used to carry items along the boardwalks from the ferry to their homes. Then comes a narrow sand road for the few local utility vehicles, and beyond that are the Co-ops, a large two- to three-story development of 100 contemporary-styled cooperative apartments.

But more pertinent to our arrival in the harbor were the thirty or so

30, 40, and 50-foot yachts docked along the left, or east side. Just as we entered Great South Bay, about five miles from The Pines, a wind from the southwest had arisen. It was chiefly from our rear and had assisted us in our trip through Great South Bay. As we entered the harbor, we were now headed south. When we prepared to go by the large yachts to our left, our handsome but small open boat was beginning to be lashed from the west. Jack, at the control, had never piloted a boat before this trip; neither had I. Jack could control our boat in the strong wind not at all. Each violent gust lurched us to the left and closer to the expensive yachts. The smiles we had shown at having accomplished our first trip disappeared upon seeing the dilemma we were now in. I observed that Jack seemed under intense stress, evidently not knowing what to do with the tiller to get a result. He was desperately moving it back and forth with no effect at all. Of course, I had no idea what to do either, and thought it wise if I remained silent.

The yacht people, most of them sitting on their decks with an unimpeded view of us and the threat we posed, became alarmed. They swung into a flurry of frenzied activity, seemingly running haphazardly to and fro on their boats, grabbing boat poles to ward us off in order to protect their beautiful assets. From various boats came simultaneous, shouted instructions that we could not decipher, or put into practice if we could.

Fortunately, a sudden gust of wind blew us the few feet still remaining toward a yacht where the owner was already waiting to stop us with his boat pole. He then managed to guide our rocking boat into the slip next to his boat, which, again luckily, happened to be vacant. Our prow hit the dock rather forcefully, but not enough to cause damage to our boat. Jack and I quickly glanced at each other and breathed a sigh of relief.

The young harbor master, all in white, frowning and shaking his head, had already rushed around to the head of the slip and stood waiting there above us. Although the slip was intended for a large boat, he wisely suggested that we stay put, rather than try to get our boat to a smaller slip along the south side. Several of the yacht owners from boats down the line joined the harbor master on the dock, muttering among themselves, and staring down at us. No one introduced himself as a fellow boater. No one welcomed us to Fire Island Pines.

We had no desire to linger in this environment and extend our ignominious debut. We gathered our beach towels and our packed lunch, climbed up on the dock, paid the harbor master, avoided looking at the assemblage still observing us, and left hurriedly for the beach. We did not look forward with pleasure returning to our boat, and occupied ourselves until about 9 PM, partly by dropping in unannounced at the cottage of Jack's friend where we had stayed a few weeks before.

Finally, we could delay the return to our handsome boat no longer. On the walk to the harbor, we noted two things: that the wind had almost totally died down, and with nightfall the air had gotten awfully cold and damp. I had on my orange nylon jacket. Very appropriate, I thought, for the sea. Jack was similarly clothed, in a white jacket, but we were both cold and getting wet in the damp air.

The harbor, so active and noisy the last time we saw it, was now dark and silent. We were relieved. Only a few street lights, spaced far apart, and dim lights in the larger boats, lighted the scene. Faint music wafted from the bar-restaurants. We saw not a person in the semi-darkness, only the shadow of a man walking along the dock pulling a wagon. We assumed that the boat people were all at the restaurants at dinner.

We let ourselves down into our boat. Jack started the engine, backed out of the slip slowly and carefully, and we putted out of the harbor into the bay with nary a soul around to notice our exit. We stopped about a thousand feet offshore, making certain we were not in the channel used by the ferry, and prepared to drop anchor. We would open our bottle of Chablis, the type of wine that everyone was drinking then, pass time reminiscing about the day's memorable trip and our arrival at the Pines, and eventually fall asleep under the stars on the folded-down seats, as per the plan. Or, we would sit there silently trying not to think about the day's memorable adventures.

The first thing we discovered was that the seats were wet from the damp air. The two blankets we had brought to keep us warm and cozy were light cotton and, alas, also wet. And, while we had not experienced much of a wind on the island, in the open bay there was indeed a piercingly frigid breeze, not strong, but icy. This was not like June in Manhattan!

We were in quick agreement that we could not spend the night here. Also, with reluctance, that our intention to spend future weekends in our open boat was not a marvelous idea. Whose idea had that been anyway? Further, cold and wet, we began to think that even owning a boat might make no sense. A moment later, the motor was fired up and we initiated the chilly five-mile journey to a closed and darkened marina on the mainland that fortune just happened to put in our path. There, we tied up our beautiful, brand-new boat, and hid the key under a seat. The following morning we called the marina and arranged to sell the boat. We were saddened but relieved to be ex-boatsmen. We would never see our boat again.

After leaving the boat, we stayed the night at a nearby B&B, and caught the first train in the morning back to warm and toasty Manhattan.

We did not put Fire Island out of our minds, however. Jack's friend told him that apartments are often for sale in the cooperative complex we had seen there. Soon we were en route to Fire Island by train and ferry, and were purchasing a two-bedroom unit. It had a ceiling in the living room that soared to 20 feet on one side, to accommodate a loft bedroom. Best of all, the apartment was on the second floor and its deck overlooked the busy harbor (where we had suffered our humiliating debut to the Pines). A weekend beach life began for a mere $7000, a bargain, it seemed to us, even then. Fire Island was an exciting place, because of its natural beauty, but also because of its people, all seeking an oasis. There were publishing people and those in advertising, like Jack and me. Models were there. John Whyte, the then-current Marlboro Man, had built a big house on the ocean. There were many from Broadway. Jerry Herman, the composer of "Hello, Dolly!" and "Mame" owned a house, and would sometimes bring Carol Channing with him for a weekend. Calvin Klein was there. No telling who you'd run into walking along a boardwalk.

Our routine was to arrive on Friday as early as we could manage to escape our jobs in the City, immediately take a walk along the ocean in bare feet, pass an hour or two Saturday at the beach, dine at new friends' houses that night or have people in, watch from our deck the mass exodus on Sunday evening, and be on board the red eye Monday morning ferry at 6:25 AM. The train would connect to the subway, and we'd go directly to our offices.

Having joined the usual procedure in the creative side of advertising of changing agencies every few years, I found that change meant the excitement of new accounts, and a bigger salary. I was now earning twice what Jack was. He was still at Doubleday, in publishing, where it would be considered undignified to bring up the subject of a salary increase. He was also still doing freelance translations of Jacques Cousteau's books.

With the influx of funds, we would buy a house a few boardwalks away, on Great South Bay, and sell the apartment. I had hepatitis at the moment when the house idea came up, the less-serious type that it seemed half our friends had. So I remained in New York and Jack went to Fire Island with the assignment to look for a house. He returned enthusiastic, with a description of a house on the bay. So we bought it, (my) sight unseen but with my total confidence in Jack's choice.

Our routine changed. We no longer went to the ocean beach; we were on the water ourselves. Jack had bought a self-help book, and, following its instructions, we began building additional decks. One we built in the shallow water by the shore, with a boardwalk, a bridge really, to it. We would remove this deck every fall, so that winter storms wouldn't wash it away, and we'd put it back in the spring.

We were unhappy with the size of the windows facing the bay, and ordered glass sliding doors to replace them. When they arrived at the ferry dock, we supported each one on our red wagon in transporting them from the ferry dock to our house. Then, following a second book, on our two-week vacations we ripped out a 30-foot wall and installed the glass doors. This whet our appetite. In the next year's vacation, we did the same thing with the other, perpendicular, exterior living room wall, facing a woods. We were creating a glass house.

We took time off now and then to go out in the bay in our tiny new sailboat, a Sea Snark, with its cherry-red sail. We made certain to stay well clear of the harbor where occurred our shameful introduction to the Pines.

We continued dinners out at friends', dinners at our house with friends. One of our new friends was a vice president and the medical director of one of the country's largest insurance companies. For a while, we wondered how it was possible that he had such a responsible job. He was such a mild-mannered guy, in our estimation hardly equipped for the dog-eat-dog New York business world. We seldom saw him without him carrying Suzy, his tiny Yorkshire terrier, in his arms. Even the little dog was bursting with gentleness. But then we saw a transformation in the medical director.

At a property owners meeting, where he was opposed to some proposal, he shouted, "One minute!" stood up, stormed to the front of the room with rigid jaw, and proceeded to give a forceful argument. He was not carrying Suzy. His demeanor was unrecognizable to us; he had shed his Fire Island persona. In time, we would sometimes go to dinner with him and his partner in Manhattan, and he would be in his New York City persona. I observed my first split personality.

It was 1967 now. As usual, Jack and I weren't happy closing our house up at the end of the summer. The ferry stopped running, but we still wanted to go there. We asked Barney, one of two plumbers who stayed all winter with their families, to put in a well. The town water, in pipes attached to the undersides of boardwalks, is turned off before freezing weather. Barney also put heat tape around all of our exposed pipes.

We arranged for a January week of vacation. Barney, with his all-wheel-drive vehicle, drove along the beach the 13 miles to the bridge on the east end of Fire Island, picked up the two of us and George, the Siamese cat, at the train station in Shirley, and drove us across the bridge and down the beach. The 400 or so houses and 100 apartments in the Pines had been vacated months before, except for the two plumbers, both living nearly a mile from our house. We would not see a soul for eight days, and didn't want to, until Barney would pick us up for the return. Our landline phone had been turned off for the winter, and, of course, no one had yet heard of a cell phone. But we were in our early 30s, and no one that age even thinks of a medical emergency.

Barney dropped us off on the narrow sand road by the harbor, two blocks from the house, on a gray, windy, snowy, or sleety, Saturday afternoon. We stood on the spot a minute, in our South Pole attire of fur-lined jackets, boots with heavy corduroy pants stuffed into them, furry hats, scarves tied around our necks, and fur-lined gloves. I even had ear muffs. We looked around.

Think Chernobyl. All the people had fled and the whole place was desolate and uninhabitable. No sane person would even think of coming here. Wild animals were moving in. While standing there in the ugly weather observing the formerly people-jammed, boat-filled, center of the Pines. a red fox casually strolled by not far from us. Are they dangerous? I noted that the cat in his wisdom made not a peep.

The two restaurants were not only dark and devoid of people standing, sipping drinks on the decks, but they were boarded up. The Boatel had each window boarded up, all the way to the 3rd floor. No chance of a sneaky winter storm squeezing into a room here.

We set off. It had snowed a little during the night, so the board-walks en route to our house were tinged here and there with snow and patches of ice. There was silence. The only sound was the crunching of our boots as we walked, and the wind whistling around us. A whisper would have seemed deafening. But this was what we wanted, wasn't it? Solitude!

As we neared our house, our heads were bent over almost to our waists to lessen as best we could the elements stinging our faces. Each of us had both hands occupied: each had a small suitcase, with George in his carrying case for me, and Jack with a cloth shopping bag for the food we brought from the City to supplement what had been left in the house when we had closed it up. Crucial were the several books each of us had, and the box with 10 packets of Carnation dry milk for cof-fees, hot chocolates, and cream of wheat early mornings. My suitcase contained the essential six bottles of Chablis.

I've mentioned that our house was on the bay. It had a narrow deck on three sides and a large deck outside the living room on the bay side. In order to get into the house, you had to walk on the narrow decks around to the bay side and enter directly into the living room. It wouldn't be until the following summer on our vacations, spurred on by this winter visit, that we would rip out a bedroom wall to make a foyer with access on the side closest to the public boardwalk.

As we went up our boardwalk approaching the house, the wind got stronger as it tends to do near open water, and the sleet and ice it was conveying became more bountiful. When we stepped onto the first deck, one of us behind the other, we both found it impossible to stand in the strong wind on its covering of ice, and we both simultaneously crashed down on the deck. I noted that, now, the cat, his carrier hitting the deck with a thud, did venture a peep.

Unable to stand on the ice in the wind, we did the only thing pos-sible and crawled on our knees and gloved hands around to the living room, dragging our goods, including George in his case, alongside us. It's not often that one is thankful that someone in the entourage smokes, but I confess my gratitude that Jack had a cigarette lighter to melt the ice covering the keyhole, so that we could insert the key and enter. All the windows facing the bay were covered with ice, too, so that the view we had created with our construction was mainly a memory.

It seemed like 50 degrees colder inside than the, unacceptable, outside temperature, probably in the 20s. But, we had a floor furnace, and Barney had seen to it that we had two fresh bottles of gas. We also had left logs piled next to the fireplace, so we anticipated that in maybe just two hours, we'd be cozy and toasty. And it happened. We were surprised the TV worked, because the roof antenna must have been wrapped in ice.

After our wicked inauguration, we did spend a nice, sometimes sunny, period there that January, and periods in winters after. On long walks along forlorn boardwalks before deserted houses, we would see many deer, foxes and maybe even a wolf or two; we weren't quite sure what they were, but we stayed clear. With wild animals roaming about, we were happy George always decided it was too cold to go outside. Besides our house, the only light we could see at night was the moon and the bright stars overhead, and the twinkle of Long Island, five miles away across black and icy Great South Bay.

We did end up converting a bedroom into a foyer the next summer, and then, doing it ourselves, started on a new bedroom to replace the one the foyer now occupied. By the fall when the Island closed up, it was well under way. We decided that we'd finish it by going there on winter weekends.

Since there is no ferry service during the winter, there was no way to get additional supplies not already on hand. But one of us had an idea, maybe me. There were a half dozen houses under construction in the Pines, each surrounded by stacks of new lumber. Need I say more?

We would creep out after dark in the pitch black and remove a few boards from each site—just a few. Not enough to be noticed, mind you, because if the lumber was missed, the suspicion would fall on us. There was no one else there that suspicion could fall on.

I don't remember feeling the least bit of guilt, though we were stealing. If my conscience bothered me, I would have put it down by saying that a few boards from each builder each weekend did not add up to much. We were spreading the losses around, a good thing.

To our astonishment, the house builders were quite adept at inventory control. So, naturally, suspicion fell on Jack and me. While we were back in the city, our property was inspected. The builders' lumber was in clear view.

When we arrived at the house the next weekend to continue work on the new bedroom, a large note taped to the front door caught our eye as we walked up our walk. Considering our offense, we were amazed at its gentleness. The builders, it said, would appreciate it if, before we went back to New York, we would stack their lumber on the boardwalk so they could pick it up. There was no mention of burning our house down, of broken legs, nor of the Brookhaven Police.

The only manual labor we did that weekend was to move lumber to the front walk. Completion of the bedroom waited until the spring when the ferry began running.

This...misdeed...was my single transgression ever, if you ignore laws against gay sex. Theft, or attempted theft, my only crime. Isn't that something to boast about?

Despite gradually easing laws, this was certainly still an age when gay people hid their sexual orientation from family, from neighbors, from employers. Fire Island was a place where you did not need to hide. On Friday nights in summer, once I stepped onto the ferry, I felt a great weight lifted from my shoulders. I became jovial for a while, almost giddy. I did not have to pretend to be interested in women. I didn't have to be knowledgeable about sports. I could introduce my partner, not as a friend—but as my partner. After the pressures of being incognito during the week, Fire Island was paradise.

As paradise, it brought certain sexual liberties that the straight world was determined to snuff out.

The Brookhaven Township police had jurisdiction and regularly would dispatch plainclothes detectives to infiltrate cruising areas and make arrests. The woods between the Pines and Cherry Grove had been a meeting place of cruising gays for years. Though isolated from both communities, it had become the location of police activity and had become too dangerous for many gays to go near. So, in the Pines, meeting areas sprung up that were small portions of dark boardwalks where few houses existed. These checker-boarded from place to place every few weeks in an attempt to stay ahead of the police. How they would learn of the latest in-spot, I do not know. A friend had been arrested on his first weekend ever visiting the Pines, charged with disorderly conduct. He was held in jail overnight and paid a fine of $500, a goodly sum then. But worse was that his name appeared in the Long Island Press with others, and for a month he worried his conservative employer would learn of his arrest and dismiss him. He claimed that his disorderly conduct had been merely loitering on a boardwalk he should have avoided.

Despite police raids on gay bars in New York City, my attitude toward policemen in Manhattan was neutral. I suppose that was because I did not go to a gay bar often, so I was at little risk of being arrested in one. True, the police frequently visited the cruisy truck area at Christopher Street and the Hudson River, but I had never heard of an arrest there. Guys just left when the police arrived, and returned a half hour later.

But I had grown to dislike the Brookhaven policemen who came to the Pines by boat. They had no legitimate business there, I thought, since there was no crime. They were not wanted there, I believed, and were merely the instruments of society's bias. They were there only to cause trouble and harm. When I would pass one or two on a boardwalk, I would look at them and sneer. I don't know that any of them ever noticed. Even so, I learned that a sneer can be as satisfying as a dish of ravioli.

One night, I approached a dark area of an isolated boardwalk near the bay on the east end, that the grapevine announced as being the latest spot. It was pitch black. Ahead, down a steep pair of steps, I could see the sparkle of the waters in the bay. There was silence. As my eyes accustomed themselves to the darkness, I could discern some men standing alone at various points along the walk, perhaps seven or eight in all, in a section about a hundred feet long.

As I stood and surveyed the scene, my thoughts were interrupted by a sharp, loud voice coming from one of the men in the shadows: "Gentlemen..." The police! I reacted instantly, unthinkingly.

From a standstill, I found myself running at breakneck speed over the 200 feet to the steps down to the bay. I heard running footsteps behind me, then the shout, "Stop! Police!" I did not stop or slow down. I did not think of the possibility I would be shot. My only desire was to flee.

I took the approximately ten steps down in two leaps, touching the wood only once before landing on my feet in the shallow water. I thought for an instant, without stopping. I would wade far out into the water until it got deep. No matter that I couldn't swim. Drowning was the least of my concerns. I could not get caught! I hoped and believed that no cop would come after me, because he wouldn't want to get wet.

It didn't matter that I hadn't broken any law, or that I had just arrived on the boardwalk and had been standing there only a moment. I had no confidence in the police. They were here to get queers, and we all were that. Maybe we were needed to meet a quota.

The water was up to my waist now. I kept going. Soon it would be over my head. No, it was still just up to my waist. I looked back to the shore. I was far out, maybe 400 feet. I could see a flashlight searching the water from the top of the steps I had come down. Ah, the cop had not followed me down. I was right! He didn't want to get wet.

The flashlight went out. I began wading parallel to the shore in the direction of my house, but it was a half mile away. I was reassured: I could see no one walking along the shore following my path in the water. They had given up!

Into my view, not far ahead, came a two-story glass house of an acquaintance of mine. No one was following me on the shore, so I angled toward the house. As I neared the shore, the water became shallower and it was easier to gain speed. I mounted the steps next to the house, my running shoes making a swishing sound and exuding water with each step. The lights were on in the house. But, through the glass, I could see no one, and no one came to the door when I knocked on the glass. I assumed no one was home.

I sat down in my dripping clothes in a wicker chair on the deck and waited. The time dragged. After about an hour, the home owner and a friend visiting for the weekend returned. They listened to my story with intense interest, and then reported that, on leaving the bar on the harbor, they passed a police boat docked there, and men in handcuffs were being loaded onto it. No doubt they were the other men I had seen on the boardwalk, none of whom, except possibly two, had actually been breaking any law. I felt a pang of guilt that I had gotten away and they hadn't. It would have been good if the distraction of my fleeing, and a cop leaving to pursue me, would have enabled some of them to get away, too. Maybe some of them did, I hoped.

By now, I was damp, but no longer dripping. The acquaintance and his guest insisted on walking me to my house, saying that the police may be looking for a single person, but certainly not for three. In their eyes, they participated in my escape. We had all scored one little victory in our tribal battle against the police.

Dear Policemen of Brookhaven Township, Long Island:
Officers, you may not remember this, but you were
in plainclothes, standing on a boardwalk in the shadows,
silently observing gay men just yards away, cruising. It

was time to make your arrests, and you began by shouting "Gentlemen..."

I took off like a rocket with at least one of you chasing after me, yelling, "Stop! Police!" It never occurred to me that you might shoot me in the back. I took the steps down to the bay with two leaps, and waded out in the water. I was right that you wouldn't follow me because you wouldn't want to get wet.

Can you imagine how frightened I was to risk a flight rather than be arrested? I don't want to think of what would have happened to me if you had caught me. You would be really mad. Would you have beaten me up?

Afterwards, I wondered how you felt about your night's work. As usual, you came to Fire Island Pines in your police boat, snuck around the community in street clothes pretending to be gay, handcuffed us one by one until you had enough to make your efforts worthwhile.

Did you wonder about the distress of the men you put in your boat? Did you see their misery? When you released their names to the paper, did you think about the jobs that would be lost, the careers halted? Did their families enter your mind? Or did you consider us animals to be culled?

Excuse me, Officers, I'm getting carried away. The purpose of this letter is not to interrogate, but to forgive. You were ignorant as society was, unaware that we were human beings like you. In fact, I would like to talk to each one of you right now, to find out what kind of people you are. I'm curious to know what you really thought of the men you were arresting. Maybe it's better that I don't know.

Time has moved on, and such police activity is greatly

**reduced. Generally, we are accepted. There are even po-
licemen who are out as gay. I'll bet you never anticipated
that. In New York City, they've formed the Gay Officers
Action League.**

**So, from one person to another person, celebrating
the new times, you're forgiven. Incidentally, thank you for
not shooting me in the back.**

**Cordially, From the Escapee,
Vincent Burke**

I really suffer in my effort to forgive the police and the writers of
the laws that brought about such pain in the gay community. Lives
were ruined. Now, large police departments have gay organizations
within their ranks, a vast change indeed. My forgiveness calls for a
massive realignment of my neurons and synapses.

I used the word battle, above, to describe run-ins with the police,
but it wasn't that at all. This was a year or two before the Stonewall riots of June 29, 1969 in Greenwich Village. The Stonewall was a battle
against the police, when police raided a gay bar and loaded a number of
men in a paddy wagon, merely for being in a bar while being gay. Such
raids occurred all the time, but the night in 1969 and several nights
after, gays actually resisted and rioted. Until then, it was all one-sided.
No battle. Capitulation. Raids, arrests, scorn, humiliation, fines, jail,
publicity, loss of jobs, family tragedies. The police held all the cards.
When I fled into the water of the bay, it was my escape from bigotry,
pre-Stonewall. Not a battle, just a flight.

When the Stonewall riots took place, it was on a Friday night in
June. On every summer weekend, I was at Fire Island. The fact is, I never even heard anything about these nights of riots for rights until they
were over. I'm disappointed that I didn't participate, although I confess
that I probably would have done no more than stand on the sidelines

urging my fellow more courageous gays on. I would have liked to see the end of words such as faggot, pansy, fruit, fairy.

When I had entered my 20s, I became certain I was included in those words, and it was apparent that the world hated me and my secret group. I returned the dislike for that amorphous mass of heterosexuals out there—with the exception of those I was meeting day to day. That included Gwen, my waitress every morning at the coffee shop, Rex, at the newsstand, Sarah, from my first job in New York, lots of people where I worked, plus all my relatives, and on and on. They constituted my surface life.

Observing the world around me at the time, the 1950s to the end of the century, it is no wonder I became biased. It was when I began working as a copy boy, and then a reporter, that I first heard the word "faggot." How many times I heard other reporters trade jokes and favorite stories about faggots and queers. They used the two words interchangeably. What they said would elicit a roar of laughter from anyone within hearing distance. I joined in, I didn't dare not to. They would have suspected that I was one of the men they were ridiculing. I participated in my own humiliation. I stayed "in the closet" in work at advertising agencies in New York, though I had reason to believe my macho guise was not always successful.

Before Stonewall, gay bars were routinely raided everywhere, and unlucky patrons were thrown into the backs of a paddy wagon and locked up overnight. Most states had statutes treating homosexual acts as felonies, and gay men were paying their "debt to society" in prisons all over the United States.

Until 1973, the American Psychiatric Association called homosexuality a mental disorder. This was despite the studies of psychologist Evelyn Hooker in 1957, in which she submitted psychological questions to homosexuals and heterosexuals. Their answers and their adjustment were then studied by experts, who found no difference between the two groups. Other research followed, with the same result.

Scandals often broke out in the federal government in Washington, and gay men would lose their high positions and reputations. They called us a security risk, claiming that we would betray our country rather than be exposed to the scorn of society.

Dear American Psychiatric Association:

In 1973, Doctors, you removed homosexuality as a psychiatric disorder. You held that same sex orientation did not meet the requirements of a mental illness, because it did not necessarily cause subjective distress, and did not affect social functioning.

Your new determination should have been made decades earlier. You are psychiatrists, yet you caused so much unhappiness. As therapists, you would know the value of an apology—if it had been offered. Think of how I felt as a teenager when you said that people like me are mentally ill. It was an attack on my self-esteem. I was young, and I wondered whether you may be right. How can I feel so normal, I pondered, when psychiatrists say I'm sick?

Prejudiced people found justification for their bias in you. Much of the bad, the anti-gay laws, the disturbed families, the ruined careers, the arrests and imprisonments, were grounded in your opinion.

Haven't you heard, Doctors, medicine's guiding maxim to first do no harm? I'd like to ask each one of you: did

you really believe we were mentally ill?

However, the correction's been made, better late than never. I thank you for bothering to make it at all.

I forgive you for the past misclassification, harmful though it was.

Sincerely,
No longer a potential patient,
Vincent Burke

Fire Island, gay as it was, was no sanctuary. As I have alluded to, under cover of darkness the police boat would creep into the harbor, and young plainclothes policemen would fan out, trying to appear as desirable as possible. Their task was to lure gay men into situations, and clap handcuffs on them. Later, the police boat would silently depart for the jail on the mainland with a few dozen "queers" in handcuffs on board. The unfortunate men would appear in court, be fined a hefty sum to fatten the township's treasury, and be released with a court record for disorderly conduct. And they would worry for a while about losing their jobs because newspapers had printed their names.

No straight person ever came to the defense of gays back then. No one questioned anti-gay legislation. Police pretty much did what they wanted. Who cared? We were all hidden, so no one thought they knew anyone gay. Our only public notice was the popular jokes.

Seeing how people regarded us, I became most comfortable in the company of other gay men. I subscribed to the oft-repeated line describing what gay men suspected was the hidden attitude of even tolerant heterosexuals toward us: "A faggot is the gay gentleman who just left the room." I became wary of even liberal straights because I wondered about their secret thoughts.

So I am now trying to lose my bias against heterosexuals, as many of them are no longer biased against homosexuals. Today, so many

Americans have no problem with acceptance. Imagine that! Anti-gay laws have been repealed. It's a new world in the 21st century, at least in the West. I should enter the century and forgive. But there are so many wrongs to forgive! No hard feelings is a hard nut to crack.

But back to the year 1970. At age 36, I was a copy supervisor at my final agency, Foote Cone & Belding. This was also the best place I have worked, despite my questions about the bias of some employees. I, and others, of course, was on the Frito-Lay account. We were the team that created the "Frito Bandito." I had an office on the 36th floor of the Pan Am building (now the MetLife building), looking south to the Empire State Building, Wall Street and the Battery. I had privileges, or took them, such as leaving at 2 PM on Fridays in summer so that I could meet Jack and get an early start to Fire Island. Jack also managed to get out early. I didn't have to travel for business much, but when I did, it was entirely first class, a luxury I had not known before.

Advertising attracts a good percentage of gay people to the creative areas. My two prior agencies, Cunningham & Walsh and Tatham Laird & Kudner, each had several fellow copywriters who were gay, art directors, and a score of others in other departments that I suspected were gay. At Foote Cone, I was aware of just one other gay male copywriter besides me, unusual for a large agency. There was a gay TV producer, however, who I had seen in the grocery store at the Pines once. He was excellent at his job, but very demanding, often filming a commercial over and over to improve it. He tried colleagues' patience, at times demanding changes in copy to fit his production better, and frequently not being politic about his requests. As a result, he was not liked by his fellow workers. More than that, he was actively disliked.

Obviously, I was not the only one at the agency who realized what the producer's sexual orientation was. Out of his presence, male employees began calling him "cockmouth." The use of this vulgar name for a gay man reminded me of the attitude I saw many years before in Cleveland in other reporters toward gays, and in the hostility of the

171

group of teenagers who had followed me and another man to a dark area, no doubt to beat us up. They had used the word "faggots." Same difference. I winced every time I heard the producer called that name.

Here I was, a writer in the gay-accepting advertising industry, in liberal New York City, yet the place where I spent five days a week had employees openly displaying a bigotry against my group. They coined no such equivalent names for the several straight men in the agency similarly disliked. Only the gay man got that distinction. Although I believe I was generally regarded well, I had to wonder whether the people I saw every day also had a pet, crude name for me, repeated only in my absence. I had already determined that it was known that I was gay. When a few of us were in New Orleans on an excursion to encourage creativity, one had offhandedly mentioned to me that he was going out that night, and added, "You'll have your own places to go to." I interpreted his meaning of my "places" as my "gay places." Now I began asking myself why not a single person had ever asked where I went weekends when I left early on Fridays, or how my weekend had gone. Somehow, they must have known I went to Fire Island, and they didn't want to talk about it.

Every time I heard that producer called that name, I felt an anger, because behind his back, he was being degraded. I also felt an unease, worried that I, too, may be being debased behind my back. What name might they be calling me? I'm gay, gays are disliked, maybe they dislike me. Once again in my life, I felt I was in enemy territory. It's the kind of mental anxiety, I imagine, that afflicts members of any group subject to bias. Pity Blacks, Latinos, Asians, and others whose physical characteristics identify their group. At least my orientation was invisible.

These co-workers of mine were seasoned and mature men in an industry that welcomed diversity as a means to broaden creativity. What excuse can they possibly give for their bigotry? That their parents indoctrinated them, that society is to blame? Well, maybe.

Dear Fellow Admen:

I worked with you at my final job in advertising. You were all fine, talented, personable people quick to smile and engage in camaraderie. It was a pleasure—almost.

You remember the TV producer who was demanding, and hard to get along with? You had a crude homophobic name for him that you used when he wasn't around.

But I was around. I believe you knew I was gay, but you were unconcerned at the effect your prejudice would have on me. I asked myself: Should I say something, object, when you called him that name? With all of you repeating the name, it made me feel awfully uncomfortable. It seemed that all of you were in league against gay people, and I was one of them.

Of course, we had little disagreements in our work from time to time. What do you think I thought about at those moments? The crude name you may have for me, that's what. I became suspicious about remarks you may make behind my back. This worry colored many of the days of the four years I was your colleague. It rather spoiled my opinion of the agency. It certainly lowered my regard for all of you. You were all city-wise, in a profession that attracts diversity. You should have been accepting.

I hope, with the majority today accepting gays, that you've changed, too, and are ashamed to be reminded of your past. If that's the case, I should be magnanimous and forgive you. I should even thank you for what I am hoping is your change of mind. But I just can't forgive or thank you until I know for sure. I would like to go for a drink with those of you I worked directly with, and find out what you really think about gays. We could go to the

Oyster Bar in Grand Central, where many of you hung out.

Until I know your thoughts, I'll hold off on forgiveness. Sorry.

Your out co-worker,
Vince

One of the other writers at Foote Cone, Nell, was on the Clairol account. She had a female partner, a public relations director for a nonprofit, and perhaps because we were both in same-sex relationships, we hit it off. She didn't look like a young woman who would be writing for Clairol. Her hair was ash brown, not blonde, and was straight, in a page boy style. Nell and I spent many long lunches together at nearby restaurants. Two-hour lunches were expected; the agency was nearly empty from noon to 2.

Jack and I invited Nell and her partner to the Pines for a weekend, and they accompanied us on the train, in the taxi, and then on the ferry. We walked the beach together, and that evening Jack cooked our favorite, shrimp creole.

We, of course, had George, the Siamese cat. A few years earlier, we had seen an ad in one of those throw-away papers in Manhattan, offering Siamese kittens for $25. On a Sunday, we took the subway to Sunnyside in Queens, and returned to our apartment with a little cat in a cardboard box.

It's a stereotype of gay people that we treasure our pets. Many of us have never been married and have no children, so... In any case, George had the unrestricted run of the Pines house, and moved from bed to bed for his naps.

I don't know that I ever told Nell that we had a cat. I do know she never told me she was allergic to cats. And, no matter what Jack and I thought of George, it cannot be denied that he was, indeed, a cat. That fact became quite apparent Saturday morning when Nell exited the bedroom. Her face had transformed from an oval to a round disk, her eyes and their vicinity appeared to be what the Red Sea sounds like: red and gushing with water. She's allergic to cats, she informed us. I made a futile, and admittedly half-hearted, offer to restrict George, but no use. The women were on the first ferry out.

The friendship was never the same again with Nell, and I don't know why. Had she blamed me for the deplorable condition of her face? Or was it I who resented her effrontery to insult our cat by fleeing? With certainty, I can say it was not a perfect weekend, and I regretted the loss of a friend. The experience taught me to cover all bases in advance before having an overnight guest, and it demonstrated how fragile friendships can be.

My social life was very active at lunchtime in Manhattan, even after Nell. I frequently saw Phil, the friend I can no longer locate. I made an effort to suppress my ego and not to talk much about my magnificent consumer accounts.

At least once a week I met Don, who I had met through Bob, Bob being the one-nighter from 1962 who turned into a good friend. Don and I made lunches a production, searching out odd places on second floors that served weird food, and big Manhattan razzle-dazzles that served what you'd expect. Whatever days in a week that might be left from our experimental lunches, I'd be at the Y on 47th Street, doing a little workout. No food at all on those days; exercise spoils my appetite.

I can't mention that Y without talking about Ed, who I met there during one of my lunchtime workouts. He lived nearby, on Third Avenue near 52nd Street. Ed had everything: looks, personality, and depth. Each of us also had a valuable, long-term relationship that couldn't be disturbed. We stopped seeing each other after a few months. Ed had come to New York with the dream to be a playwright. I'd love to learn he succeeded.

At the agency, I was on interesting accounts. Despite my worry about bigotry, I liked most of my workmates; I was paid well; and my job had oodles of status—but I still felt discontent. Essentially I just didn't want to go into the office anymore. Was I never satisfied? Jack and I would rise early on workdays so that we could put off going to work for an hour or more, sitting on the sofa with the view of our big grand piano, having cup after cup of coffee. I did not like our conversations to end, and my workday to begin.

Jack was feeling the same way. So we hatched a plan. We would save all the money we could for two years, then quit our jobs, move to the Hamptons, and buy rental property — that, we thought, would enable us to live as gentlemen of leisure. The first thing was to give up our expensive duplex. $365 a month was, incredibly, a high rent then.

We rented a modest-sized apartment on the parlor floor of a brownstone on West 13th in the center of the Village. We still could not consider giving up our bartered-for grand piano, although it had not been played since we had it. Somehow, we must fit it into our smallish living room. On the day we moved from the duplex, out went the piano and down the 16 floors on the outside of the building that it came up two years earlier, and into a truck provided for it alone. We wondered about our decision to keep this handsome musical friend when it consumed perhaps 40% of the new living room. Our living room furniture was big; it was during the Spanish decor craze. The piano was awarded prime place. Actually, any piece of furniture that takes 40% of a room takes prime place, and everything else was crammed in around it.

During the next two years, our morning conversations centered on the good life, i.e. the idle life we would lead as gentlemen landlords. Jack was planning on free-lancing book translations from French, and we thought I could type as he dictated. We didn't think we would need a large amount of money. We both had simple tastes: no Rolex watches, no dinners at Michelin restaurants. Our only extravagance after giving up the duplex was Fancy Feast daily for George, the cat. It was more expensive than other brands, but we couldn't ask our cat to economize because we wanted to join him in idle retirement.

CHAPTER 11

Night Swim.
Hazards of the
West Village.

LIVING IN THE Village, the temptations were walking around everywhere. One evening, I found myself at the west end of Christopher Street at the Hudson River, where young men gather and roam around the trucks that park there for a few hours or overnight. It was the same area where I first encountered Jack a few years before.

Despite the darkness, I could see that the trailer of the semi nearest me was backed up to within a foot of the deep drop off from the bulkhead into the river. There were maybe six other semis parked in the same fashion, their drivers grabbing a few beers at a seedy bar on West Street, or enjoying a little conversation with a fine lady at a by-the-hour hotel nearby.

Young gay men regularly took advantage of the opportunity to mingle among the trucks in the dark and come upon someone to invite to his apartment, or to join him in the back of a truck. I was one of about 20 that night. We had come from the center of the Village for some alfresco cruising that was likely to a better result than an hour or two in a stuffy bar.

I rounded the back of the trailer, being careful of my footing in the small space at the edge of the dock above the murky water. Not knowing how to swim, I always try to avoid bodies of water, let alone filthy water on a cool night.

I looked up in the half-darkness at the back of the semi from the dock pavement. One of the two doors of the truck was closed, its mate on the left side fully open and hanging out over the water perpendicular to the truck. Standing in its opening was a young man I discerned in the limited light to be good-looking, of sturdy build, and about my age. On seeing me studying him, he nodded. I concluded I was being summoned to come up.

I did not need coaxing. The truck bed was several feet off the ground, but I saw that the closed door on the right side had a handle within easy reach that I could use to pull myself up. This would be simple. I clutched the handle with my right hand and began pulling, my left hand lightly supporting my body on the edge of the door, but nearly all of my strength assigned to the task of pulling myself up, using the handle.

Suddenly I was aware that the door and handle were moving. The door was opening. It hadn't been locked, merely loosely shut. As it opened, it quickly overtook the short distance the truck was from the river, and transferred me, holding the handle with my one hand and my body moving with the door, above the dark water.

Before I could even think, I was no longer clutching the handle of the door. I was going down, down, deep into the water. I remember the depth, how very deep it seemed. Was it 20 feet? Was it 50 feet? Strange, I recall thinking that I was going to die—drown—but I wasn't alarmed. I took the time to suppose that my body would probably wash up far from Manhattan, maybe in Brooklyn, and I felt uneasy about that possibility.

As this thought was occurring, my body bumped into the side of the dock. Better yet, I found myself against a pole supporting the dock. I quickly shimmied up the pole—astonishingly, just about 5 feet—until I thrust my head out of the water. I looked up. In the ambient light, I could see, staring down at me from about 10 feet up, a long line of young men.

One of them shouted down: "Can you swim?" "No," I yelled back. Without a moment's delay, he jumped into the water himself, fully clothed, landing right next to me with a splash. Without a word, he boosted me up to the extended hands of men lying on their stomachs on the dock in order to reach me. In my excitement, after being pulled up, I neglected to identify or thank the man who jumped in.

When I got home, Jack looked at me and my sopping-wet clothes and asked, "Is it raining out?"

Recalling the cliché that when a horse throws you off, you must get right back on or you will never ride again, I changed clothes and went right back to the trucks. I was not interested in cruising. My aim was to try to find the man who had jumped into the water. I was extremely grateful to him, and I was feeling very guilty that, after my rescue, I had not sought him out to express my thanks. When I returned to the trucks, there was no one around in wet clothing; so I concluded that he went home to change, and maybe called it a night. That week I placed an ad in the Village Voice thanking him, hoping he, or a friend he told the story to, would see it. I have no way of knowing if he saw my "thank you," but I hope he did.

In my memory, I was under the water a long time. I had time to wonder where my body would be found. But it couldn't have been long, because I did not swallow water or even run out of breath. It must have been merely seconds, no time at all. And I thought I sank down deep. That 20- or 50-foot depth turned out to be just maybe five or 10 feet at the most. Was I about to drown? Probably not. Not with a slew of guys staring down at me, and one of them willing to jump in for me.

So I continued my life with adventures, and with problems. A frequent discussion between Jack and me was my hair, or rather my diminishing hair. I'll call it what I suppose it is, male pattern baldness, although I can hardly hear that b-a-l-d word without feeling a little queasy to my stomach. When I was a teenager back in Uniontown, a barber cutting my thick black hair volunteered that I never was going to have trouble with losing my hair. I was happy with his remark and stored his words in my mind to be recalled again and again. He was wrong. What a charlatan!

My disappearing hair was what I thought frequently about in the years from about age 20 until 40, when I finally threw up my hands and gave up. When I was in my early 30s and at my last agency, Foote, Cone, I saw an ad for a powder to fluff into your hair that guaranteed the look of thicker hair immediately. I bought it right off, and was quite happy with the result. Indeed, my hair looked thicker, though with a whitish cast. But as with most things in life, this product gave with one hand and took away with the other. A serious caveat was that, in a wind, my head was in a cloud of powder. I looked like Pig-Pen in Peanuts. And my shoulders were frequently speckled with this elixir that had forgotten its job was up on my head.

As the months went by, sometimes just weeks or days, I suffered periods of desperation. One day another ad appeared, this time for a procedure called hair weaving. As I understand it, real hairs—from a lucky someone who has sold a batch of spares—are attached to the weak on-the-way-to-death hairs left on one's pate, by knotting them on with a thread. So it's 100 percent real hair you'd have, except for the thread, permanently attached as though it grew there. Sounded good to me. It's painstaking work, and time-consuming, attaching one hair at a time. Everyone has these sickly little hairs when you're still relatively young. That's why if you want a clean head, you must shave it, even if you're technically b-a-l-d.

What a yokel I was. I was in advertising. Didn't I know you talk about the good points and forget the bad? First, the powder, now this. So, one day after work, I took the subway up to a salon on 125th Street in Harlem, the first time I was in Harlem, run by Black people. (The process seems to have been developed by Blacks.) Several hours later, I emerged with the coiffure of a 20-year-old. Jack, on seeing me, seemed a little reserved in his complements. But he had a full head of hair, so he couldn't appreciate my relief now that I had a full head of hair, too. I had to drag complements out of him by asking him questions about my metamorphosis.

I was happy. Then came the next day.

The receptionist in the agency's reception room started greeting me, but stopped after the word "good," as she stared at my hair. She finally managed to get out "morning." My hair, indeed, looked quite different from when I left work the day before, now being thick and wavy, and piled three times as high. It was luxurious; instead of being thin, straight, and so low to my head that it was in danger of exposing scalp here and there.

Then there were a few giggles—snickers—from the secretarial pool as I passed. I settled in my office. I noted that there was heavy traffic of the young feminine type past my open door. As usual, my secretary, a tall slim blonde named Libby, in a white blouse and tight navy skirt, came into the office, after giving one knock on the door frame of the open doorway.

"Your hair looks...different," she said after our good mornings, without the usual small talk.

"It should," I answered. "I went to a hair stylist."

"Oh, I see. Can I touch it?"

I was astounded at this request. It was peculiar. But, on the spot, I couldn't think of any reason to refuse. I felt her hand press down several times, and felt my sumptuous bouffant springing up and down.

"It feels funny," she now commented. "Like straw."

I was getting annoyed now. This was too much. I thought quickly.

"I loaded it down with hair spray this morning," I explained. "Maybe too much."

I hadn't realized before this encounter that the hair did indeed feel like straw. I'm still not sure why. Maybe it's the knot of the thread on each hair. I was familiar with my hair feeling stiff from hairspray, albeit not like straw. For the past two years, I had been using a lot of hairspray to keep the wind from baring a bare spot.

Libby added a weak "Oh," and we went on to discuss business. I noticed to my irritation that she just couldn't keep herself from glancing up frequently at my generous mane.

On Jack's advice, that night I washed my hair, and then in the morning, I wet it down, or soaked it, so thoroughly that its height dropped by 50 percent. I got no further questions at work, no one stared or giggled anymore. But I soon was on to a new solution to feed my obsession.

That evening, with good humor and a chuckle, Jack mentioned that he had never met someone as vain as I was. I did not take his comment lightly, pointing out that he, with full, thick hair, could never understand. I looked up the definition of vanity: "excessive pride in or admiration of one's own appearance." Was I excessively proud of my appearance? Certainly not. I was concerned, rightly so, about my appearance. Did I excessively admire my appearance? No, I was worried about it. I concluded that I was not vain. I was not proud of my appearance, i.e. my hair; nor did I admire it. I was merely obsessed, and for good reason. I would be the object of this same good-natured comment, or criticism, decades later, in identical words, from my second long-term partner. And, again, I would study the definition and deny that I was vain.

What I learned here is that if your—obsession—is going to bring you to experiment, for goodness sake wait until you're starting a new job, or better still, wait until you're moving to a new city.

In no time, our two-year lease on our small apartment was coming to an end. Jack had already left Doubleday, and was freelancing translations as per the plan. At the agency, I wanted to finish a submission to a client that would take the team several months to complete. Jack and I did not want to renew our lease, since we wanted to begin our lives as gentlemen landlords in the Hamptons. We would give up our apartment.

We got rid of our furniture by selling some and donating some. The new tenant for our apartment was a young man who said he had practically no furniture, as this would be his first apartment. He even once played

To economize, we gave up the duplex and moved into a 1-bedroom on West 13th Street. We were in the apartment on the parlor floor right above the restaurant.

the piano. He was eager to take our beloved grand piano, and have 40 percent of his room occupied by it, as it had ours. Our beautiful piano friend was getting an appreciative owner, and wouldn't even have to move.

So, with no apartment, where did we go until I left my work? We rented, by the month, the luxurious penthouse suite at the Fifth Avenue Hotel on lower Fifth Avenue. Don't ask how this fit into our plan to economize. We passed a lavish, three months there, with a very large suite, a mammoth terrace, and daily maid service. Just what one does when starting a new life where economy is the watchword.

After several months, I gave my notice at work. I hesitate to recall the following period. I told the creative director that I was leaving because my widowed mother had decided to provide me with a large sum of family money, and, therefore, I was retiring. This, of course, was absurd. My mother was working as a bookkeeper, and there was no "family money." Why did I do that? Was I harboring in my subconscious a sense of inferiority because my family had been poor? Did I feel my status would go up with people I would probably never see again in being from a wealthy family? The story, the lie, just popped out, as though I had no control over what I was saying. Why not just tell the truth: that I was quitting to move to the Hamptons and buy rental property? Most people are not in a position to be able to risk all for a new life. Maybe my advertising colleagues would have even found it admirable, and enviable. But I lied, not the only time in my life I have. How does occasional lying, and for no discernible reason, affect the rating of a life?

Before I left, we all went out to LA for a week to develop a campaign. The client was not located there. Not unusual, the trip and a new location was meant to inspire us to be more creative. We stayed at the Chateau Marmont in Hollywood, where as copy supervisor I had a suite, but we met by the pool at the Beverly Hills Hotel for our working sessions.

We wrapped up a campaign by the end of the week. It would be based on my idea that the associate creative director was enthusiastic about. The group was remaining in LA through the weekend, but I had never been in San Francisco, with its large gay population. So I went there for the weekend. Someone I met served as a guide and showed me all around: Fishermans Wharf, the Embarcadero, the Castro area. We had brunch on the water in Sausalito. A nice weekend.

But I faced a rude awakening when I got to the agency Monday morning. Everyone had liked my idea for the campaign when I was with them, but not when I left. The campaign had been seriously changed in my absence. I was outraged, and did not even consider whether it had been improved. I went into a pout. How old was I? Eight years? I realize today it was totally reasonable that the group would continue to talk about the campaign while they were still together, and improve it if they could. I acted like a baby. However, maybe it was my stifled resentment over the bigotry I had observed that had surfaced.

Because of my behavior, my last days at the agency were unpleasant. That experience taught me that I cannot always trust my spontaneous reaction to a changed situation, and that I must be objective. Stop and think! Avoid a bad exit. How low does this put the rating of my life?

Recently, I looked up the email address and saw the photo of my former supervisor at Foote Cone & Belding. I was never close to him when I was working, my departure was not the most glorious, and, despite 48 years having passed, I decided to email him a line: "Don, I hope your life is going well. You're looking good.—Vince Burke" I'm not sure why I didn't stop myself from contacting him, given my ignominious parting. He did not reply back to me, and it's just as well. Let bygones be bygones.

Southampton was charming.

So, goodbye to Madison Avenue advertising, to the luxury of our Fifth Avenue Hotel penthouse, and we were off to the Hamptons. We rented a neat ranch house In The Springs, a wooded community just outside pricey East Hampton. Our suddenly-found economy excluded us from most of the restaurants in East Hampton, but we, the former penthouse men, found an inexpensive diner that was good enough.

Although I risk eyebrow-raisings in saying it, we didn't care much for East Hampton. The businesses in what there is of a town center are lined up on either side of a wide road, the highway that goes on to Montauk at the end of Long Island. There are big old trees and some charm with a number of storefronts, but, in our opinion, the town lacked intimacy.

The case is very different with Southampton. It oozes both prosperity and charm. You're on Main Street to shop, not to pass through. It's lined with architecturally-handsome low-rise businesses that are inviting. So, after seeing its town center, Jack and I decided Southampton was where we wanted to be.

We learned an important fact. North of the highway, as townspeople refer to the Montauk Highway, prices of houses are about half per square foot of what they are south of the highway. South of the highway, there are a few less expensive streets before the estate area begins with its 25-room "cottages" on large tracts bordered by tall hedges, and the ocean at the south end. I don't know that the streets south of the highway that we could afford conveyed status with property ownership, but the streets to the north came with a lack of status. So, it goes without saying, we looked only to the south. And we found the ideal rental property, two 2-family houses, one behind the other on a deep lot, on Meeting House Lane, a handsome street right off charming Main Street. It was perfect, one of the two multi-family properties on the street. The front house was a natural-shingled colonial with wood shutters that we painted sky blue.

Both the lower and upper floors were vacant. We moved in upstairs. In the back house, the two apartments were occupied year-round by elderly sisters.

The property required no updating, which fit in well with our aim to be gentlemen landlords. But then we faced the cold fact that the rent of a furnished apartment to someone from Manhattan for four or five summer months would far exceed the annual rent to a local resident.

So, the gentlemen idea was tweaked, and we found ourselves, 12 hours a day, in the downstairs apartment painting, wallpapering, furnishing.

Jack picked up the "Southampton look" from the windows of the

Our first property in Southampton, at 105 Meeting House Lane. A Gold Star mother was a neighbor.

trendy shops on Jobs Lane, and it served us well in this and other rentals. Basically, it's an airy look with a lot of white, lime green, bright yellow. We rented the apartment immediately.

Across the back of the property was a privet hedge about six feet high when we moved in. Many houses in the estate section have their large properties surrounded by privet hedges that have grown to 20 feet. They inspired us to decide to let our 75 feet of hedge grow as high as it would. That would hide the house behind us that fronted on the next street, and provide a curtain of greenery.

Several months later, one early evening there was a rap on the front door downstairs, rather than the ring of the doorbell. I flicked on the light and went down and opened the door. Standing on the stoop in the light was a petite late middle-aged woman with grey hair and a heavy grey coat to her ankles.She introduced herself as the neighbor in the house behind ours, and then proudly added, "I'm a Gold Star mother, you know."

It quickly went through my mind, going back 30 years to World War II, that a Gold Star mother was a woman whose son was killed in military service. I didn't know what to say in response to her announcement, but she didn't wait for me to comment. By now, Jack had joined me at the door, as she continued.

She explained that she observed that we were not cutting the hedge at the back of our property, and that she wished we would, because the tall hedge was ruining her view.

"But the only view you'd have if we cut it," Jack intervened, "would be of our houses."

Our neighbor lady thought quickly. "But it makes me feel closed in, and I'm a Gold Star mother," she concluded. I was not kind, explaining that we wanted to block out her house and see greenery instead. Jack interrupted me to say that, nonetheless, we would talk about it and consider it. The next day the hedge was cut back to its former six feet. An accommodation for a Gold Star mother.

No sooner did we have this property under our belt that the realtor who sold it to us, spotting an easy mark, showed up with another listing down the street. This property was the other multiple-family on Meeting House Lane. It had a 3-story house with an apartment on each floor that had never been updated. The elderly woman who owned it and lived there was moving in with her daughter. Every surface needed attention. There were also two ramshackle cottages in back. Not the cottages of the estate area nearby, but wee one-bedroom ones, where every surface needed help, as in the main house.

How could we resist? We bought it.

CHAPTER 12

DIY Landlords.
The best laid plans...

WITH THIS PURCHASE came an end to our dream of being gentlemen-landlords. With diminishing funds, we would have to do much of the work ourselves. We hired two young men to help, contracted out electric and plumbing, took up hammer and nails and especially paint brushes, ourselves. (Yellow shutters this time.) No longer gentlemen, we were now do-it-yourself landlords. A major tweaking of our plans.

Our two helpers, who called themselves handymen, were not really so handy. They were young guys eager to work, and willing to try things they hadn't done before. Jimmy was about 30, and arrived promptly every day in his beat-up old van—except for the days he came in his girlfriend's car because his van wouldn't start. The other was P.J., a 20-year-old with floppy reddish hair, who had temporarily dropped out of college (later to return and get his BA). He took his Irish heritage to heart, sometimes lapsing into a pseudo-brogue.

We paid them every Friday, and occasionally, by invitation, would accompany them to a bar. Jack made no effort to hide from them our life partnership, and they seemed to accept it nonchalantly. But I was always suspicious of the hidden thoughts of heterosexuals. My past experiences had warped me. My attitude was not unusual with gay men, my bias toward heterosexuals, because I fear they are biased against me. I must forgive and forget.

At the newly-purchased property, we were rushing to get all five units ready for the summer season, and congratulated ourselves that the property no longer looked derelict. Its former sad state had almost spoiled the look of the large white Georgian colonial right next door, owned by a prominent local architect. And, one morning, the architect came calling.

I was on a ladder on the front porch of the house, painting the ceiling, when he stepped onto the porch. I got down from the ladder to introduce myself. He gave me his business card.

Then he made a statement I hadn't expected:

"I don't see a permit posted."

"Uh..." I replied.

"You converted the garage of the back cottage into a room?"

"Uh..." I replied.

"I've seen tradesmen here. New electric and plumbing?"

"Uh..." I replied.

He smiled. "Well, you're doing a good job. Happy to have you here." And he was off, never to be heard from again.

I wonder what would have happened if the architect had not been satisfied with our changes, and reported to authorities our lack of a permit and our flouting of the law. We were at a critical point, nearing completion with the renovation, and anticipating, for mortgage payments and the necessity of eating, the much-needed rental income from the summer rents of these five units. The certificates of occupancy could have been pulled pending elaborate, time-consuming inspections and revisions. And I ask myself why we did ignore the law. Certainly, we were aware that a building permit was required. The only explanation is that, as gay men, we were daily violating the laws which forbad almost our very existence. Disrespect for the law in one realm engenders disregard for it in other areas.

It was a good summer season in the Hamptons. The central location of our properties, plus, I like to think, our talent in decorating and furnishing, enabled us to rent all five of the newly-renovated units, and the vacant apartment under ours down the street. Financially, we were in good shape. We were feeling quite confident in ourselves, when the same broker who sold us our two properties arrived with yet another,

The property he presented this time consisted of ten substantial two-bedroom cottages, or little houses, and a main house with an apartment and office. The all were well-spaced on five acres shaded by a number of weeping willow trees lining a circular drive. The development was north of the highway, but, because it was a little beyond the town limits, we didn't think it qualified as low status. Besides, you would never get five acres and all the cottages in town.

So we snapped it up and closed in early October. Later that month, OPEC embargoed the sale of oil to the US because of our support of Israel during the Yom Kippur War. Gasoline became nearly impossible to find.

Our plan was to re-do the cottages and main house over the winter for the next summer's rentals. After that, we would offer them for the winter, having researched and found that there was a winter market, at modest rents. We hired Tommy, a third worker, and set to work installing ten self-standing fireplaces backed up against... asbestos, for protection against fire, and many other improvements. (This was before anyone knew of the danger of asbestos.) We contracted for a furnace for each cottage.

The race was on to have everything completed by the spring, so that summer rentals would replenish our dwindling funds. We had sold our first property, where we were living, to pay for improvements, and we were living from cottage to cottage, moving just as renovation began. George, the Siamese cat, and Cat, Jack's cat that he had when I met him, could hardly keep up. They were always napping in one cottage behind our move.

In March, we were ready. The final touch, the new stone gate posts, crowned with large lantern lights, and bearing our new name, "Willow Square," in large bronze letters, had been installed. We placed ads.

In our long winter work days as do-it-yourself landlords, we had not followed the news closely. In March and April, we became aware that there was very little gas available. It would be a drive of 85 miles from Manhattan to find a summer rental. When the shortage eased, somewhat, the cost then quadrupled. Practically no one was driving anywhere, worrying about the scarcity of gas and the cost.

No renters were coming to renovated Willow Square. The need for mortgage payments continued, but income did not. We did rent four of five units at the second property in town, because they were in the first tier of offerings: desirable properties in the heart of Southampton. You could walk to the beach, restaurants and the supermarket. You needed a car to go anywhere from Willow Square. Once would-be renters managed enough fuel to drive out from the City, they wanted to park their car and save their gas to get back home to Manhattan.

Jack and I went to the house on Fire Island for the summer, and we took turns going to Willow Square on weekends for an "open house" for prospective tenants. It may have been an open house, but it was always an empty house. No one came. On a Sunday, I may observe, from the porch of one of the cottages, a single car enter, roll around our circle road shaded by willows, and exit between our exquisite new stone gates with the lantern lights on top. Fortunately, the rentals of the apartments in town on Meeting House Lane enabled us to keep current with the in-town mortgage, and continue eating.

However, there was big trouble at Willow Square. All summer we were getting nasty and nastier letters about the unpaid mortgage. By the fall, the bank, eager for a payment, or four or five of them, was making unfriendly foreclosure noises. Our next hope for an influx of serious money was the next summer — and the bank made it clear it was not willing to wait to see if the next year would be a better season.

So we did what the bank suggested, "suggested" not being quite the word. We turned over the keys and walked away, obligations-free. And nearly assets-free, too. Gone forever was the almost $100,000 spent over the past winter on renovations.

Dear Arab Members of OPEC (The Organization of Petroleum Exporting Countries):

How imprecise it was of you, in 1973, to impose an oil embargo on the United States. You aimed to hurt the country that supported Israel in the Yom-Kippur war.

But did you think of the individuals that it would injure? Like Jack and me, who were eagerly awaiting summer renters for our just-renovated Willow Square. With no gas, the renters couldn't get to us from Manhattan. We waited in vain at our open house for the cars and renters that did not come. No gas, no renters, no mortgage payments, no property.

But what government, or kingdom, ever bothers to worry about repercussions? To think about the effects on real people is just too petty. You're too big for that. So, two guys 7000 miles away lost their property. Tough luck.

Surprisingly, I can consider thanking you for your boycott, painful as it was with no prospective tenants arriving. We lost the property, due to you, but that sent us to profitable Manhattan real estate.

Forgiveness, however, is what's on the table right now. OPEC members, my memory of our stress during your embargo is still too strong for a letter of forgiveness. Maybe next year.

Sincerely,
The (former) owner of Willow Square

But at our darkest hour, there appeared a ray of sunshine in the form of an article in the Sunday New York Times. It reported that real estate in Manhattan was in desperate straits; in fact prices had collapsed, reflecting the flight of Fortune 500 companies from Manhattan, and the approaching bankruptcy of New York City. Real estate was going for a song! Was this our second chance to be gentlemen-landlords? On Monday, we put our 5-unit property in town on the market, and on Tuesday we were on our way to the Taft Hotel on Seventh Avenue.

We didn't need to look at many properties. Our primary criterion was location. It served us so well in our first two properties in Southampton. One, or rather two buildings offered together as a package, filled our location requirement above all others. The better building was at 107 East 63rd Street between Park and Lexington Avenues. You can hardly get a better address. It was a 7-story dark red brick building with 15 2-bedroom apartments, with just a 25-foot frontage. It had an elevator, putting it in a higher class. The other building was at 246-248 East 51st Street between Second and Third Avenues, a good location, too, but more commercial. It was a 6-floor walkup, a no-elevator tenement building, but had the saving grace of having four street-front commercial spaces. The two buildings were on the market at about 4 times the rent roll, the annual total of all rents. In a good market, they would be 10 or 12 times the rent roll.

Our building at 107 East 63rd Street. Prime location, early financial woes.

It's easy to understand why the owner, who was British and living in London, wanted to sell.

There are two types of rent regulation in New York. Rent control, the original one, came into existence just after World War II and covers all apartments built up to 1947. More recent apartments fell under rent stabilization. The two programs are similar in that any rent increases are dictated by city boards. The boards set a percentage increase based on the original rent when the unit entered regulation.

And that would be our difficulty. The original rents were not set at market rents, as they should have been, but we were stuck with them. Another similarity in the two systems is that they give a tenant the right to occupy an apartment indefinitely, with very few exceptions. Long after our time as landlords, New York City would abandon regulation in freshly-built buildings. By 2020, only about 50% of apartments would still be regulated.

Despite the low rents, we would soon discover that our shabby building on East 51st Street held a hidden treasure, due in part to the non-action of the former managing agent, the same one for the two buildings.

Rent regulation is what Jack and I confronted in 1976 upon buying the two buildings, with only a vague idea of its terms. We hoped to change the economics of the premises, first by eliminating the 10% management fee, then by—we were not sure what. Maybe in time, a controlled tenant would move and the new free market rent, the initial

246-248 East 51st Street.
Good location, difficult ownership.

stabilized rent, would be several times the controlled rent. In New York City real estate, landlords loved to see rent controlled tenants vacate, so that the new rent could go to market, where it would enter the stabilization system.

The East 51st building, being a tenement, would never have the class of the elevator building on 63rd. The advantage with the East 51st property, however, was that the four retail shops, being commercial, were not subject to controls of any kind. Both buildings were losing money. We would be managing the properties ourselves, so that this saving alone could mean that we'd come close to breaking even. Or so we anticipated. We really didn't have lofty ambitions for big profits. Happiness would be in paying the bills.

We sold the remaining property on Meeting House Lane in Southampton almost immediately, gritted our teeth at our big loss at Willow Square, and thought only of our coming life back in Manhattan.

A bonanza on East 63rd was that there was a vacant apartment that we could move right into. So, one late September evening, the gentlemen landlords arrived in their getting-old Pontiac station wagon with a box spring and mattress tied on the roof, to take possession. Fortunately, no tenants were around. Bedding on the car roof doesn't do much for one's image.

But anyway, tenants would think we were just new tenants. We had rented an office service on Fifth Avenue, and would use that address for mail and a phone. Tenants had been notified in writing of the new ownership and of the procedure to contact us. No tenant in the 63rd Street building would ever know that the landlords lived there.

It didn't take us more than a couple of days to realize that our cover was blown. It was just after October 1, the starting date where the law requires that the temperature in apartments be no less than 68 degrees. We noted that the law said nothing about the heat being on: it merely referred to temperature. The outside temperature dropped suddenly with the arrival of an early cold wave.

We had not yet turned on the heat, aware of the feeble financial condition of the building. A quick check at points in the building found that nowhere was the temperature less than 70 degrees. On lower floors, it was even higher. No doubt being sandwiched between two other buildings contributed to this circumstance. Maybe we were using our neighbors' heat. So with temperatures within the law, we decided we need not turn on the heat.

That evening at about 10:00 there was a loud pounding on our door. Jack and I looked at each other, and turned down the TV we had gotten that day. I hesitated, and was relieved when Jack went to the door. When he opened the door, there stood a large rotund man well over six feet, in his early 50s, with a ruddy, reddish face, and casual white t-shirt and pants that hung on him as though they were made for an even bigger man. He hadn't bothered to comb his greying, unkempt hair.

His eyes were flashing with anger, and without introduction or preamble, he began shouting, repeating over and over "Turn on the god-damn heat!" Jack attempted to explain that the temperatures were comfortable, and above requirements, but his voice was drowned out by the man's shouts. Finally, Jack forced the door shut with it slamming against our tenant's foot that was trying to block it. We heard a few additional, now muffled, shouts about the heat, and then silence. How did he know we were the landlords? We wondered whether we'd have to move to some other landlord's building to have peace.

The same pounding on the door and outburst was repeated a few evenings later, when the elevator was out of order. The tenant would not acknowledge Jack's assurances that the elevator maintenance company had already been notified. The imbroglio concluded in the same way as before: Jack forcing the tenant's foot out of the doorway, and slamming the door shut. We had to do something about this tenant, or we could not live in our building.

The next day, a Wednesday, our attorney had the tenant served with a complaint for harassment, scheduled to be heard in court the following Monday. Late on Friday afternoon, we withdrew the complaint, but because of the intervening weekend, the tenant could not know this. We heard that he arrived at court with his attorney, only to learn we had discontinued. It was unfortunate that the tenant spent the weekend anticipating a Monday court appearance. Our serving the complaint, and its withdrawal, served the purpose we intended: the tenant never came to our door again. In fact, when we occasionally passed, we acknowledged each other politely.

Our first months were spent worrying about paying bills. We had relied on cost savings from our managing the buildings instead of paying a fee to an agent. But, even so, we discovered that there would be a deficit. We had no funds in reserve, after our ignominious exit from Southampton, and rents could not be raised. Each month we would collect the buildings' bills and determine which ones to pay and how much. Electricity, fuel oil, the elevator maintenance contract, and mortgage, which included taxes and insurance: these all were non-negotiable.

At the closing, the buildings' financial condition had led the real estate attorney we had hired to tell us that we must be "crazy" to be buying rent controlled buildings. It was not a comment to inspire confidence on a day we were planning to go out and celebrate with a nice dinner. But we were innocent, and nothing could blacken our feeling of joy and accomplishment.

The tenement building on East 51st Street was about to prove that our attorney's bleak assessment was misplaced—and save its problematic self, as well as its superior cousin on East 63rd Street.

The 51st Street building, six stories and no elevator, had a wide street exposure for a small building, 50 feet. A center door opened into a long hallway to the stairs, in the rear. On the first floor on either side of the center door was a retail space, and below these, open to the public sidewalk by a wide well with stairs, were two more retail spaces. We had been collecting the rents for these four retail units as per the rent roll provided by the seller's agent. By now, we had researched commercial rents in the area, and determined that the four stores were grossly underpriced, the same managing agent at work again. We asked ourselves, when do the leases expire? We were about to be thankful for the managing agent's negligence.

Leafing through the slew of papers we were given at the closing, we found all four leases. And to our befuddlement, lo and behold, each lease had expired months before we bought the building. The failure of the prior managing agent to have the stores execute new leases was indeed a treasure. No doubt, he would have continued his practice of below-market rents.

We had planned to bring the rents to market when the leases expired. Thanks to the former managing agent, we saw that we could do it right away. None of the proprietors expressed a word of discontent at the terms of his new lease, no doubt expecting a new owner to discover the low rents, and Jack and I sighed with relief at the thought of the increased revenue. We would be able to pay bills.

One would think I would harbor fond memories of this life-saving building. I do not.

Each month I had to stop by the stores on the 1st to collect the rents myself. We learned that we wouldn't get the rents if we relied on the tenants' mailing their checks in. Even my personal visit didn't always work. One store was occupied by a shop that sold small occasional furniture. Each month when I collected the rent, I would run to his bank to have the check certified. If we merely deposited it into our account, by the time it reached the tenant's bank for payment, there often weren't sufficient funds left. Apparently the store owner would write more checks than he had funds to cover, and the first creditors whose payment checks reached the bank got the money. Having the check certified on the day I collected it put us ahead of everyone else.

There was a fortune teller in one of the lower spaces. I would call on the husband of the woman. He would insist on discussing a rent reduction on a lease that now had several years to run, tell me what repairs he wanted me to make even though commercial leases provide that the tenant makes his own repairs, and would finally conclude by saying that he would have the rent tomorrow. So maybe I'd get the rent tomorrow, or the following tomorrow or two. I grew weary. When we were selling the building and knew the closing date, I made the man's day by agreeing to make the repairs he wanted—beginning on a date that I knew we would no longer own the property. I'm not proud of such a trick, but it fell within the guidelines of my conscience.

CHAPTER 13

Nightmare on East 51st Street

BUT EVEN THOUGH getting the rent was often like pulling teeth, the four stores were our salvation.

The nastiest experience on 51st Street concerned a young woman in her early 30s, a rent-stabilized tenant on the 4th floor. She was a short, too-thin woman, with coal black hair pulled back tautly into a pony tail. Her face was sharp, chiseled, and her skin the whitest white. She wore no jewelry and used no makeup. Her plain dress and her appearance reminded me of a younger-aged version of the woman in Grant Wood's "American Gothic."

There was a plumbing leak in the kitchen of the apartment above hers. There had been water in that apartment, but also in this tenant's apartment. We had had a plumber in on an emergency call. He determined that the entire cold water line, from the ground up, was in deplorable condition and must be replaced. (The building dated from the early 1900s.) Holes in the kitchen walls were made in each kitchen from the 1st floor to the 6th in order to install the replacement line. This work was done on a Friday, but it wasn't until Monday before we could get a plasterer to restore the kitchens.

At that point, our 4th floor young woman began withholding her rent. And started calling building inspectors.

It is admitted in New York that tenement buildings are often neglected, of necessity, I believe. The reasons for this are that the rents are held to a very low figure, and that the buildings are old and poorly built. Fifty-first Street I regarded as being in a class above a typical tenement. Being in Midtown, it had been built more recently than those in the earlier-developed lower East Side. Our apartments weren't railroad flats. They were well laid out one-bedrooms with bath and large windows. The kitchens and baths were old and looked it. It was also unique among tenements, because the stores were paying the deficit from the apartment rents, as well as helping 63rd Street. Landlords with New York tenements don't often have that advantage.

Building inspectors always come running when tenants call, and over a few months came running repeatedly at the behest of the lady on 4. In a short time, we went from zero to 43 violations; the tenant had been quite busy. Many were minor, but the most costly was the order to repaint the six flights of fire escape, front and rear. The fire escapes would have to wait until we won the lottery. Meanwhile, we'd get to work on easy ones, since, in order to get the 7 1/2% annual increase on controlled rents, 80% of violations must be corrected. To have 43 violations was extraordinary, Jack and I thought, but soon learned that there are tenement buildings in the city with hundreds.

The tenant's rent was in arrears now three months. We hired a Landlord & Tenant lawyer. That's what the field is called, but the attorneys specialize in either representing landlords, or tenants, not both. I suppose that avoids fights breaking out in the waiting room. We had a date in L&T court. Just as there are tenant lawyers, there are tenant judges, jurists who are reputed to favor tenants in their rulings. (I never heard of a landlord judge; the best a landlord can wish for is a neutral judge.) Our judge was going to be a judge well-known to favor tenants.

On the day of the trial, we met our attorney, a spirited young woman, at court, and came prepared with evidence that the rent had not been paid for three months, and documentation that nearly half of the slew of violations had been corrected in a short time. The tenant was sworn in first.

Her testimony and exhibits shocked us. She swore that for "weeks and weeks," her apartment had been virtually uninhabitable, and to prove this, introduced photos of her kitchen, apparently taken on the weekend that the new plumbing line was installed and the wall had yet to be repaired. The photos showed several holes up the kitchen wall, with the gleaming new water line visible in them. Then she introduced a printout of the building violations: not the 27 at this point remaining, but the high of 43 after her series of calls to the building department. I noticed that the judge did not verify, on his direct link to the Building Department, the record of current violations.

I was eager to take the stand to rebut this misleading testimony. This perjury. But as I headed to the front of the small courtroom, I heard the judge shout at me, and this is an exact quote that I have not forgotten to this day: "I don't need to hear your side!" From behind me, I heard our attorney strongly protesting, but the judge's voice over-shouted hers: "Three months rent abatement. Case continued for three months."

The court decision wiped clean the last three months of rent, and probably guaranteed that we would not get the next three months. And, presumably, the summoning of building inspectors would continue. The violations, now down to 27, would be coming faster than we could cure them, and the annual raise for the rent-controlled apartments, conditioned on curing violations, was becoming a distant dream.

Jack knew what to do, and intuitively seemed to know how to do it. Our attorney provided us a pass giving us access to a private legal library. Jack drew up a complaint against the tenant for harassment, that we filed in New York Supreme Court (despite the name, the lowest state court in New York). This complaint gave us the opening to serve an interrogatory of over 50 questions on the tenant's employer, a publishing house. We hoped to make life unpleasant for her at work, as she was making life difficult for us. We hoped our retaliation would persuade her to stop her attacks on us, and leave us the (expletive) alone.

The plan worked better than we anticipated. She was dismissed from her job at the publishing firm where we had served the burdensome interrogatories, and a few weeks later vacated the apartment.

Dear former tenant of the 4th floor:

What did Jack and I ever do to you to make you so angry that you withheld rent and got a slew of violations against our building?

I am thinking that something in the past happened in your life that made you bitter. Maybe you had terrible parents who treated you badly. That may explain things. We're all products of our genes and our environment, and much is out of our control.

We were new landlords in Manhattan, just arrived, bright-eyed and bushy-tailed, and yearning to succeed. Your efforts to undermine us produced the result you wanted. We became disgusted with the property, and ended up selling—but that was after we succeeded in getting you out. Things didn't really turn out great for either of us, and we both should have tried to stop the runaway train before the wreck.

Perhaps at the start, I should have dropped in on you, and tried to make friends. I could have tried, but I suspect that you were a cold person and it would not have worked.

Would you have invited me into your apartment to talk? More likely, you would have slammed the door shut. I would even like to see you today, sit down with

you over coffee, and find out what your intentions had been.

In any case, I don't hold you responsible. It's the way things were, and neither of us could change it. In fact, your harassment encouraged us to sell the building you lived in, and the proceeds enabled us to undertake renovations of the better building on East 63rd, and increase its value considerably. Strange how things often work out.

I forgive you, and hope you're having a good life.

Yours truly,
Your former landlord

We never collected her rent, but we couldn't care less, so happy we were with her departure. We then put the building on the market, which had been rising for the three years we owned it. We sold it quickly, "subject to violations," at far more than what we paid for it. The higher rents on the stores helped. I was glad to say goodbye to East 51st Street. Not only had the woman on 4 soured us toward the building, but we were disgusted at having to plead with the commercial tenants for their rent each month.

We now had a pocket full of cash for East 63rd Street.

I should say something here about the accounts I relate of our interactions with tenants. I have tried to keep them objective, but I'm not sure that's possible. Rent regulations and landlords' fights to turn a profit, or at least to not be seriously losing money, have created an antagonism between landlords and tenants. The whole affair began after World War II when wartime rent controls were continued, ostensibly until a certain vacancy rate was attained, a goal never reached. And the tenant has the absolute right to continue in occupancy, as long as the tenant wants, unless the tenancy falls into one of several loopholes. The law favors the tenant. So, even though I attempt to avoid it, my animosity could be coloring my interpretation of events. You see, I was a loathsome landlord; that accounts for any bias.

I suppose that there's an argument that Jack and I, without sufficient funds in reserve, had no business buying two mainly rent-controlled apartment buildings in the first place. The mere elimination of management fees, despite our hope, would never make them profitable. Without a management fee, ten percent of total rents, the buildings would just barely be out of the red, but only so long as there was no unexpected expense. You could call us naive. To buy such property you must have resources. That would be true especially of East 51st Street, in need of serious repair when we bought it, repair that would cost more than the value of the building. It was a building whose situation mandated a landlord to find every legal means to turn it around. Otherwise, it would just continue its decline. The 43 violations the tenant was able to get placed on the building speak to the building's condition. We were babes in the woods at the start, but educated ourselves quickly.

The building on 63rd, however, was a different story from the tenement. It was constructed as a substantial building. In fact, it had once been a men's private club. But by the time we owned it, it had been in years of decline because the income was insufficient to maintain it. Most of the tenants had taken occupancy just before rent control was instituted, when the rent was appropriate for a building just off Park Avenue. There was a doctor, two lawyers, a psychiatrist, a producer for a major TV network, two interior designers. These were prosperous people who profited from a system that I believe was intended to help the poor. Our tenants were much better situated financially than Jack and I were, yet we were subsidizing them.

Our long-term plan for 63rd was to correct the previous management's lack of attention — we considered it neglect — in applying to the rent control authorities for increases allowed by law. Then it was our hope, in time, to have a few apartments vacant that could be renovated and re-rented at the market rent where stabilization would kick in.

It seems incredible, but the market rent was eight to ten times what some of the controlled tenants were paying. Therefore, getting market rent from just a few of the apartments would turn the building around dramatically. We did spend a little on extras for the building. We ordered an elaborate glass and decorative iron entry door, and to satisfy my desire for a fancy building, Jack acquiesced and we had an entry awning installed with the number 107 on it.

Examining tenant files, our attention centered on a controlled apartment with a rent just over $400, easily the highest rent of a controlled apartment in the building. The apartment was occupied by a late middle-aged psychiatrist and his wife, a freelance writer who was regularly published in prominent, elitist magazines. We had been made aware by other tenants that his was a Collyer apartment, a condition where the occupant accumulates goods and even junk that he is incapable of discarding. Collyer is the family name of two brothers who lived in a house in Harlem in the early 20th century. On their deaths, 140 tons of hoarded goods and debris were found to fill their rooms. Jack, for a reason I can't remember, had been in the apartment of our tenant and observed his wife sitting on a chair in a tight clearing in the living room surrounded by piles of trash, eating half a grapefruit. There was just enough space for her chair and a narrow path to it. The rest of the room was filled wall to wall with newspapers and unidentifiable junk to a height of three and four feet. There was also a narrow path through the debris — or treasure, as the tenant considered it — to the kitchen. The stench from the rubbish permeated the apartment, and the entire floor and beyond, whenever the door to the apartment was opened, a situation that several tenants had complained to us about.

I will not comment on the irony that this issue concerned the residence of a psychiatrist. Jack and I considered it a fire and health hazard. And the odor emanating from the unit threatened the good standing of the building. Living under such conditions is grounds for eviction, even in New York City, but in New York any attempt at eviction is time consuming.

However, we found a quicker route. In a rare move, the rent control department had decontrolled any apartment whose legal rent on January 1, 1965 was $250 or more. The records we received when we closed showed that the rent on that date of the psychiatrist's apartment was $265; the managing agent, no surprise, failed to file for a decontrol order. So we applied for a decontrol order now, years after the date. Rent control refused to acknowledge that we had filed an application, until we got a court to order the city to issue a decontrol order. The market rent was six times what the psychiatrist had been paying, so he and his writer wife opted to move, with every last piece of treasure from their apartment. We had our first decontrolled flat.

The records of the building at the rent control office did not include the value of the superintendent's free apartment — an item that can be passed on directly to controlled tenants. One of the tenant-attorneys protested that there was no certificate of occupancy for the super's apartment. That was a fantasy on his part; we got the increase.

In the first few years when our financial condition was weak, we learned how to virtually guarantee that we would get the annual 7 1/2% increase on rent controlled rents. It was conditioned on the landlord curing 80% of the violations on the building. East 63rd never had many. But, to avoid having to correct expensive ones, prior to the approximate date the building inspector would likely be visiting, we created situations that we knew would get us violations—but easy and cheap ones to cure. So we'd remove the numbers on each floor outside the elevator, leave a bucket on a staircase, and so on. Then we would correct these violations, and ignore the expensive ones that would fall in the 20% not cured. As years passed and finances eased, we abandoned this subterfuge and cured all violations. We had become proud of the condition of our property, and had the funds to maintain it.

A tenant asked that we paint her apartment. This would be a reasonable request under normal market conditions where rent is not artificially kept low. We figured the job would cost about $3,000, the tenant's rent for a year. We would almost have to decide between the paint job and a month of heat for the building. So we stalled, hoping that the tenant would forget the whole thing. Not so. We received from Rent Control a copy of the tenant's complaint, saying that "the landlord has NEVER painted my apartment." We were trying, unsuccessfully, to think of a way to answer the complaint, when another form arrived from Rent Control, dismissing the tenant's complaint. It seems that the statement that the apartment had never been painted signified that painting had not been one of the services included in its rent controlled status. We would wait in vain for Rent Control ever again to rule in our favor.

Interior designers in two apartments advertised their businesses as being at the building address. A city ordinance specifically mandates that, in such a circumstance, the landlord must institute eviction proceedings. We did, and one moved before the case came up in court.

The other, a gay man probably in his early 30s, was a different story. He hired a well-known law firm that accepted only tenants as clients. It soon became clear that the strategy of the tenant's new attorney was to delay an order of eviction as long as possible by elaborate legal maneuvers. We were being served motion after motion, each one requiring an answer. This policy may have served prior clients of the attorney, by exhausting a landlord financially. But our legal fees were nil, since we were doing our legal work ourselves. Scholarly Jack had become proficient in answers and briefs, and my appearances in court required hardly more than my body being there. It was not us, but only the tenant incurring legal expenses. Almost a year went by before the tenant's attorney contacted us, suggesting a payment of $100,000 to have the tenant vacate at once. The law firm was eager for a settlement, because the tenant was in arrears to it of $45,000. We wanted an end, also. The tenant, even though stabilized and not under the stricter rent control system, was paying under $500 because, when the apartment was decontrolled and went into the stabilization system, the first rent, as usual, was set far too low. With just a little renovation, we'd be able to easily re-rent for $2000, or $18,000 more per year. Buildings were now selling for 10 times the rent roll, so re-renting this apartment would add $180,000 to the value of the building.

We weighed the settlement offer, considering how long the tenant could continue the delays while already being in arrears with his attorney. Influencing us also was our inability to raise his rent more than a few percentage points with each new lease, the immediate value re-renting would add to our property and to our monthly receipts, and how unpleasant we found this protracted litigation. I was eager to say goodbye to my court-day stomach cramps. Just at that point, we were served with a Notice of Appearance from a new attorney. A new firm would now be representing the tenant—or was this merely a straw man to push us to settle?

Entering into our decision, too, was that, surprisingly, we had the money, from a recent refinancing. So after going back and forth with the tenant's earlier attorney, still on the scene, we settled at $70,000. The tenant vacated with about $25,000 in his pocket, his attorney got his sought-after $45,000, we got an apartment that we re-rented for $2400, and the building's value increased by over $200,000. Nonetheless, the outcome left me with a feeling of annoyance that we paid a large sum to get possession of our own property.

It wasn't that the $70,000 was sitting in the bank waiting for us to buy a Porsche. The borrowed money was intended to finance future apartment renovations.

Jack and I felt that the tenant's attorney had treated his client badly, by running up his legal fees with motion after motion. When he realized we were representing ourselves and bearing no legal expenses, he should have adopted another tactic, or so we thought. The only one who suffered financially from excessive motion practice was the attorney's own client. With the settlement, the tenant's payout would be eaten up quickly by a higher rent wherever he was going. His attorney got most of the settlement money, plus whatever the tenant paid before falling into arrears. We wondered whether this attorney was working for his client, or just for himself. Of course, we could be biased, as he had been our foe.

So, out of the need to operate a building in the black, and our desire to increase its value, we had joined the battle that rent control and rent stabilization brought to the city. In our defense, I want to point out that we were selective in our enforcement of loopholes in the law. In a former doctor's office-apartment on the first floor lived the doctor's elderly widow, paying a low rent. We were fond of this woman and treated her kindly. Never did we look for any reason to raise her rent. She reminded me a little of an older Mrs. Paulo of Uniontown, who cared for me when my father disappeared. Another flashback to Lemon Street: I wondered if our good treatment of this woman was a lesson I learned from our landlord, who cut my mother's rent when my father disappeared. Apparently, the widow was aware that we treated her differently than other tenants. When she died, we were among the heirs to her estate. Her residence became an expensive doctor's office.

Another elderly widow wanted to move to California near her son. Her sister, who lived a few blocks away, would move with her. But her sister owned a condo that she hadn't been able to sell yet. Here was a chance to aid another elderly widow, while, at the same time, helping ourselves. We bought her sister's condo to enable our tenant to move, and for us to get another decontrolled apartment.

We would renovate before returning an apartment to the market. The funds for all of this renovation activity came from the sale of 51st Street, and by refinancing the building's mortgage. As we got decontrolled apartments, the rent roll increased, and so did our ability to refinance.

Setting the initial rent when an apartment passed from rent control to rent stabilization, which would affect the rental increases permitted in the future since they were percentage increases, required great care on our part. We recalled that the initial stabilized rents were set too low in both buildings before we bought them. We were not going to make that mistake. The first stabilized tenant, although having signed a lease, has the right for 90 days to challenge the initial rent to the Rent Stabilization Board, on the grounds that it exceeds the market rent.

The way we devised to protect ourselves was, after renovating a vacant apartment, we would rent it to a tenant, usually a business executive or his company, for the time the executive would be required to be in New York, usually four to six months. We insisted that the tenant rent furniture independently of us so that furniture would not become an essential service of the apartment. Since the tenants for such units were busy executives in the city for just a short time, it would be unlikely they would challenge the initial rent. No one ever did, and we locked in high initial rents. How do these maneuvers affect the rating of my life? Were we astute or were we greedy? Did Lemon Street have no influence here? Our landlord on Lemon Street: would be disapprove of such a tactic?

We never let our private lives be neglected in favor of time spent trying to turn the building around. Right away, we established a routine, whereby, each morning, we would exit the building at 8 AM, walk the block and a half to a cafe at Lexington and 62nd for what we called breakfast, but in reality was just whole wheat toast and coffee. We were always served by Gwen, a lady who quickly caught on that our order would never change. So, our so-called breakfast appeared each morning without ordering. In truth, the "cafe" was a Burger Heaven, but at breakfast time, it was close enough to being a cafe to suit us. I don't know that in the years we were home on 63rd Street, that there was a day when we interrupted this routine. We sat at our two-person table against the floor-to-ceiling glass, watching the city go to work. It's a good feeling to watch others go to work.

Our cafe was a friendly place where everyone knew our name, as the theme for the TV comedy "Cheers" went. One older man, a daily customer like Jack and me, arrived every morning with his own box of dry cereal, evidently a type the restaurant didn't offer. He'd sit at the counter, give the box to the waitress, and she would pour a quantity into a bowl and add milk. I can't imagine the charge, since it was the man's own cereal. What's the price of a bowl and a little milk?

On the way home, we would stop at the newsstand for the Times from Rex, and for my daily chocolate-covered cherry packaged individually, a holdover from my boxes of them at movies in my youth. Then would begin the not-too-strenuous workday. Finally, dessert right before bedtime. Begin and end the day with something sweet has been my maxim.

We saw friends from Fire Island in the city, taking turns visiting them for wine and appetizers before going out to dinner, and them visiting us. As time went on, the appetizers became more and more elaborate, each set of hosts surpassing the prior get-together. The hors d'oeuvres became so generous that they were ruining our appetites when we finally went to dinner. We agreed to put on the brakes. Another amusement: Jack and I saw almost every movie that came out. That was before Hollywood aimed so much product at teenagers.

A weekend off-season, we went to Provincetown, on Cape Cod. Early in the 20th century, writers, painters and other artists began gathering here to make the little town the summer Greenwich Village. Provincetown is also known for its large gay population. (According to the Town Hall in Provincetown, today 66% of the residents identify as LGBTQ.) There weren't many people around. We had a chance to admire the charm of narrow Commercial Street and smell the pungent salty, and fishy, sea air. We had already gotten into the habit of stopping to look in the windows of real estate agencies at the listings of properties for sale wherever we happened to go, just in case. We went further this time. We actually went into an office, found a 200-year-old Cape

Cod on the West End, and signed a contract contingent on our selling our house at The Pines.

We had been growing a little bored with Fire Island. Friends had moved on, some to the Hamptons, a couple to Vermont. Most of all, the Island had changed, in our opinion not for the better. The Pines was now almost totally gay, which was not a problem. But the new gay men were crowding into rental houses, and partied, loudly, from the moment they arrived on Friday night until they left. We missed the quiet little get-togethers at friends' houses. The friends were gone, the quiet was gone. We just didn't like the new people. It was time for us also to be gone.

The house sold quickly to two men who liked all the glass we put in ourselves, the resulting wide views of the bay, the series of decks we built in steps down to the water, the portico we designed and nailed together. And we would do the same sort of thing all over again in Provincetown.

At Cape Cod, we returned to having dinners in and out with new friends, including one friend, Ed, who lived near me in Fort Lauderdale four decades later. He had a sweet partner, Rich, a small, youthful blond man. Ed and Rich owned a motel when we arrived there, and later expanded by buying a large hotel with restaurant and gay bar. The marvel about Rich was that he'd phone Jack and me at 5 PM with a dinner invitation for 6 PM that evening. When you sat down at his table, you would swear he had worked on dinner all day.

Rich died in the wave of deaths from Aids in the early and mid '80s, before doctors had an effective treatment, and what they had, it was discovered years later, was administered in such unnecessarily high doses that the treatment itself could be fatal. Those were depressing years in P'town, watching so many young men get sick and die. From that period on, lesbians have held a special place in my heart. Gay men were stunned and immobilized, but lesbians stepped forward, helping dying men whenever they could.

When we were at Fire Island, we did have a few lesbian friends, even though it seemed to me that lesbians prefer to stay to themselves. Even so, there is a sort of comradeship between gay men and women, as shown in Provincetown when lesbians became Nurse Nightingales. The proportion of gay women to men at the Pines is quite small, perhaps 1 to 5, maybe less.

But Jack and I did snatch up two of them, a couple, as friends. One was older and retired, the other was a clinical psychologist maybe 20 years her junior. For three years at the Pines, we would take turns at issuing dinner invitations. We saw them in the winter in the city, but less frequently. The friendship came to a screeching halt when the women broke up. We couldn't decide which one to see, or both separately, so we saw neither. Not the perfect solution.

During our decades together, we were friends with a few male couples who broke up. After much thought, we came up with the same non-solution: see neither one. I imagine that when a straight couple breaks up, friends don't have a problem. The man stays friendly with the man, the woman with the woman. That's the gender solution, impossible when both parties are the same gender. I don't have much experience with straight couples breaking up, so I'm guessing at some of this.

Now to one of our renovations in Provincetown: Jack was tearing down the wall to expand his second-floor bedroom into the eaves. I happened to be out somewhere at the time. When I returned, he managed to restrain himself. "There's something I want to show you," he said quietly, as he led me into the dining room. There on the rectangular glass table was an orderly spread of several hundred pieces of sterling tableware: 12 demi-tasse spoons, over 20 teaspoons, 18 table knives, three kinds of forks, elegant serving pieces, and so on. Next to them on the table sat a large black leather chest, obviously custom-made to contain all the silver. In tearing down the bedroom wall, the old chest had been revealed where it had lain for perhaps a hundred years.

Across the street from us lived a man who was an auctioneer at Sotheby's. He estimated the value at $25,000. Almost every piece had a different marking. He surmised that this was because the pieces were cast into silver over a long period, as a family, not trusting banks in an earlier age, accumulated wealth gradually. We benefitted, but, nonetheless, it was pitiful that the owner had died without his rightful heirs ever knowing of his scrupulous saving.

We were at Cape Cod 12 years, passing April to October there, and the rest of the year in our apartment in Manhattan. On 63rd Street we had succeeded in having a number of apartments decontrolled, which had greatly increased the building's value, as the rent roll grew. In addition, by luck, we had bought it at the very bottom of the market, when the city was threatened with bankruptcy. The city was back on its feet now, if you can use that term for a city. Each year prices were rising 25%, 30%, 40%. We were not accustomed to being so... rich.

But suddenly this asset brought a big worry. The figures on real estate prices were released for the preceding year. To our dismay, in 1987 there was no fantastic increase. What goes? The change, year to year, was just about nil. We nearly panicked. If the figures were flat that year, what next? Serious drops? 25%, 30%, 40%? We couldn't chance it. Although it was extremely unlikely to happen with rents as high as they were, we could not help reflecting on our traumatic exit from Willow Square and our surrendering that property to the bank after a winter of expensive improvements.

We put the building on the market, and it was under contract within a month. We felt it was important to sell quickly, because who knew what the market would do. For us, it was the safe thing. But I did a foolish thing that I would not do today. Older and wiser? What happened was we were offered below our asking price, slightly below, but still 13 times what we paid for the building 12 years earlier. Our work to increase the rent roll, and a rising market, paid off. We did, however, have the proceeds from the other building, on 51st Street, invested there. Despite our good offer, I insisted on risking the deal by demanding $45,000 more, a figure I pulled out of a hat. I felt that with the buyer already paying so much, a little more wouldn't bother him. Whew! Luckily I was right, but my greed could have just as easily lost us the sale.

Two years after our sale, our realtor phoned us in France and said we could buy the building back for one-half of the price for which we sold it. We didn't accept. Jack was dead set against it, and I wasn't eager, either. We were enjoying life in France. But, today, I look back with regret at our decision. Manhattan prices would again recover, as they always do.

In the year before we sold, in 1987, while I went to Cleveland for Christmas, Jack went to France to find an apartment for us. His French family ties, and having gone to university in Paris, made him eager to live there, and it would be an adventure for me. He found a condo on the Mediterranean in Nice, at 161 Promenade des Anglais, that was cheap by New York standards. The street's name, translated as Walk of the English, attests to the number of Brits who relocate there. Years after we sold in Nice, a terrorist would drive a rented cargo truck down the narrow street next to our former building, enter the Promenade, jump the curb and roar down the wide pedestrian walkway above the sea. With his 19-ton truck as a weapon, he slaughtered 86 people, there to watch the fireworks display that celebrated the July 14, 2016 Bastille Day.

Before the closing of the sale of East 63rd, the buyer offered us an interesting proposal, presumably out of the goodness of his heart. If we opened a bank account in France, he could transfer the proceeds of the sale directly to our new account from his account in a London bank. This way there would be no financial record of the transaction in the US. Our attorney raised his eyebrows at this, but said nothing. We declined the offer, fortunately. A year later the IRS contacted us in France, asking for details of the transaction. We were not the ones being investigated.

Right before the closing, alone in the apartment with Jack already in France, I collected the few items we were shipping. Things we could not give up. One was a handsome chest with a maroon marble top that my mother and sister bought for me for $60, after we found it in the basement of an antique shop — or rather a used furniture store — on Second Avenue. They had visited me at my first apartment in the Village, and saw that I had barely more than a bed and a TV set. I was also shipping two paintings of pilgrims we found in Southampton, and a slop-jar, or, more politely, chamber pot, engraved in gold from the former Astor Hotel on Times Square. Our apartment furniture was included with the building sale, but these were things we couldn't let go.

So my partner and I took up residence in Nice, France, along with Fred, our latest Siamese cat. Nice is a beautiful city of seafront, flowers, outdoor restaurants and cafes, and friendly but sometimes strange people. They think differently than we do. The ambitions of the average Frenchman, I found, is to have his own little house and little car — and big vacations. "Le weekend" goes by the English name, and is revered. La retraite, retirement, comes early, putting an end to a short work life, and is pretty much guaranteed once you're established, without regard to performance on the job. As you see from my proud display of French words in the preceding sentence or two, I did learn some French, having attended an immersion course in Nice. But Jack and I always spoke to each other in English, and any French acquaintance insisted on trying his English with us, so I got very little practice. I got to the level of being able to read French newspapers, and to understand the nightly news on TV, but I was lost in a French movie where dialogue is fast and filled with colloquialisms.

One day, unprovoked by us, we became involved in a financial "complication" that I'm sure is rare in the annals of economics. We were collecting funds in the hope to soon find a chateau we would buy. We asked our mutual fund to transfer $100,000 in US funds from our account to our French bank account. The mutual fund would sell equities and direct its bank, a large multi-national firm, to make the transfer.

Nothing happened. We made a second request of the mutual fund. Still nothing, despite faxes and phone calls. And then a third multi-faceted plea. This time it worked, in spades. Two deposits of $100,000 each, instead of one, appeared in our bank account. We weren't sure what to think. Did the mutual fund sell $200,000 instead of $100,000? No. A call to the fund indicated our balance was down just $100,000.

We had been thinking of changing mutual funds because this one was no longer performing well. This would be a good time to do it. We transferred the balance to a competing fund. And the $200,000 in our bank account, $100,000 more than debited at the mutual fund, became a topic of delight and of worry and woe. Months passed. We investigated the large multi-national bank responsible. Its profit each year was in the billions. Its CEO was paid in the millions. No one at such a bank would even notice the paltry deposit of an extra $100,000.

We were wrong. Six months after the double deposit, just as we were beginning to forget the episode, came a certified letter with the fancy logo of the bank in the upper left of the envelope. Both of us were nervous as I opened it and read the short letter, in English, from the regional manager. The bank had made an "unfortunate error," and it wanted its money back "forthwith." We were "required" to go "immediately" to any branch and deposit our check into an account with a given number. The letter was abrupt and demanding, and lacked the courtesies usually found in French business correspondence. Its arrogance annoyed us; it had been the bank's mistake, not ours. We weren't bank robbers.

We found it curious that $100,000 happened to be the same amount we lost in Southampton when another bank demanded we surrender our property.

After long discussion, we composed a letter to the regional manager that we sent certified. We took the typical politician's way out and ignored the real issue, the accusation that we had the money. Instead, we scolded the bank for its admitted negligence in misplacing or misdirecting such a large sum, and pointed out that its carelessness may be of interest to the Financial Times. Our letter gave us a feeling of satisfaction, not to jump when the bank ordered us to jump.

We received no additional communication from the bank. It seemed to be a closed issue so far as the bank was concerned. The bank had an absolute legal right to get the money back, and it may have been the fear of nasty publicity that kept the bank's attorneys at bay. But we still asked ourselves many questions.

Should we continue to keep the money and just get over the guilt? Should we write to the columnist on the local paper, who answers questions on ethics? Should we open an account at this big bank under our own names, and deposit the $100,000 there, so that the bank would at least have the use of its own money? Should we select a charity and donate the money, and, if so, should the donation be in our name or the bank's? Or should we shock the bank and do what it commanded, and return the money? The bank had a branch a mere ten-minute stroll away. Anyone who has followed my life so far in this book may be able to make a good guess as to whether we took that ten-minute walk.

We continued our hunt for a chateau, and we would soon purchase the Chateau de Malvaux in central France, and we'd eventually buy a house in Fort Lauderdale for winters, so our nice Nice apartment would go. Too bad. You can be only one place at a time. I've never understood how very wealthy people have seven or eight houses all over the world. It would drive me nuts trying to decide where to go.

The following section treats a typical period at our petit chateau during our years there. As you'll see, that ended also. Life is full of sad goodbyes. But let us first say hello to the center of France, the people, and our wonderful property.

CHAPTER 14

The Chateau. A man's home is his castle.

WE ARRIVE AT the Grand Café for our morning cafe au lait at precisely 9 AM. The familiar line of older men, farmers or retired in bib overhauls, are standing at the bar with their glasses of morning red wine before them. On our entry, all of them look our way, some of them nod slightly, and a few of them mutter something in French, almost under their breath. Is it a Bonjour? I hope so, but I'd rather not know. Ignorance is bliss.

We have been coming here for the eight years since our purchase of the Château de Malvaux nearby. We are known by townspeople as either les Americans, or les chatelains, which means, roughly, château owners, and in France still carries a certain panache 200 years after the revolution and the fall of the aristocracy. I don't believe many people know our names. The men at the café surely do not.

Jack and I each pull out a wooden chair from a little wooden table, and sit down. The proprietaire nods to us from behind the bar. Soon will appear on our table two small porcelain cups with hot café au lait— about $3.00 each in US terms, no refills.

Before it arrives, I leave the bar and go to the patisserie next door for our croissants, following the suggestion of the café owner on our first morning years ago, when we learned the café served no food. "Apportez vos croissants ici," he said enthusiastically, and for eight years now I have been buying our breakfast next door, and bringing it over to the café to have with our coffee.

Thus starts the typical day for us in Culan, France, a town of 800 with a declining population, in the middle of rolling farmland. Our Chateau de Malvaux is a mile away. The chateau has as its address St. Eloy d'Allier, a tiny place in the center of France about 180 miles south of Paris and near a few charming old French towns holding onto their 18th century look.

Culan is not one of those charming towns. The main street is a departmental (county) road passing through, with graveled parking before a small post office, grocery, a bread-baker, the small pastry shop and the Grand Café. There is a good restaurant, and a few, rather sizable, and handsome houses. Everything is gray stone. In front of these buildings there are newly-planted small trees, plane trees, I believe. They will one day be larger than the buildings. All of the buildings look very old. The town looks old. It is old. Many of the houses are medieval.

What Culan does have is the Château de Culan, a gigantic chateau with three towers, on a small river. Constructed in the 12th and 15th centuries, the lord here ruled over all the chateaux in the area, including Malvaux.

The Grand Café is really not all that big or great, the usual meaning of grand in French. Its address: 9, Place de Grand Croix. The place was not so much a square as a triangular parking area. Is there a big cross? Yes, it's over there behind that truck, Stone, now almost black from age. Not all that big, though, perhaps six feet high.

Despite the obvious age of the café building, you enter it through a new sliding glass door, with the bar perpendicular to it, so that the

*The Chateau de Culan. The lord here ruled over a number
of chateaux in the Middle Ages, including ours.*

curious customers at the bar, never anyone but men, can view arrivals
from the time they park, all the way through their entry.

For my partner and me, American owners of a chateau, I suspect
the layout did provide the chance to comment, not so much to greet
but to acknowledge our arrival, and for a few to grumble under their
breath. Camaraderie we did not experience with the men at the café.

It must have been obvious that we were two men sharing their
lives together, but never did we see, on the surface at least, the slight-
est hint that anyone noticed it. We talked about this, Jack and I, and
concluded it was the same as the privacy, or disinterest, that the French
accord their politicians; their private lives are not discussed, at least not
in public.

The French legislature did pass same-sex marriage in 2013, two
years before the US. In truth, the law in France was beset with contro-
versy, as the issue is in the United States. I was surprised, and disappointed, that there were French who were opposed to marriage equality.
I expected such an attitude in the US, but somehow, when I lived in

France, I felt the French took to heart their national motto: liberté, egalité, fraternité (liberty, equality, fraternity). Paris is one of the gay capitals of Europe, with perhaps 40 or 50 bars, B&Bs, saunas. One of the outdoor cruising areas is the right bank of the Seine near the Louvre, primarily at night. In Culan, I did wonder about the attitude of the men at the cafe, particularly the ones who mumbled a greeting that was incomprehensible.

Some of these men at the café, I'm sure, are among the farmers who would from time to time block the route nearby with burning tires, tractors, whatever, to protest against the government's level of farm subsidies, I jump to the conclusion that the subsidies were generous, because the European community was always objecting to them, maintaining they gave French farmers an advantage in pricing over other European farmers. But here I am, reaching a conclusion when I'm not well-enough informed.

In addition to the bar, which is about 15 feet long and of natural dark wood, probably walnut, there are maybe 10 square wooden tables in dark wood, each with four dark wooden chairs, on a dark wooden floor. In addition to the glass door, there is a window, but so much dark wood gives the café a gloomy look even though there is ample natural light. There is never any artificial lighting provided at breakfast time.

We have been there only first thing in the morning, so I cannot say whether the tables are ever occupied at other hours. Jack and I have invariably been the only clients at the tables. But the bar has always been virtually full, with 8 to 12 Frenchmen chattering, going over the racing sheets, and ordering glass after glass of red wine.

We determine that today there is no need to go into St. Amand Montrond, the idyllic little town of 12,000, 10 miles away. No need today for the supermarket. St, Amand is also a town of good country restaurants, tree-lined streets, spotless pedestrian areas, and the efficient speedy trains into Gare d'Austerlitz in Paris.

Instead, we drive directly back to the chateau, down the little

*Colza is an important crop in France.for its oil. Its
cultivation makes a beautiful yellow countryside.*

country road cutting through the rolling hills covered with bright yellow colza, whose oil, used as a lubricant for machinery, makes it an important French crop. Then the long driveway shaded by old oaks. We remark that the iron gate to the parc, the landscaped lawn in front of a chateau, is open, meaning that elderly Monsieur le Jardinier is here today. We see him on the mower.

Apparently he will not be spraying Roundup today, nor regaling us with the glories of it and all American products, and deploring the shame of everything French except French wine and French women. He is a good man, if not a little garrulous on this subject. His wife, a spitting image of the bloodthirsty women depicted at the revolution, our part-time housekeeper, is close-lipped at the chateau, but, we have heard, loquacious when she returns to Culan.

The property of the chateau has been whittled down to just about 12 acres, from 3000 hectares, or 7400 acres, centuries ago. Generation after generation had the need to sell off pieces of land to bolster finances. An aristocrat would never go to work. Localities a distance away still carry the Malvaux name in their title.

Jack and I have been together many years, decades by now. After leaving our careers, there were the renovations in the Hamptons, the stress of apartment buildings in Manhattan, and the reward of retirement at a fairly young age. I was 58 when we left New York. Jack was 61.

Being from a Louisiana French family, as a youth Jack acceded to his father's wish that he familiarize himself with his heritage by attending the Sorbonne in Paris. He earned doctorates in French history and in languages, and became Dr. Bernard as an instructor at the University of Montreal. After a time in New York, Jack wanted to return to France—and I was eager for the adventure. So that is why we are here. We first bought the apartment in Nice. It was an almost perfect city, protected from harsh winters by the mountain range just to the north. We would purchase a chateau as a country house, and sell Nice when we decided to spend winters in Fort Lauderdale.

One summer, I was dispatched by Jack to Fort Lauderdale to try to find a house. We had two friends there, a couple, and Ed from Provincetown, so it seemed like a good place to spend the winter. By now, having owned several properties in Southampton and two buildings in Manhattan, you would assume we were experienced in real estate, and I thought we were. We put a ceiling on what we would pay for a house in Fort Lauderdale, which would buy a fairly nice place. I looked at a very handsome house with a pool, 10 percent above our maximum price. However, we would not consider budging from our maximum price, no matter what expensive amenities the house offered. Instead, I ended up arranging the purchase of an inferior house within our limit—and in the space of six months, we put in a pool, that the other house already had, and, eventually, we would spend far more to give our new house the allure of the house I had foolishly rejected because it was over our limit. Our schedule would become six winter months, plus at least a day or more in Florida, to make us eligible for homesteading, and six months less a little in Europe.

We were there during the winter when my mother and sister were at our house, and my mother reached her 90th birthday. We decorated the living room with huge cutouts of the figure "90" that greeted her when she entered the room. "I can't believe I've reached this age!" she exclaimed joyously. My mother would go on for almost five years more.

I suppose most people believe their mother was the best mother that ever lived. I believe that of my mother, and she really was. Having never worked in her life when my father disappeared, she got a job as a housekeeper, went to school, became a bookkeeper, and kept our little family together. Although she never finished high school because of demands at home, her voracious reading equipped her to speak authoritatively on many subjects. She was interested in politics and people, and, early on, became a member of the Sierra Club. She was adventurous. As late as age 92, she was traveling alone to our chateau in France. I remember one time, when we were meeting her at Charles de Gaulle Airport in Paris, that there had been a gate change and confusion, so that, for quite a while, we could not locate her. Then we spotted her: sitting in a waiting area with her nose in a book, totally unconcerned. "I knew you'd find me," was her comment. "I thought it wise to stay put."

We were driving from the chateau to the apartment in Nice once, when my mother and sister were visiting. After stopping for lunch in Marseille, we were leaving the city, my mother and sister in the back seat, when we stopped for a red light. Suddenly, the rear door on my mother's side was pulled open from the outside, and one of two teen-aged boys on a motor scooter roughly yanked my mother's shoulder bag from her body. As they fled, Jack pursued them, blaring the horn. They were not dumb. They turned into a pedestrian walkway too narrow for us to follow. For some months after, this harrowing experience enlivened my mother's conversations. She spoke of looking into the eyes of that "desperate and frightened boy." Never did she assess any blame, only pity, for her young assailant. That is the kind of mother I had, her empathy unlimited, and carrying over to showing her love for me as I am, and having affection for my partner Jack, too.

But we still had Nice when we found the chateau. I recall our first view of it and its medieval towers. We had been looking in chateau country around the city of Tours, where most of the former royal chateaux are. We were finding nothing, and followed an ad to the center of France, and met with an agent.

The Chateau de Malvaux is one of a ring of small chateaux that defended against marauding enemies beginning from the 12th century, including against England during the Hundred Years War. Chateaux from that era are generally called, in French, château fort, meaning, in English, fortified castle. These fortresses were defensive structures with two-foot thick stone walls, with battlements, perhaps a crenelated tower, sometimes a moat or wall, sometimes guard houses. A chateau

Our Chateau de Malvaux.

fort can be distinguished from a building called merely a château. A château does not have defensive characteristics, and is much more recent, often 18th or 19th century, and was built to be a residence, after the need for local defenses ceased.

Malvaux is a typical chateau fort. The towers have their origin in the 12th century. The chateau consisted of a square stone tower crenelated for defense. It was where the lord lived. At Malvaux, it is five stories high. The square tower, called a donjon, is on one end of the overall structure. A round stone tower is on the other end, and has three stories and a tall cone shaped slate roof. This round tower has the openings, arrowslits, that narrow toward the interior for protection when launching arrows. Falcons have noted the protection feature. Each spring, these arrowslits become a falcon nursery, open to the exterior via the slit, closed to the interior by recent glass.

Between the two towers in the early ages was an open area for soldiers, with a thick wall and a cellar for protection. It was on the ancient

The Grand Salon, the largest of the 26 rooms.

stairs, carved into the centuries-old wood, that we discovered the eroding but still intact initials of a soldier, "D-L M," with the year carved, 1353, no month. Nearly 700 years have passed since this man's successful effort at immortality.

In the late 15th-century, after the Hundred Years War and when local wars were less likely, with on-site soldiers no longer needed, a building about 70 feet wide and three stories, with a steep, sloping slate roof, was constructed between the towers as the residence, with the towers, of the lord and his family.

This building and the two towers, modernized many times over the centuries, was the chateau my partner and I acquired. There was also a small building, once the kitchen, next door, in another structure for safety against fire. This small building had a two-foot high cross deeply carved from outside into the stone between the two floors, indicating that a family member was fighting in the Crusades. The Crusades were fought from 1095 to 1291.

A memory of the Crusades carved into stone.

A drought one year revealed buried structures at the chateau until then unknown by us. The grass in the parc had turned yellow and brown because of lack of water—except in areas where there were underground stones that held moisture that kept the grass above green. It became apparent that the chateau had once been surrounded by a moat and wall with two round 10-foot diameter guard houses.

When we bought the chateau, it was empty of furniture, save for a beautiful antique billiard table, surprisingly in the grand salon on the main floor. We had it moved to the huge 20 foot high grenier (attic). The chateau had been owned by a chemical company in Marseilles, and used for employee holidays. Considered a petite chateau in the land of Versailles and Fontainebleau, the chateau nonetheless had 26 rooms and six baths. The heating system was the fireplace in every room, which may have been a godsend in the 15th century, but I tend to like thermostats. Electric heat would be coming.

On the ground floor, the rez de chaussee, was a wide center hall, a foyer really, since it was ten feet wide. Here we would put a large crystal chandelier, one of six on the main floor. Ahead was a long oak staircase that turned and continued to the third floor.

The double door from the outside was almost 10 feet tall, and had in the lock the largest key, iron, that I have ever seen. It was 10 inches long, and it worked. I don't know what era the key came from, but it was old. It couldn't be from the fortified age, when it was necessary to defend against armed groups roaming about. The lord surely didn't just lock the door to the enemy. There had been a moat and guard houses. I'm sure they counted on stopping intruders then and there.

On either side of the center hall foyer were two large square rooms, extending through the chateau to the rear. On the left, the two rooms were separated by an opening where we would install double paneled doors. The front room would become our morning room, as the English call it, with leather sofas. Americans might call this room a den. Here was a TV, hidden in a cabinet, and a game table. It became the room we spent the most time in.

The rear room on that side would be the dining room. Each room had two large French windows, and each room had a fireplace.

The kitchen and a half-bath were off a small hallway off the dining room, in the square tower. As I said, the original kitchen had been in the ancient house next door. It was still there, but unusable. A new kitchen had been installed in the square tower. It was merely adequate; however, it was attractive, dominated by a large stained glass window. We had planned to resurrect the old kitchen as the elaborate room it once was with a large fireplace. It had to be eat-in. I wouldn't want to be running between the kitchen and the château dining room, even if we found an unobtrusive way to connect the old house to the chateau. I was thinking about an all-glass corridor. Using all glass was good enough for I. M. Pei for his Pyramid at the Louvre. Malvaux and the old part of the Louvre are about the same age. It works at the Louvre, so it should work at Malvaux.

On the other side of the entry hall, the right side, when we bought the chateau, were two rooms similar to the left side. The rooms had French windows and fireplaces more elaborately decorated than others in Malvaux. The front room was called the grand salon, the living room to us Americans. We would have the entire wall torn down between these two already sizable rooms, install two columns, and produce a grand salon about 55' x 25', with two fireplaces.

The two back windows in these rooms would be replaced by French doors opening onto a very sizable stone terrace the width of the building. We had this terrace, about 70x25, constructed at the same time as the French doors that would open onto it were installed.

It was determined that I would get the front east bedroom on what we call the second floor, but the French call the first. The bedroom was larger than I ever had, or seen, and would eventually hold, besides the usual bedroom furnishings, two sofas in a seating area centered on the fireplace. The room, with two French windows overlooking the chateau parc in front, had a spectacular bath in the round tower, with stained glass windows.

Jack's was the rear west bedroom of identical size as mine. Fireplace, as in all rooms. Similar windows. But an ordinary bathroom, nothing like mine. The bedroom had a view to the rear and would overlook, in the future, the croquet court, when we got to making one. Here I want to mention that Jack, though his quarters with the small bath may have been a little inferior to mine, made no complaint. He was an author and avid reader, and for these reasons pretty much monopolized the library, a glorious cherry-paneled room in the round tower off the grand salon. When I couldn't find him, I looked in the library.

The only part of the chateau I want to mention a little more is the square tower, the donjon, as I said, from the 12th century. It is where the lord originally lived, and was a chief defensive structure. When we arrived, the laundry was on the ground floor, the kitchen on the main floor, a bedroom and bath above that, and a partially open room on top, protected by battlements on all sides.

I didn't mention the 12-foot high room under the top room. When we looked at the chateau with the real estate agent, she said there had been a recent fire. It turned out that this room, the chateau's former chapel, still had remnants of that recent fire, but the "recent" was the 19th century. It's a matter of perspective. With an ancient building, perhaps the 19th century just happened.

It was our plan to restore this chapel or, rather, since the room was totally empty, install a chapel. Neither of us is religious, quite the contrary, but all ancient châteaux have chapels, so we wanted one, too. We found a handsome old holy water fountain at an antique shop as a modest start.

There are many religious stores around Place St. Sulpice in Paris, and we collected items there various times, not old, but nice. The big things were yet to come; the altar, pews, confessional box were still for the future.

We were surprised to find so many religious supply stores in Paris. While recent polls reveal that 81% of the French declare themselves to be Catholic, 40%, obviously some of the declared Catholics, claim to be atheist, an unexplained paradox. Although Catholicism is the official religion, from 1905 the law established secularization. Today, politicians on the left do not reveal their religious beliefs, and others are often wary of doing so.

We could easily claim that our chateau is located in the precise center of France. There were three towns within 30 miles in three directions, with elaborate markers making the claim. Why not join the group? We were in the center of the centers. However, recently, through modern techniques the real center was determined. It was none of the three towns claiming it, nor our chateau, but little Vesdun, a tiny village of fewer than 600 souls a couple of kilometers east of Culan.

A big advantage for me of the chateau's location was the ease in getting to Paris by car or by train. Jack and I went there often. One time when I was in Paris alone, an elderly woman walking in front of me on the rue Royale tripped on a curb. She would have fallen had I not been quick enough to grab her. I complimented her attire, and said she must work for a fashion house, choosing the present tense as a subtle compliment. She lit up, and said that, yes indeed, she was retired from Chanel. She was eager to talk now, and I heard the word Chanel several times as I walked her the dozen or so blocks to her grand building on Parc Monceau. I missed much because, in her enthusiasm and animation, she spoke so rapidly. It was obvious that she had been pleased with my complement, and, in turn, I was happy at her reaction. When we got to her building, perhaps recalling the pleasant teas served me as a child by the woman of the Victorian house in Uniontown, I hoped that my new friend would invite me in for tea, even though I could barely understand her French. I should have known better. I was no longer a 10-year-old boy. So I bid the Chanel lady a "Bonne journée, Madame," and reluctantly departed.

I reflected recently on this episode, and I wonder whether my compliment of a woman's attire would be proper in the current atmosphere of accusations of sexual harassment. Perhaps it would be accepted by an elderly woman, but not a younger one. That alone would speak to the rarity of any recognition of beauty in age.

Now being older myself, I like to think that there can be beauty in age, I'm not thinking only of inner beauty, which certainly can exist at any age, but physical beauty, as well. I believe it's rare in an older man, but frequent in an older woman such as the Chanel woman I just described. Women have more possibilities. They can have their hair styled. They can apply makeup judiciously. They can dress smartly. But to me, it has to be more than window-dressing. Now I am referring to inner beauty. I think it can be apparent in many older people. Looking into an elderly person's eyes, I can see, or at least I imagine I can see, the depth of years and experiences, joys and suffering of a long life, the aspects that make living sometimes difficult but always wonderful. It is the majesty of life that is beautiful. Both genders qualify for inner beauty, but perhaps men are at a disadvantage when older for physical beauty. The first possibility for improvement, styling hair, leaves me, for one, cut off from the start. You can't style nothing.

Back to the chateau. Our first encounter at the chateau was not with the French, but with Johan, from The Netherlands, a tall, blond, young farmer with land next door, and whose house lights we could see at night across our 12 acres. We would invite him once a year to dinner: he would invite us. He was alone most of the time and said he liked it. However, every other weekend his male partner from Amsterdam would join him.

Johan had dairy cows, black and white Holsteins. A small truck would arrive at his house every morning about 10 to pick up the milk. Johan had an arrangement with our predecessor-owner to graze his herd on part of the chateau property, an understanding we continued. In return, he kept an eye on the chateau in our absences.

There had been robberies at other chateaux in the area. We had an absolute trust in Johan that time only reinforced. We were lucky. There was the story that the manager of a chateau not far away, in the owner's absence, had all the trees of an exotic wood cut down and sold, before he himself vanished.

Johan's use of our land for his dairy cows did not include the parc in front of the chateau, separated from the other land by an ancient stone balustrade, and then a short fence across an abandoned driveway. One day, part of the fence fell or was trampled down, and 25 or 50 black and white cows were gorging on virgin grass in the chateau parc, when Monsieur le Jardinier arrived.

The poor man became apoplectic. Running around, arms flailing, he was trying to impress the sizable creatures with his small, thin body, screaming and shouting "Les vaches dans le parc! Les vaches dans le parc!" He wanted to get them back through the fence, clapping his hands at them and yelling, but mostly scaring the poor beasts as they almost tripped over themselves to get away from him. All was returned to calm after Johan arrived and ushered his animals out. Afterwards, I sympathized with the gardener when he pointed out the numerous holes the cows' hooves had made in the sod.

Fred, the Siamese cat, the successor to George from our earlier days, was with us. We dragged him all over the world. Fred gladly became a chateau cat, using most of the 26 rooms, and becoming impossible to find. He was a wise cat: he treated the cows with respect. They weighed 1500 pounds. He didn't weigh 10.

As time went on, the characteristics we observed in the French became stereotypes, maybe not of all French, but at least of country French. They like Americans, even though their government often opposes ideas from anyone not French. They are wary of Americans, or maybe everyone. The ones we met were friendly, but even young people were reserved. They were dignified and proper. I will repeat the word "proper," meaning mannerly, fittingly dressed, behavior suitable to the place and occasion. America a half century ago? Kind of. However, the young people we encountered seemed to lack the driving ambition of our youth. The English word "holiday" must be the most common word in France.

Perhaps the French we met had little drive, compared to Americans, but one particular happening surprised me. By now, we had set up the croquet area on the grass behind the chateau. One day when he had stopped by, we invited a neighbor, who had once been a soccer star on the local team, to play a game. To my astonishment, I won. He appeared crushed. I was flabbergasted at my win because I had participated so little in sports in my life. The next day, the ex-soccer star returned to the chateau, challenging us to a rematch. There was a sense of competitiveness. With clenched jaw, he weighed and mentally measured his every shot. To my astonishment a second time, I won. The former soccer star never asked for a game again.

Generally at Malvaux, we read a lot. After starting just about every morning at the café in Culan, we then stopped at the store for the French paper and the Times of London, and picked up anything we might need. That always included a baguette, freshly baked. Our satellite TV enabled me to watch Sky News from London, while Jack sequestered himself in the library. We'd have lunch, and in the afternoon maybe go into the towns Montlucon or St. Amand, to the supermarket. I had several pots of petunias on the back terrace that I would deadhead, that is, remove the wilted blossoms. That's supposed to keep petunias healthy and productive. Well, there won't be a whole lot of prizes in line for Malvaux should there ever be a competition.

I devoted a lot of energy and worry to roses. When we bought the chateau, within view of the chateau there had been a long rectangular area enclosed by a low privet hedge on three sides, and on the fourth side was the wall of the stable. The rectangle seemed to serve no purpose, since there was no access, as the privet had no break in it. So, I made a break about two feet wide and, going all out for chateau style, on either side of the new opening I put a pedestal with an urn on top. Inside the area, I planted red climbing roses all along the stable wall, and in front of them, about a dozen or so bushes, mostly floribundas, with roses in various colors.

I did everything the books had directed in order to grow perfect roses. They were in total sun. They were mulched. They were fertilized. When watering them, I was careful not to get water on the leaves, and once a week I dutifully sprayed them with a powder for black spot. Actually, it could have been called a powder FOR black spot, because some of the bushes got so much black spot that the powder could find

Our fancy animal enclosure.

My rose garden and number one worry.

hardly a virgin leaf to treat. I exaggerate a little, but it was a constant battle. At this time in my life, I had no particular stress, so my worry over the roses filled the void. I must admit, however, that, despite all the concerns I had, the roses often looked pretty good.

Tonight Jack and I are going into St. Amand for dinner. We drive past a building that was a wonderful château before they built the A71 highway just on the other side of it. The owner must have been there for some time. When you buy property in France, your attorney conducts a search and guarantees that no public facility is in the planning stage in a two-mile radius for the next five years. This chatelain would never have bought it if told of a future freeway.

The A71, as all French highways, is a madhouse of speeding demons. The speed limits are similar to ours, but cars frequently go the equivalent of 100 mph. When you go to pass another car (rare indeed) and clear your movement to another lane by looking in the sideview mirror, a speeding car can be right up on you when you pull out. It had appeared for enough back. Good roads everywhere, but frightening.

Further toward St. Amand, we pass a semi pulled off on the side of the road. As we have seen many times, the truck driver is having his dinner à la francaise. He has spread a white tablecloth on the grass. On it is his china dinner plate, his bottle of wine, and his stemmed wine glass. Is that a cloth napkin? Yes! Dinner on the road in France. Just because you're a trucker doesn't mean you're not cultured.

Having dinner out in France, we are prepared for a long evening. The restaurants in these little towns apparently do not plan on more than one seating per evening per table. Dinner begins about 8 o'clock. We usually start with the platter of crudités, raw vegetables sprinkled with a vinaigrette.

Then follows the plat du jour, the main course, the dish of the day, of which there are several on offer. A main course isn't called the entrée in French, as that word comes from "enter" and is the appetizer. Then the waiter holds the cheese platter for your choosing, then fruit, dessert, coffee... After the silver coffee pots are placed on the tables of various guests, the entire waitstaff invariably disappears. The others in the restaurant, French, are busy chattering and, evidently, are content to remain a long while. No way for us to get the check. The attitude in the country: "Don't rush off, spend the night." But don't they know we're Americans?

Sundays, we frequently have afternoon dinner at the small but elegant hotel in Herisson, a beautiful town close to us, dominated by the overwhelming ruins of a massive chateau fort on a hill. The hotel's restaurant is grand but cozy, and busy. My dessert is usually Charlotte Royale, a light cake with strawberries and raspberries baked inside. There was no point in looking for cheesecake, a favorite of mine. No one seems to have heard of it, even though France is the land of a million cheeses. Oh, by the way, Herisson is one of those three towns allegedly in the very center of France.

The chateau of Georges Sand (not a chateau fort), where she spent time with Chopin, is nearby. She's buried in the garden. We bought a dozen plates at the store there depicting scenes from the French Revolution, some of them almost too gory to serve food on. Nonetheless, we do.

Often we would take a few days to drive to a nearby city and almost always we would observe small French idiosyncrasies—not at all the right word if you are French. Oddities isn't any better. As examples: a small store may have just one escalator, set to go down, not up; a door into a supermarket opens automatically when going in, but you must use a non-automatic one when exiting with your cart or packages; peanut butter is in the gourmet section; drivers start with 10 points on their licenses and lose points, and their license, when infractions lower their number of points to zero. To me, it makes more sense to start with zero, a clean slate. The highway billboards warn, in French: you only have 10 points! (So, drivers, you can relax. It's a long way to zero.)

A disappointment to me in national elections here is that there are no long, nervous hours of returns on TV to become engrossed in. On national election day, a Sunday, at exactly 8 PM, an announcer appears on TV and informs the nation who its new president is. No following the returns state by state, or in France that would be department by department, to sometimes a breathtaking conclusion. No drama at all. Are my hopes for drama unreasonable here? It must be considered that the country has just one time zone, and the polling points all close at the same time. Sad. To me, the French miss the best show of every four years.

Returning from Bordeaux one day, Jack driving, a siren sounded behind us and a motorcycle policeman pulled us over. As he walked to the car, we asked each other what we could have done. The first words out of the policeman's mouth were, in French, "You're from New York?" No doubt he had spotted our New York license plate. We had our car shipped over. He then engaged Jack in a conversation about whether Jack liked New York, that he himself wanted to take a holiday there, what Jack thought about France… There was no infraction.

On the same return to the chateau, we stopped at a restaurant in Aubusson, the little city of rug fame. While eating, we observed three young men, perhaps 14 or 15, enter the restaurant with two shopping bags. The maitre d' summoned the chef, who began laying out the contents of their bags on an empty table: mushrooms of all sizes and varieties. There was a whispered negotiation, and the teenage boys left the restaurant all smiles with euros in their pockets, in return for their morning work. The French are crazy about mushrooms, and the season sees cars parked along country roads, with the fields dotted with people searching. The newspapers join in on the excitement, with pages devoted to the most desirable mushrooms and the ones to avoid.

On our arrival back at Malvaux, we discovered there had been a leak in the steep, slate roof. We figured this was no small thing. The roof rose at a 45° angle at quite a height. And our observation from the ground indicated there were about a half dozen spots needing attention. The Euro equivalent of $10,000, I estimated.

There was actually a roofer in our little neighborhood town of Culan, who said on the phone that he'd be there the next day. He arrived in the morning, set up scaffolding outside the three floors and on the roof, did the job in a few hours—and presented a bill of about $200. Because of our shock, he explained that this is France. There are steep slate roofs everywhere. Pas de probleme, Monsieur.

As our eighth year at the chateau was winding down, we began to reminisce about our joys thus far in France, and our disappointments. There was the obvious interest in us by the country people because we were Americans and chatelains. That was good for my ego. There was the wild applause for the US Marine Corps band at the Bastille Day parade one year in Nice. That filled me with pride at being an American. There was the bus driver in Nice who, when a poorly-dressed woman was fumbling in her ragged purse for the fare, just waved her on without a word. His concern for that woman touched me emotionally. I had observed the desperation of the water department workers to finish a line to the chateau, so that we would have water on the weekend our well ran dry. There was the well-dressed older couple stopped on the sidewalk, earnestly talking to a homeless man sitting in a doorway, apparently wanting to help him. Where, despite the crotchety older men at the Grand Café in Culan, people smiled at you, appreciated my attempts at French, stepped back to let you go ahead. We knew now that we liked the French. Maybe not those in Paris, who can be abrupt like some New Yorkers. The French of everywhere else.

But, we had made no lasting friends. The French country people, polite, respectful, had a different background, a different culture, and a different present. We concluded that, if there were just some Americans nearby, or some Brits... The only foreigners nearby was a community from The Netherlands. We were lonely in the country. And what were we doing in the middle of the country in the first place? We were from Manhattan!

We had been investigating the UK, and that's where we would go. We agreed that Johan, the farmer next-door, ambitious and not French, would place an ad in an Amsterdam paper to sell the chateau, completely furnished. His ad brought a buyer and Johan earned a commission. The chateau would be the home of an older Dutch couple with lots of grandchildren. They would love Malvaux as we did. They set up a website. Their photos today show the chateau as on the day we left it, furniture, decorating, my little rose garden, all. A consolation.

The understanding in the purchase was that the equivalent of about $250,000 of the sales price would be paid upfront, in cash. This was at the request of the buyers, and it suited us well, because it would avoid an elaborate collection of receipts for capital improvements such as electrical heat installation in 26 rooms, a stone terrace with balustrade, expanding window cuts and installing French doors, and on and on. Evidence of these improvements would have been required for the French fisc (the French IRS) for us to avoid taxes on any sale figure above our purchase price.

The day before the closing, the buyers arrived with the money, in cash, in a beat-up brown gym bag. It was in British sterling, per our request, and Jack and I sat with the buyers at the dining room table, counting a sample of the packets of 50-pound notes. We stopped in Paris for the weekend after the closing, and I took the gym bag with us everywhere we went, afraid to leave it at the hotel unattended. On Monday, I would rent a safety deposit box at a branch of Credit Lyonnaise, and empty the contents of the gym bag into it. Fortunately, the boxes at the headquarters on the Boulevard des Italiens near the Opera, where I went first, were all taken. The interior of the elaborate, 19th-century building was destroyed by a fire a month later. To avoid any possible questions by British customs, still monitoring entries at that time, it took me perhaps eight day trips from the UK to Paris to collect, little by little, the cash from the safety deposit box in batches. I was being cautious about the amount I carried, because I remembered

TV news reports of US customs confiscating large sums on the possibility they were profits from illegal activity. It did not occur to me to carry the closing statement with me, to substantiate the money's origin.

On the morning of the closing, I felt depressed. I got dressed, had a cup of coffee with Jack, and said barely a word. Every room, every item that fell within my sight, I realized would be my last view of it. Over there was the marble-topped chest my mother and sister bought on Second Avenue for my first apartment. The two paintings there, each of a pilgrim, Jack and I had found in Southampton. And there, that is the hand-painted china chamber pot from the long-ago Astor Hotel on Times Square. The Astor Hotel name is painted on it in gold. We had shipped these things to France because we couldn't let them go. Now we were letting them go.

We drove past my rose garden, through the tall iron gates, down the long driveway with its canopy of old trees, to the public road. With heavy heart, I turned and looked back through the trees and saw the tops of the two towers, glistening in the morning sun, the square tower and the round tower. How beautiful!

And how sad. I was leaving France. I was leaving the French. I was leaving the chateau. I would never have a French château again.

Then the towers were lost from my view.

CHAPTER **15**

The Sofa. 3500 miles.

NOW, JACK AND I have relocated from France to England. We are in Brighton on the English Channel, to look for a rental for the summer, and possibly to buy a condo if we like the city. We had read in the Times of London that Brighton had many Victorian-style houses. This meant to us, charming, 19th-century neighborhoods. Brighton was a favorite place of Queen Victoria. King George IV built a handsome Indian-Chinese-style palace, a tourist attraction today, called the Royal Pavilion. In more recent days, the city acquired a shady reputation

as the favorite weekend trysting location for many a CEO and their curvaceous secretaries. The Times article also mentioned that Brighton is one of the gay centers of the UK. That meant that we would feel comfortable, and, maybe, make a few friends.

We didn't settle in one of those charming Victorian neighborhoods that we discovered do exist. Instead, we rented an apartment on the seafront, in a condo above what was then a Hilton Hotel, and is now a Holiday Inn. Before the summer was out, we would buy an apartment in the same building, on the 12th floor, with a sensational view of the sea and the Brighton Pier. In the distance on the curve of the shore can be seen the White Cliffs of Dover, as in the World War II song.

The Brighton Pier is not a grand affair. Near the street is a large domed building with restaurants and an arcade. The pier thrusts out over 1700 feet into the English Channel, and is occupied in the final section by amusement park rides. There is a Ferris wheel. The Brighton Pier is one of the things that attracts the masses to Brighton from London.

The beach is not covered in silky sand as it is in Fort Lauderdale. Just as in Nice, it is a pebble beach.

Every nice day, I would walk from the apartment to the Brighton Pier, about a half mile away. On September 11, 2001, Jack and I started the day as usual, going to the nearby cafe, the Regency, just after 8:00, for coffee and a croissant. After, I darted up Prescott Street to the newsagent for the Times and the Telegraph. I left for my walk after noon, or after 7 AM New York time.

I became lost in the view and sound of the waves. I usually walked to the very water end of the Brighton Pier where the rides are, and I did so that day. Then I headed home along the sidewalk on Kings Road above the beach and sea. I was almost home when an English man in a tan summer suit, walking toward me, veered from his route to stop me. He seemed excited. "Have you heard?" he asked, "A plane, a big plane, just hit the World Trade Center in New York!" He could supply no more detail than that, so I hurried home to tell Jack. It must have been just after 1:46 PM in Brighton, because the first plane hit the north tower at 8:46 AM, New York time.

Jack had still been reading the papers, and in stunned awe we watched on TV the second plane hit the south tower just after 9 AM in New York. We sat there on our brown leather sofa in the comfort of our living room, 3500 miles away, watching the grotesque nightmare as people jumped from windows to end their lives, as the buildings where 50,000 people worked fell to the ground, and as just under 3000 people met their deaths. That evening we ate an abbreviated dinner off of trays that we held on our laps as we sat on the sofa in front of the TV. In retrospect, I am astonished that we could eat while watching such horror. In the days that followed, I was particularly saddened to see the hordes of people roaming about the city, to hospitals and police and fire stations, posting photos of their missing loved ones in the vain hope that they may still be alive somewhere.

Eventually, life at such a distance from New York returned to normal. We contracted for a conservatory on the seafront portion of the balcony, to make use of an area that was, until then, usually off-limits because of the incessant strong winds from the English Channel. Although this was a condo building, we required no approval for the design, virtually all glass, from the condo board of directors. Respecting owners' ownership, condos in most of Europe do not have the strict oversight you find in the US, that we call the freest country in the world. The result is that buildings above the ground level will have apartments with exposures having many variations. I did not find this appearance of versatility unpleasant, and I admire the respect of individuality.

The winter before buying in Fort Lauderdale, Jack and I rented a house for the season on a lake in the very center of the city, off Las Olas Blvd, a grand street of royal palms, canals, and expensive shops. The house was a little dated, but, heck, so were we. And here again, like the time when I quit my job in New York and said I was retiring to wealth, I created a lie for absolutely no reason. I seem prone to that. Past lying does not help when you go to rate your life.

247

Several years before, when we were still in France, I applied to the Irish consulate in Paris to be recognized as a foreign-born Irish citizen. Ireland considers you a citizen if your grandfather was born in Ireland, no matter where you were born. My grandfather was born in Cork, so, after the submission of documents, many documents, I received the Irish document certifying me as a foreign-born citizen. I then obtained an Irish passport that I use in Europe, though I could not enter the US with it, since immigration here requires Americans to use a US passport. I do like being an Irish citizen, and the song "Danny Boy" touches me emotionally.

But in renting the house, I claimed to the landlady that I was from Ireland. I had my Irish passport visible on a coffee table the time she dropped by. I remember her remarking that I had "very little" Irish accent. Actually, I had none at all. I explained that many Irish have very little accent, which is true, and that I had spent so much time in the "states" that I had lost most of what I had.

So, again, I went out of my way to lie. Why? I suppose I yearned to seem a little exotic, rather than just being another American. Is being from Ireland exotic? Maybe not, but it's all I had. Or didn't have.

After confessing that I have in the past not infrequently fibbed, I stop here in order to affirm that everything I am putting down in this book is the truth. It's quite some time since I've told a lie of note. Maybe I'm over it. Maybe I'm finally mature, at age 87. But just as a witness in the stand in a court case who lied to police lacks credibility, my believability may be under a cloud. I ache to redeem myself.

But let's go on. Jack and I continued life six months plus in Florida, six months minus in Brighton. Fred, the pussycat, is no longer a player, having died some time ago in France, age 18. Wherever we were, we continued our practice of going to a neighborhood cafe each morning for what we called breakfast, just a croissant or bagel or toast and coffee. In both England and Florida, we were in populated areas where people-watching was fun, so making friends seemed less important than at the chateau. In England, we made no friends; we didn't seem to need to, although this had been an earnest desire in foreign-like France.

The invitation went out to my mother and sister to visit us in Brighton, but they were less enthusiastic than when they accepted invitations to the chateau in France, and they never came. England just was not as exotic to visit as France, and an apartment could not compete with a chateau. My mother and sister both had accepted my minority lifestyle and, as I've said, became fond of Jack. Never having been close to his own mother, he readily reciprocated. My mother and Pat did visit us in Fort Lauderdale. Not exotic either, but closer to Cleveland than the UK.

CHAPTER 16

The Jailbird: The crime of disobedience.

I NEVER REVEALED to my mother and sister the disaster of their last trip to Florida, never told them a word about my ending up in jail. If my mother learned about it, she'd somehow try to blame herself. She always thought it was her fault when I was in difficulty.

When they were leaving at the end of their visit, Jack and I took them to the Fort Lauderdale airport for an early morning flight to Cleveland, Jack driving. He dropped the three of us at Departures. Since standing even for a short time was prohibited, he would drive around in a loop while I helped with their luggage and got them to the check-in line.

I said goodbye to them and returned outside to wait for Jack. Even though traffic was light, to make myself conspicuous, I stood in an area forward several feet of the walkway, in a zone painted with parallel lines meaning, I presumed, No Parking. A Broward County sheriff's deputy approached. "Get back on the walk!" he shouted at me. I felt offended by his rude tone, and embarrassed that there were a few people nearby to witness my scolding. My pride was under attack.

"I'm waiting for someone to pick me up," I tried to explain, but he cut me off, still shouting: "I said get back on the walk!" I observed Jack's car in the distance, approaching. "Here my ride comes now," I interjected. The deputy was now next to me and grabbed and held on to my upper arm. "You're under arrest!"

As I was led into the terminal, I was aware that Jack must have witnessed my dilemma. In passing the crowds in line to check in, I could see my mother and sister now at the check-in counter, evidently having cleared the line. I was relieved that they did not look back to see me being led through the terminal, held tightly by the arm by a uniformed deputy. We went down the escalator to the baggage claim area, and into a narrow hallway on the side. The hallway ended at an office, where I could see desks and several deputies. Before we reached the office, the deputy holding me pulled my arms behind my back, and clamped handcuffs on my hands. He pushed me down until I fell on the floor, unable to brake myself because of my handcuffed hands. "Wait there," the deputy commanded, as he continued to the office. Of course I had no alternative but to wait there. While I was sitting on the floor, a few other deputies came down the hallway, observed me below them, stepped around me, and continued on without saying anything.

After ten or 15 minutes, my deputy returned and ordered me into the office, being kind enough to help me to my feet. He took a chair at a desk, and I sat in front of it. He asked for my ID. I told him it was in my left pants pocket. He got up, came around, and removed my small wallet himself. "I guess it's too late to say I'm sorry," I offered meekly. He did not reply, nor look up from writing and checking my driver's license. He asked: "Does your middle initial stand for Paul?" I lied. "Yes." Actually the P is for Patrick, and it flashed through my mind that it would be a Vincent Paul who was arrested, not me. I was grasping for straws here. Is it against the law to lie to a sheriff's deputy? I know it is if you lie to the FBI.

Then I was led by another deputy, with my hands still handcuffed behind my back, past a crowd waiting for their bags at a carousel, outside past the taxi line, and pushed, gently I must say, into the back seat of the marked car, and driven to the jail. The sheriff's deputy-driver was sympathetic. "This is nothing, you know," he assured me. "You'll be out in a few hours."

In jail, I spent four hours in a holding cell with about 20 others, until Jack, who was busy on the phone trying to learn my precise whereabouts and how to "spring" me, could post the $100 bond. Food was the last thing I wanted when our lunch trays arrived. I generously gave my lunch to a ravenous fellow prisoner whose appetite, apparently, was unaffected by his circumstances. He ate his own lunch and mine too. I learned that I had been charged with three offenses: disorderly conduct, resisting arrest without violence (I had questioned why I was being led away.) and failure to obey the lawful order of a police officer. They were throwing the book at me! A month later, I pled no contest, was given a $500 fine and a year's probation. My attorney arranged that the monthly reporting, as part of the probation requirement, could be done by mail, so that I could go to Brighton for my six months. The judge agreed to issue an order to expunge the record, but ten years later my record was still there.

Jack and I were living a good life, with our time in Europe and America. One December, when I returned to Florida after spending Christmas in Cleveland, we decided to fly to Paris for New Year's Eve. We were there on a chilly Pont Neuf at midnight as fireworks exploded around the top of the Eiffel Tower. We hadn't been in France in the couple of years since we relocated to England. It was good to be back. Home sweet home, almost.

By now, to be closer to us, my mother sold her house in Cleveland, and my sister her condo, and relocated to a brand new house in Coral Springs, a 40-minute drive from me. They would spend holidays at our house, with Jack cooking a traditional dinner, and me serving as busboy. I would go to their house every Sunday, and we would go to a restaurant. My mother and sister came to our house maybe every month or two. My mother was enjoying Florida immensely. I remember one Sunday going into a Chinese restaurant, walking next to my mother, her diligently pushing her triangular walker. In mid-walk she stopped, looked up at me, and exclaimed: "I can't believe I'm living in Florida!"

But as the years were passing, time was taking its toll on my mother: 93 years old, 94 years old. There was sometimes a little mental confusion. After an apparent but minor stroke, she was admitted to the hospital near my sister's house. More mental confusion than before. I visited her. I crouched low to her bed to talk to her. From less than two feet away, I studied the deep, gentle eyes that I knew so well after a lifetime. I was taken aback. I was not certain I was seeing my mother. She returned my look intently, without blinking. Was it without comprehension? I told her how much Pat and I loved her. She continued to look into my eyes, but said not a word. A sadness such as I had never felt came over me. I would never know if my mother understood me, nor if she knew who I was.

The following day I didn't make the 40-minute drive, but my sister said things were about the same.

CHAPTER 17

Exits. Gloom.

THE CALL FROM Pat came at 2 AM the next morning. I said to Pat; "It's better this way. She wouldn't want to be in this condition." I did not believe what I was saying. Our little family lost its guiding star. All I could think of, then and from then on, is that I didn't go to see her on her last day.

Mother, your job is officially over, the work you willingly took on, of raising your two children and keeping our little family together. I proclaim your life a success. We have been a family trio all these years, wonderful years, thanks to you. Pat and I are both doing well in life and are happy, because of your careful grooming. You are the woman I admire most in the world. Not Eleanor Roosevelt, not Mother Teresa. It is you, mother. If Pat and I have any good in us, it comes from you, our idol. Please forgive me for any troubles I caused you, and I'm sorry I did not give you grandchildren. You have understood that part of me that prevented it, and thank you, thank you for that. You have accepted Jack and treated him as a second son. You were a remarkable, loving woman. I wish desperately that I could have just a half hour with you to tell you all these things I should have said when I could.

Mother, I hope I'm wrong about there being no God. Because you deserve Paradise forever and ever.

Pat and I purchased four niches at Our Lady, Queen of Heaven Cemetery. I carried the urn with our mother's ashes to the pavilion, my sister right next to me, the three of us together one last time. A priest said a short prayer, the door of the niche was closed, and we left.

My mother always had a good time.

Rest In Peace, our beloved mother.

Life in time returned to normal for Jack and me. Our schedule in Florida: we tended our yard, as always went out for breakfast each morning, ate out about two times a week, and both in Florida and in Brighton were leading an enjoyable and quiet life. In both places, Jack devoted his leisure time to his books and his music, always classical. He was also enjoying cooking. Jack had the ability to create dishes by combinations of foods that had not found their way into a recipe book.

Then one day, Jack returned from his primary care doctor with concerning news. He reported to me that tests showed an aneurysm in the groin area that could not be surgically remedied. The prognosis was that one day, without warning, it would rupture and end Jack's life. He was stoic. He said that he was now 71, and continued that he certainly would not be taken in the flower of youth.

I was overwrought, but optimistic that we would continue on for at least another ten years before the worst happened. I told myself that he would be the exception to this dire prognosis. We had now been partners for over 39 years. We would barely make it to 40.

Jack was declining noticeably, being extremely winded after expending just a little energy. We were in Brighton now, and I had decided to fly back to the US for my 50th class reunion. I would be gone for only five days, but I still had to make sure that Jack would be comfortable while I was away. Both the supermarket and the newsagent were up a hill, a climb that Jack could no longer easily accomplish. I made certain that every food he could possibly want was on hand in the apartment.

I've mentioned that Jack spent a good part of each day reading the newspapers. This was, of course, before they were available on the internet. The newsagent agreed exceptionally to deliver the papers daily himself to Jack while I was gone. I also hid a number of small treats—Jack's favorite things like Pringles potato chips—around the apartment, and would reveal a hiding place in each of our daily phone calls.

The following year, on the plane back to the US from London's Gatwick Airport, Jack felt suddenly sick and weak. I was in an aisle seat across from his aisle seat, and I was concerned by his paleness and his difficulty in raising himself up. Obviously, however, it was no sudden rupture of the aorta. We tried to tell ourselves he was coming down with the flu.

We went to his doctor in Fort Lauderdale right away, and she ordered him to the hospital at once. Jack had gotten so weak that I had to use a wheelchair to get him from her office to the car, and I drove straight to Holy Cross Hospital. We faced the possibility Jack would be there a few days.

The next morning I answered the phone, a call I will never forget. The doctor identified herself, and bluntly said the following: "Mr. Burke, I don't think Mr. Bernard is going to live through the day." This was a shock, the first inkling that Jack would not get over this quickly. At the hospital, a counselor discussed Jack's condition, futile, with me in a closed room, and said she would arrange for hospice at our house or at the hospital. She was consoling, apparently recognizing our relationship. This being a Catholic hospital, I was surprised at the compassionate treatment.

Jack, too, was told of his hopeless situation. Not surprisingly, he chose the option to return home for hospice care. I drove home, and he would come by ambulance.

I was waiting at the head of the driveway next to the house when the ambulance arrived. It parked in the street and did not enter the driveway. As the stretcher with Jack on it was removed, he looked toward the house and saw me waiting for him. He smiled at me, and despite his weakness, pulled himself part way up on the stretcher, extended his right arm full length, and waved at me. I can see Jack and this scene, him smiling and waving, as I write this. This image will never leave me.

In the week Jack was back home, we had a brief talk in which, of all things, he said he didn't deserve me. I believed the opposite was true, and said that I was the luckiest man in the world to have been with him. And I was. Later, I called Jack's brother in Louisiana and told him of Jack's condition. Jack and he were not very close, so I discouraged his offer to come.

Jack had been home several days, with hospice caring for him 24 hours a day, but he was sleeping all of the time. One night before going to my room to go to bed, as usual I went to his room, where he was sleeping. The aide was sitting reading something. I said "Good night, Jack." He seemed to awaken, and in a strong voice replied, "Good night, Vincent." I would never forget those simple words. They would be the last words Jack would ever speak.

I couldn't sleep, and returned to his room a short time later. Jack, apparently in a coma, seemed restless. I asked the hospice attendant, insisted, really, to increase the drug administered to make breathing easier. She did so.

Jack died shortly after, with me and hospice there.

The last formal photo of Jack.

After, I knelt beside his bed, and told him of my desire that we'd be together again one day. Now I think of so many things I should have told him in that final week or two. If I had a precious hour with Jack, I'd thank him for 40 years, 365 days each, of pleasure in living with him, and of my admiration of everything about him. If I had an hour...

I carried the urn with his ashes to the niche, with my sister, Pat, right next to me. A priest said a short prayer. The door of the niche was closed, and we left. Two of the four niches were now occupied.

Rest In Peace, my beloved partner, Jack.

The death certificate gave the cause of death as COPD, not an aneurysm. That's logical; Jack was a smoker. In the early '70s, he switched to Carlton, the lowest tar and nicotine brand. That was the time when we believed that would make a difference, and I was enthusiastic about his concern for his health. Jack had never told me anything about having COPD, perhaps feeling guilty that he had brought this on himself. He needn't have felt that way. I acquiesced in his change to a so-called light cigarette, and was relieved that his smoking was now safe.

It's been hard for me to write details of my mother dying, and Jack dying. After many years, it's still painful. You never get over the death of someone you love.

CHAPTER 18

Solo. Single senior

NOW A LIFE alone.

I've written earlier that I'm an introvert. I read. I work crossword puzzles. I watch TV, but not a lot. Chiefly the news, but in the past I was a fan of Cheers, Seinfeld, and Frazier. I hardly have looked at anything but news since those programs are no more. Further back, I liked Mary Tyler Moore. Oh, yes. I do often get hooked on a Masterpiece Theater series such as "Upstairs Downstairs," "Downton Abbey," "The Palisers." I even watched "The Sopranos." I putter in the yard. I grow some flowers. I go to a restaurant once or twice a week, but don't like the group I'm with to be more than four people total. I hate parties and being with a lot of people. I like movies, but I'm careful to go only to those meant for adults. I've watched Amadeus three or four times. I prefer that my close friends be counted on the fingers of one hand. Perhaps that's a face-saving mechanism, because, in fact, I don't believe I've ever had the opportunity to have more than a few friends.

With Jack gone, my nature had to change. I was alone. I was utterly depressed. I no longer wanted to be in the house that Jack and I had shared. Reading, puttering in the yard, watching the news—I no longer could do any of that because all I was doing was thinking. How many times I went over in my mind the last week, the last day, the last hour, the last minute.

I had to get out or I'd go crazy. I went to my sister's house and spent some nights there. How lucky I was to have Pat. I started seeing a psychologist whose name I found in a gay paper. He was a help. I had never been to the Gay Center in Fort Lauderdale. I now went there and attended the men's discussion group on Wednesdays. I went on their Thanksgiving week cruise. That was a disaster for me, because I was so lonely in my single cabin, and I was unwilling to participate fully in group activities.

I went to the monthly dinner sponsored by the men's discussion group at area restaurants. I even, eventually, positioned myself to be responsible for arranging the group dinners. This was not me, but it was getting me away from the house I feared.

The group planned on going to a concert at a church that was welcoming to gays. I happened to see the flyer promoting advertising in the concert's program. I noted that a half page ad was $50. When we entered the church and sat down, I leafed through the program for my ad. There it was, a half page with just two words on it: "For Jack." I stared at the two words silently for a while. When the music started, I folded the program and put it in my pocket.

I yearned for companionship at home, something to stop the silence, so my sister and I answered an ad in Boca Raton for Siamese kittens, and I got one. I still have him, 18 years later. I named him Nigel, a typical English name and a tribute to Jack and my good times in the UK. And, what they say never to do without long reflection, I did right away. Less than two months after Jack, I was in Brighton selling our condo.

But slowly, with the help of Pat, the psychologist, and Nigel, I was coming out of my gloom. I began liking the new less-introverted me. I liked the groups at the restaurants. I was interested in the discussions at the weekly men's group. I was recovering.

Then occurred a life-altering day.

It was the usual Wednesday meeting of the men's discussion group. The moderator always did a round robin, giving each man a few minutes to say anything he wanted to. And, hopefully, set off a boisterous discussion. Usually, though, each man merely reported how his preceding week had gone.

My good friend Nigel

Mine, no surprise, had not been newsworthy. Jack had died a year ago now. I had made no intimate friends. I did see Ed, the friend who moved here from Provincetown. I attended, arranged. all of the group dinners. I had been seeing, from time to time, a man from the discussion group who made it clear he was not looking for a partner. Maybe he was not looking to me as a partner. Nigel had grown into an affectionate presence at the house. But I was still lonely. I had spent most of my life with a partner, and my affectionate cat with the sapphire blue eyes didn't fill the bill. When my turn came to speak, my desperation must have been apparent. I should have been ashamed of myself. "Does anyone want to go to dinner with me?" I implored. "If so, please see me after the meeting." I did everything but beg. There were about 30 men in attendance who heard my plea. There was no stampede to get in line to see me. Thirty men did not appear before me after the meeting. Just one did. One was enough. It was Frank. Frank Grant would become my partner, eventually my spouse, 18 years so far, and make me, for the second time in my life, the luckiest man in the world.

Frank reminded me of another aspect to our first meeting. He recalls that in my short soliloquy, I reported on sending $50 a month to a prisoner in a state prison. In addition to accepting my invitation for dinner, Frank thought it urgent to caution me about such an arrangement, that prisoners take advantage of gay men. Defending myself, I told Frank it was not quite as black and white as it would seem on first hearing of it.

John, the prisoner, had been the pool maintenance man for a company servicing our pool for several years, when he was convicted for the type of drug offense that, with liberal laws, no longer carries a prison sentence in some jurisdictions. The amount being sent to John was modest; enough for hardly more than a candy bar each day. Importantly, when Jack was dying, he asked me to continue the payments, and I promised that I would.

Neither of us recalls much, or anything, about that first dinner. We don't remember where we went, what we talked about, even what impression the other person made. So it was not a coup de foudre first meeting. Certainly, I had to explain to Frank the $50 a month being sent to John. But, astonishingly, a few days later it was Frank who called me, and not the more likely opposite, desperate me phoning him.

It seems that Frank had parked in a drugstore parking lot while he went to the library. He asked an employee in the store whether it would be ok, and the man, evidently with no authority, said "Sure." Well, it wasn't ok. When Frank returned, his car was gone. A call to the police informed Frank that it had been towed.

Frank was brand new in Florida and knew no one else but me to call. I gladly provided transportation to the city pound, and as much sympathy as I could muster to calm Frank — and to bolster my standing with him. I wanted to impress him; I liked his personality so far, and liked his looks. He was maybe an inch shorter than me, and I'm 5'8" when I stretch and try my best. He's slim and in good shape. He has a waking-up routine of exercises.

Frank is Italian on both sides of his family, but when he visits Italy,

Italians guess his nationality as everything but Italian. His most obvious and best characteristic is his beautiful, thick, silky, dark blond and grey hair that must have the same number of producing follicles as when he was 20. Loss of hair, as I said earlier, has been my curse, so you can guess how I admire Frank's. I would be happy with one third of his number.

People we meet often ask if we are brothers. Frank's the brother who got all the hair.

Almost as soon as Frank arrived in Fort Lauderdale, he bought a large apartment in a heavily-gay development a little drive from the center. He also owned a house on 26 acres near Richmond, in a Quaker-humanist community of about a dozen homes. He had become disillusioned living there due to disagreements among neighbors, who Frank felt were betraying their professed beliefs.

The week after the towed-car rescue, Frank returned to the Virginia house to put it up for sale, pack up, and move his belongings to Florida. At that point, my wooing project was hatched. Helping him out with his towed car would be small potatoes. I volunteered—insisted— to help him pack, and before he could much resist, I had arrived at the Richmond airport. Frank was impressed, as I expected him to be. My selfless effort paid a big dividend. Even today, my trip to Virginia gets star billing when Frank tells anyone of our early days.

My advice to anyone looking for a partner: look for someone about to move.

On knowing Frank, I soon realized that he is a different kind of person, and that is his charm. I will go with the positive adjectives unique and individualistic. He is enthusiastic about just about everything. Going out to dinner or staying home and cooking in. Going to a movie, or skipping it and reading a book. Inviting two friends in for a drink, or 30 for a party. He doesn't like the status quo; change to him is always an improvement. Perhaps a fault is that he's too eager for change, and can be impulsive. I will often treat an idea presented by him with caution that I like to think is practicality and logic. Frank has sometimes dubbed me, "Mr. No." I hate that handle because it's accurate.

What does annoy me about Frank is that he's up at 6 AM with the energy of a dynamo. He doesn't do like I do, spend an hour over coffee. He immediately jumps into some project, whether it's working on a review of a book, or tending his tomato plants. I feel awkward sitting there while he's working. When I was with Jack, we got up about 7 AM, had coffee for an hour, and then went out to breakfast at 8:00 for another hour. Work, when we did any, was put off until late morning. It's true that, under Frank's schedule, he finishes early and has the rest of the day free. But for me, it's hard to get started without my hour of wake-up coffee.

What I admire about Frank is his wholehearted devotion to good causes. He was once a Quaker and subscribes to values like peace and simplicity. He talks about the environment and climate change a whole lot. He reads every book on it, and even makes notes to send to friends. He writes reviews for environmental publications. He writes and calls the offices of senators and representatives whenever he gets upset about a pending action. Which is frequently. Can you imagine: the White House is on his contact list! He also spends time doing research for presentations to local senior centers on subjects such as nutrition, sugar, salt, fat, sitting-down exercises. He tutors, too, and is always looking for an immigrant or a slow-learner for English instruction. Just writing about his activities right now has exhausted me. If I were putting a rating on Frank's life, contribution to society alone would give him a high one.

It is the "singularity" of Frank that makes it impossible to compare him with Jack, and that's a good thing. I say that is desirable, because I bet that many widows and widowers do compare a new partner or spouse with a former one in their own minds, or, perhaps, even to the other party during a heated argument. That cannot happen to me, because Jack and Frank are disparate people, so cannot be compared. Each had, or has, qualities that I appreciate. Sometimes, I wonder if Jack and I, being of like mind, weren't a little boring. At the same time, I wonder whether Frank and I, disagreeing on many things, doesn't lend itself to uh...turbulence.

Jack was steady and reflective; I found that comforting. Frank is creative and spontaneous; I find that fascinating. With Jack, we were on the same wave length and each of us reinforced the other and added to his thoughts and ideas. With Frank, we are sometimes far apart in our thinking, and each person makes his own individual contribution. With Frank's creativity comes sensitivity. I must monitor my words to avoid an offense should I not be enthusiastic about an idea of his.

Like Jack, Frank also has a PhD, his in Psychology. (No, a doctorate was not my prerequisite for a partner.) When we met, he had just retired as a psychologist from the Washington, DC schools. In his career, he has been associated with all ages: as the head of training at a psycho-geriatric hospital, and conducting training in an anti-drug program for the US Navy in the Mediterranean. He lived in Italy several years.

You do not know Frank long before you know that he is an artist. I think he sort of exudes the aura. He works in mixed media. In other words, he puts into his paintings anything he finds interesting. He has a painting made up entirely of men's neckties, arranged in a circle and finished in a way that only an artist could devise. Another painting, round and painted bright yellow, incorporates a few dozen gloves he found on the street over one winter. He has paintings of bright-colored or

This is Frank Grant. I'm fortunate to have him as a partner.

quiet-toned blobs, geometric patterns... He has had shows and has sold some of them, but mainly he is an artist for self-fulfillment. He loves to see what he can create, but has never promoted his work. I am the beneficiary. Our living quarters will always be enhanced by his unusual work, large and small. I'm sure Jack would have liked his work, and I know he would have appreciated Frank's individuality.

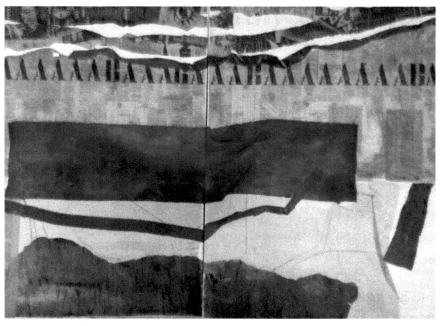

After I first met Frank, I bought this painting of his
at a showing. Now, anything I want is free.

CHAPTER 19

Second Chance.

FRANK AND I, after a few let's-end-it-all arguments and subsequent patch-ups, agreed that Frank would rent out his condo, and move into my house. Finally the pool would get regular use.

Even though his name is Grant, it had been Grandinetti, and on the strong advice of his father, before he graduated from college, he changed it to a less ethnic name. His father, although a vice- president of his company, felt that his own progress had been slowed by his ethnic name.

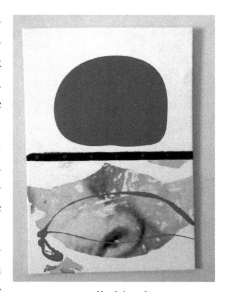

I really like this.

I could not match Frank's Italian heritage, with all of his grandparents being Italian, but I boasted that my maternal grandfather was Massimo Filippi from near Trento, Italy.

Twenty years earlier, my mother and I went to Trento for the first time, and one morning drove the few miles to Gardolo, her father's little town. My mother wanted to find her father's house. He had told her about looking out his bedroom window as a child and seeing snow on the Dolomite Mountains. My mother was eager to relive his story.

We figured that the local priest may know of the family and perhaps the location of the house. So, we went directly to the rectory of the big church on the central square. The priest, an Italian Barry Fitzgerald look-alike from the movie "Going My Way," sitting at his desk, listened intently, but without comment, as I told him the story of my mother's family and her father, Massimo Filippi. "One minute," he interrupted, and got up from his desk. "I'll be right back." He returned five minutes later with an Italian-looking woman appearing a little younger than my mother, who had been at work at a nearby store. The priest introduced her as Clelia Filippi. "Clelia is your cousin!" the priest triumphantly informed my mother. Many tears and hugs followed between the two women who had not known the other existed. Clelia and her husband not only showed us the house of my mother's father and his view of the snow-covered Dolomites, but assembled various unknown relatives for a gala introduction dinner that evening.

Shortly after meeting Frank, I became aware of his liking for West Virginia. Before Frank owned the property near Richmond, when he was working in Washington, he had built a house on 30 acres in Berkeley Springs, West Virginia, two hours from Washington. Berkeley Springs is a pleasant little place, a former spa town that has become an art center and weekend getaway for Washingtonians. There, Frank was introduced to the folk heritage of the Mountain State and its people.

So when we discussed the possibility of getting a house for summers away from the heat of South Florida, Frank concentrated on West Virginia. There haven't been too many people who have moved into Appalachia, rather than out, but I was becoming accustomed to Frank's singularity. I consented. He told me to select a city, and I did: the state capital, Charleston, a city neither of us had ever seen. Frank consented. My stated reason was that there was an airport, making a flight to Fort Lauderdale easy should my sister, in iffy health, need me. Another reason, unstated, was that I didn't want to be spending our time in some ramshackle backwater that fit my stereotypical vision of Appalachia. The capital. I thought, should be the best of the state. As Frank agreed on Charleston, he got his beloved state, and I got its nicest city, a give-and-take to be repeated in many other matters through the years.

I found Charleston a surprising place, because, being West Virginia, I didn't expect very much. A wide river with a promenade along it, quaint downtown streets with brick walks, replica-lantern lighting, and a sweet little park here and there. There was a new Federal Building and an FBI building underway. Senator Robert Byrd, who was still alive, was doing wonders in encouraging federal investment in his state. A huge downtown mall with a glass roof would have been welcome in any city. Restaurants were plentiful. There were three Indian-Middle Eastern restaurants run by their natives, who somehow found their way to West Virginia. Frank knows pizza, and there are two pizza places that out-pizza any pizza Frank's ever had. All that in a city of just 50,000. My stereotypical view of the state was crumbling.

We walked the East End Historic District, a few very long blocks, in fact the two longest blocks in the country, with preserved houses from the early 1900s. Most of the houses were large, with big front porches, and there, people still gathered in good weather just like I remember in my old neighborhood on Lemon Street. We decided this would be a good area for us: picturesque and an easy walk to downtown.

Frank is not shy. As we walked along, we noticed a man loading the trunk of his car with a few boxes containing what appeared to be household items. Frank went right up to him. "Are you moving?" Frank asked eagerly. Approaching a stranger is something I would never do, but Frank does. Frank was eyeing the man's house as our future home. Or, maybe, the items the man was loading, to use in a work of art. Who knew? The man replied that he was not moving. Frank wasn't finished. He introduced the two of us, not reticent to call us partners to a stranger. I, of course, would have preferred to be called friends, maybe brothers. By a lucky coincidence, the man also had a male partner. Frank made this man, Roger, a friend that we had for many years.

Then we spotted a "For Sale by Owner" sign in front of a handsome house with a wide porch. It was large: 4 bedrooms and 2 1/2 baths, split between two apartments.

The owner was a woman who had inherited the property, and, another coincidence, like Frank was an artist. Frank would buy the house and take her as a friend. He would make major changes to return it to a single family rather than a two-family, and the three of us, Frank, Nigel the cat, and I, would live contentedly there for three years. Until we spotted another "For Sale by Owner" sign.

The house in Charleston, WV. From 3 apartments down to 1 big house.
From a business standpoint, maybe not the best idea.

Just three houses up the street from the first house was a rather neglected large Georgian colonial, built in 1910, that had been converted into three apartments before the historic district was established. There were three floors, an apartment on each one. We would want to do away with the apartments and return it to a single family. There was also an apartment over the garage at the rear, a good rental that would not interfere with our privacy.

The apartments were vacant, and the owner was the local YWCA, having recently inherited it on the death of the long-time owner. When he was 90, he had negotiated an arrangement with the Y. If the Y would agree to care for him in his house the remainder of his life, in payment they would get the property on his death. I assume that the YWCA welcomed this plan; after all, he was 90. So they found a couple who occupied one of the apartments, and provided services.

What no one counted on, I'm sure, not the elderly man nor the Y, is that he would live another 16 years, to the age of 106. The Y dutifully cared for him during that extended time. Now, Frank and I appeared as potential buyers to reward the Y for its long devotion to service. I don't mean to imply that the YWCA considered it a burden to care for this man. From conversations with employees, I have seen that the people of the Y really liked him and were saddened at his death.

I'm not sure why we bought this house. It was the lure of having a large, grand house. The main house was 4500 square feet. And it had all the detail of construction from a bygone era: a wide mahogany staircase rose from a large foyer; there was a marble fireplace in almost every major room, seven fireplaces in all; the future dining room had a paneled ceiling and chair rail. And the Y had set the price commensurate with the building's scruffy condition.

We figured all we'd have to do is put in three new heating/air conditioning systems, one for each floor; a mostly new electrical system; a revamped plumbing system; remove at least one kitchen and renovate another; remove plastic tiles from ceilings and repair plaster; restore a good deal of the old moldings; install new baths, a large two-story addition on the back... We got some estimates, made others ourselves, added everything up, increased the total estimated cost by 50 percent in anticipation of nasty surprises. A piece of cake. We felt we could do it, and not have more into the property than we could one day get out.

We went back and forth, the two of us, for a week, trying to decide yes or no to the purchase. Finally, one day, a yes day, we signed a contract. One day later, it might have been a no day. It was going to take a lot of money, and a lot of work.

So, we started on the house. Our only real problem was of our own making. We refused to let our six months in Florida be interfered with, so in the middle of work, with workmen hammering away, we and Nigel, the cat, got in the car and drove away, even though a good chunk of our assets was sitting there behind us.

While we were gone, in the dead of winter, the crew would be building the sizable, mostly glass two-story addition to the rear that we were calling a sunroom. Frank's penchant to recycle used objects into his paintings had migrated into architecture, and we had purchased a number of French doors, tall foot-wide windows, and a bay window from the ReStore, operated by Habitat for Humanity. These were items that builders may have ordered, but were the wrong size, or might have been in a building being torn down. We had a collection of these in the garage, and even though I was the one my college entrance aptitude test said was suited to be an architect, it was Frank who pulled together a design using unrelated elements that was quite novel and handsome. An architect then had drawn up the plans for submission to the Historic Preservation Review Board. We were given approval for the addition because it couldn't be seen from the street.

It seems that the architect's measurement was off. The bay window we had collected would not fit. So the contractor, or the architect, or both, apparently not wanting to disturb our basking in the Florida sun, substituted two very conventional double-hung windows. A loss to the design. But Frank and I concluded that mistakes such as this will happen when you're not on site, and spending six months in Florida was worth it.

Frank is passionate about reusing and recycling items instead of discarding them. We have a crammed storage room that attests to this devotion of his. I am merely an amateur at it, still in training. It's part of his mania for preserving the environment. Although we moved to a state where coal is the biggest single employer, he is opposed to coal-fired power plants, as I am. When Barack Obama was running for his second term, billboards appeared all over the state with the line, "Obama's war on coal." (I wonder who paid for those.) Frank joined OVEC, the Ohio Valley Environmental Council, and I put my name in, too.

I want to point out that, even before I met Frank, on my very own without encouragement from anyone, I had joined the ACLU and the Human Rights Campaign. As a gay man, I am avid about protecting every minority's rights. There were too many times in the past when police abused mine. I belong to PETA and the Humane Society. I believe that animals have rights, too, that we must not harm them because we're more powerful. Isn't that why we have fought wars? To protect ourselves from those who deemed themselves powerful? Frank joined me as a member of animal rights groups.

Many people would say that I go overboard in respecting the lives of bugs and other insects. I avoid killing them, and try to shoo them outside. So far as I know, there's no organization with the mission to foster the well-being of tiny creatures. When there is, I'll join.

It is so difficult to get through life and be proud of some aspects of our species. There are major and minor things that, despite their varying degrees of importance, sadden me. Cruelty to animals distresses me. At the other extreme, there's war. Not only are young people snuffed out, but so is the happiness of their loved ones. I hate to see a disabled person, because it almost breaks my heart. I look away from them, since I don't want them to think I'm staring at them due to their disability. And poverty in the world is so disturbing. TV shows people starving in Africa, small children so malnourished you can count their ribs. And here I am, having just finished a big meal and put leftovers in the refrigerator.

Our supermarkets are a shame to our America, with aisle after aisle of every food imaginable, while little children across the world are desperately foraging for a morsel to eat. You almost have to inure yourself, or you wouldn't be able to cope with life.

Let's go to something less depressing. Charleston is serious about its recycling program. Everyone is provided with a bright blue plastic carton where, once a week, it can be put out with your recyclables inside for pickup, at the same time as the normal trash. We were both very good at adhering to the rules. We found that recyclables generally amounted in volume to twice regular garbage. Paint cans can be put out, but they must be empty or, if not, have kitty litter or sand added to the paint. A city worker told me that before that rule, the trucks would leave a trail of paint down the street.

I find it disgusting to see a motorist toss a piece of paper or other trash out the window. Frank carried his disapproval to an extreme. One day, a driver in Charleston in front of our car threw a small piece of paper out the window. Frank pulled up next to the car at a red light, blew his horn, and motioned for the driver, a teenaged boy, to lower his window. "Hey, you dropped something back there," Frank shouted. Without comment, the boy rolled up his window and looked in the other direction until the light changed. I would estimate that this boy would think twice in the future before littering. But, as I told Frank, he could easily have pulled out a revolver and shot Frank dead. West Virginia is one of many states that permits concealed weapons.

Chastising someone, even if you're in the right, is at your peril. It's the kind of thing I would hesitate to do, but Frank does such things not infrequently. With a piece of trash dropped from the window of a car in front of me, I would moan about it to someone in my car, or "Tsk, tsk" it to myself, but not say anything that might do some good in the future. I would like to say my lack of action is because I'm an introvert, or shy, or mind my own business. But I have to put it down to my lack of bravery. Or, maybe it's because I abhor a scene, and will stifle myself to avoid unpleasantness. I like that reason better than lack of courage.

Several people have described Frank as "determined." They certainly had the right adjective. He could not let the boy who threw the paper out of his car window go scot free, no more than he could ignore a hit-and-run. When he reads all those books on the environment and on climate change that come along, he does it with determination, in a day or two—and as I've said, he makes notes and emails them to as many friends as he can think of — or maybe now, former friends.

While Frank was worried about the future of the entire human race, I became concerned about what could happen to my own sub-species: gay people. At this period, and to the present, science sections of newspapers were publishing announcements of DNA identification, manipulation, editing. I could hardly look at the articles.

In August of 2019, scientists identified the gene responsible for muscular dystrophy and for ALS, terrible diseases. Recently, we began to be able to find out whether we are likely to have Alzheimer's disease, years in advance. The source of various cancers has been identified as mutations in specific genes. All these discoveries, it is believed, make progress to treatments probable. We are perhaps at the beginning of the end of these scourges. What advances!

There is so much in genetics to generate hope—but as a gay man, so much to anticipate with foreboding.

The publications reporting on the advances in genetics relating to diseases, have also told of scientists' belief in the existence of a "gay gene," and the discovery of its location. For example, Newsweek on May 13, 2017 carried an article with the headline "Is there a gay gene?

Researchers think so." Frank himself was in a group study by geneticist Dean Hamer that reported as early as 1993 significant linkage between the Xq28 chromosome and same-sex orientation.

In contrast, on August 29, 2019, the New York Times reported on a large study, appearing in Science, that contradicted some other studies, and concluded that there was not just one gene involved in same-sex orientation, but many genes. If confirmed in the future, it will make gay gene elimination decidedly more difficult, but not impossible. The same study said that social and environmental factors also have an influence.

With gene editing, some have expressed concern that many couples will request designer babies, those that will grow up tall and slim, with perhaps a programmed talent for music, or math, or whatever. It is my fear that, given the choice, complex though the procedure may be, non-gay couples will virtually always opt for babies who will have the same sexual orientation as their own. And it appears that science will one day give them the opportunity. I worry that future generations will know gay people only from history and sociology texts. If the study reported in the New York Times is correct, that many genes are involved, it will be complicated to snuff out same sex orientation, but perhaps worth the effort for those determined to do so.

The Newsweek article summarized a three-year analysis by the Academy of Science South Africa, of studies conducted in many countries in the last decade. The conclusion was that the gene chiefly responsible for sexual orientation is in the X chromosome. It has been called the Xq28 factor, and has a complex interaction with other genes, and the environment, before and after birth. Therefore, these studies do not seem to be entirely in opposition to the New York Times report of the involvement of many genes. They explain why identical twins, with identical genes, have the same sexual orientation, straight or gay, two-thirds of the time, but differ about 1/3 of the time. (Curiously, most research on sexual orientation is limited to the study of males, and rarely includes females.)

Scientific American, in an article on April 25, 2017 titled "Cross cultural evidence for the genetics of homosexuality," while not specifically citing a gay gene or genes, discussed a study of an indigenous people in Mexico that presents compelling evidence of homosexual heredity.

I found it interesting, but having nothing to do with a gay gene, that other findings show that sexual orientation is passed through the mother; that a mother with a gay son is generally more fertile than other women and their female relatives are also more fertile; and that it is more likely that a younger son will be gay, rather than his older brother.

I thought about all this research into sexual orientation. This is being done while other scientists are busy working on gene identification and editing with the goal to treat and cure terrifying diseases.

While the latter scientists occupy themselves in such a socially-rewarding enterprise, we have some scientists using their research efforts and resources to locate gay genes. Apparently, they, too, believe that their work may result in a contribution to civilization. They search, just like the scientists seeking to treat and cure diseases, to treat or cure being gay.

I worry that such a treatment or cure would be welcome. Who can blame straight couples for choosing in their offspring their own sexual orientation? It is to be expected. What father doesn't want a chip off the old block? What mother doesn't want to impart her empirical wisdom about men and marriage to her daughter? Who doesn't dream of a child having a glorious—heterosexual—wedding with bridal gown, bridesmaids, flower girls? What parents don't want grandchildren and great grandchildren to brighten their old age? Warm family gatherings at holidays? What family doesn't want its name continued down generations?

But even some of these now can be obtained by parents with a gay child; for example, when a surrogate is used.

Many of us have "come out" to our parents—with mixed results. A minority of parents has greeted a child's announcement with equanimity and acceptance. Some children, when they speak to their parents, are ostracized, shamed, and even ousted from the family home. Fathers not infrequently separate from their sons, and sometimes a rapprochement never occurs.

As I have said, my mother was in the minority of accepting parents. She became very fond of my partner, Jack, who I met several years after telling my mother I was gay. But she never had a grandchild, and I have no doubt that, given the choice, she would have elected that I be straight, and give her grandchildren. Not that she would have ever said that. She never said a word, and that said enough.

So in future generations, if all goes as planned, the world will be free of some of our worst diseases—and, with couples having a choice, being gay will be a rarity indeed. Right now, studies say that gay men and lesbians make up no more than 4.5 percent of the US population. From my participation in the gay world, I believe that figure is much too low. But, of course, I would think it to be much higher. I just called the environment I occupy the gay world. However, many Americans, when polled by Gallup in 2018, seem to agree with me, arriving at an average estimate of 23.6 percent.

When quizzed by a pollster, many gays will not readily admit their, let's call it, alternative orientation. Jess Stevens' 1961 book, "The Sixth Man," maintains that one in six men have had homosexual experiences, which does not necessarily indicate that they are gay. The Kinsey Report way back in 1948 said that one in ten men lived an exclusively gay lifestyle for at least three years. That would be more of an indication of the percentage.

Someday, if through genetics gay people become less common, I fear discrimination will return with all the fury of past times, even in areas now relatively free from prejudice. The smaller the minority, the more helpless it is. The impetus for less discrimination in the present day was gays coming out, so that society realized we were a substantial number and the people next-door. Prejudice was brutal prior to the acceptance of today. I would hate to think that gay men and women of 2050 would have to hide in the closet as my generation did.

With the manipulation and editing of the gay gene, or genes, in order to eliminate, "cure," same-sex orientation, be careful of some unplanned results. Other characteristics may be killed along with the unwanted orientation. There might be talents lost. A future Michelangelo or Leonardo could be erased. A Sondheim, a Bernstein, an Elton John. Excuse the stereotype, but I foresee a shortage of interior decorators and hair stylists.

It is peculiar that I am so apprehensive, so gloomy about such a future, where gays approach extinction. It will happen over generations, so I won't be here to see it. However, I believe I am on to my reasons.

It's because being gay is a lifestyle that I have lived and liked. It is friends that are dear to me. It is belonging to a group drawn together by the ostracism of others. It is a special society, and I feel the way straight men may regard the Rotary or the Elks. It is the sense of a private club, and the warm feeling of going to a new town and being welcomed by fellow members. It is a partner that I admired for his scholarship, and my spouse today, who I admire for his uniqueness. For me, it is the life that I would not want anyone destined for it by nature to miss.

With so many scientists devoting their work to gene manipulation, the continuation of the gay species may lie with the small number of gays themselves who have children, and certainly will not be manipulating a gene that has an influence on sexual orientation. Gay survival may also rest with the even smaller number of straight couples who would welcome a child with whatever sexual orientation nature has provided.

Perhaps with society's growing acceptance of diversity, this group will swell.

Wherever we were, Frank and I never allowed ourselves to be so busy that we didn't have a social life. Both of us liked to confine any work to the mornings. Frank, of course, to early mornings. Even appointments, medical or dental, we scheduled before noon. I preferred an appointment at about 10 AM. This way, I had enough time after I got up for a leisurely cup or two of coffee and whatever I would have with it, like toast. Frank got into the habit of serving each day a mixture of plain yogurt with various fruits and a few nuts mixed in. The fruits would be cut-up peaches, apples or pears, or he would throw into the mixture a handful of blueberries, or raspberries. This was about the healthiest breakfast I can think of. For me, it is almost the only way I get any fruit, as I seldom go to the refrigerator for it myself.

Likewise, all my vegetables come from Frank's maneuvering. If it were up to me, I'd eat pasta every day. No meat, or very little meat. I do like hot sausages. I would get plenty of whatever vitamins are in tomatoes, because my pasta has to be served with tomato sauce, and lots of it. Forget fettuccini alfredo. Then I'd have an enormous dessert: chocolate cake, or cherry pie, oatmeal cookies, a big bowl of ice cream. The ideal is a combination of a couple of these. After, I'd opt for health by taking a vitamin pill before going to bed.

I had to adjust to Frank's serving vegetables. Actually, I'm now habituated to it, but not really adjusted. He's stopped serving squash; I hate it. Spinach is close behind squash, but I'll take it raw, served as a salad with dressing. He buys for himself various bitter dark green leaves, chard, collard greens; for himself, because I won't touch them. I do like eggplant and the various ways he prepares it. I'll also take broccoli, cauliflower, a few other things. Not too eagerly.

What I do like is to add hot sauce to just about everything. You'd think that fire would burn the lining of the stomach, or the intestines. But I remember about ten years ago reading the results of a study. A diet of hot spicy food did nothing bad. In fact, my research disclosed a wealth of information saying that hot peppers extend your life. I'm going to live forever!

By noon, if things had gone right, Frank and I would be finished with whatever chores we had, such as tending to the yard, sweeping the porch, going to the supermarket. In the afternoon, we'd usually read. Sometimes we'd watch an old movie on TCM, Turner Classic Movies. We went through a long period where we were checking out TV series from the library, some having so many episodes it would take us a few weeks to watch them all. That's how I watched "Upstairs Downstairs" a second time, and "The Sopranos," the first time. You don't have to read a book to use the library these days.

We were beginning to meet people. The East End Historical District is a neighborhood of many liberals in Charleston, in contrast to most of West Virginia. The Charleston City Council, way back in 2007, did pass an ordinance on non-discrimination, specifically with protection for those with same sex orientation. It has since been copied by many cities in West Virginia. We had no difficulty meeting and being accepted by other residents, especially with Frank willing to chat with people walking by.

On one side of the house was the CEO of a Japanese chemical company, who was overseeing the construction of a new plant. On the other side was an elderly widow of a pharmacist, and her daughter, who directed senior programs for the county; we became good friends. A few houses down the street was a young gay couple, male. Across the street was a musician who played the oboe and carted that large instrument all over the country. Frank, almost eagerly, introduced us as partners. I was pulled out of the closet. Everyone we were meeting seemed to accept us as a couple without batting an eye. I don't mean that all of our neighbors, in a red state, were liberal, but you could see, from the many placards on lawns before Election Day, where sentiments lay. With some people, we avoided saying any word about politics, because we did not want to risk a friendship by being awakened in our divided America.

The first year we were in Charleston, we decided to collect all of our new people together on a Sunday afternoon for a party, serving mostly wine and hors d'oevres. We invited 35 people. If I remember right, 38 showed up. Everyone's always eager to go to a party — but don't count on being invited to a party in return. Guests are easy to come by; hosts can be a rarity. Everyone seemed to enjoy themselves, but we were a little nonplussed that the dozen or so gays seemed to segregate themselves in a group in the foyer away from the non-gays. That wasn't the feeling of community we thought we had been feeling. I made an effort to circulate among the straights and engage as many as possible in conversation. I wanted to distract them from noticing that they were being ignored by the clannish gay men there, that they were not being accepted. Actually, I felt an affinity for my gay clan, but I was also comfortable with the straight people. After all, I had always led a surface life and an undercover life.

Some of the gay men at the party belonged to Prime Timers, an international gay organization that we, also, had joined. Its name, Prime Timers, is an inviting cover for the older men it aims to attract as members. No doubt, it's more enticing to them than if it had gone with my suggestion for a change in name to "Old Timers." My mere mention of that name was greeted by the local group with a stony silence. Most everyone in the group is at least in his 60s, so it would certainly fit better than Prime Timers. How about "Past Prime Timers?" (Sorry, fellows, I'm just joking.)

Charleston is one of 76 chapters in the US and internationally. Locally, the group goes to restaurants, movies, concerts, has an annual picnic. A group of members travels to the Columbus, Ohio area for that local group's summer pig roast. A few go together to the national convention in a different city each year.

We had a difficult time feeling at home with this area group. We always felt like outsiders. Well, we were outsiders. Very few people immigrate to West Virginia. The traffic's in the other direction. It's a shame, because it is a beautiful state. The motto, "Mountain State," suits it. In retrospect, I realize that Frank and I made little effort to be anything but outsiders. Not one time did we join group members in a trip out of the city or out of the state. With a little effort on our part, we may at least have had experiences to share and to talk about. The problem we failed to overcome is that in Charleston, being a small city, everyone has gone to the same schools, passed their lives in the same neighborhoods, know the same people. Anyone who has gone to college, went to West Virginia University in Morgantown.

Frank spent years in Washington, and I lived in Manhattan. Both of us lived in Europe. These are alien places to many of the people of this state, and we are foreigners. An astonishing thing to us: a good many West Virginians pride themselves at never having set foot out of the state, even brag about it. God forbid we mention a foreign country. Some people would have no idea what to say, and the conversation would fizzle. What to talk about here? If only we had gone to Capitol High or WVU.

At our party, when I observed that the gays were not associating with the straight neighbors, I was perplexed. "Why aren't they mixing?" I asked Frank. For me to be disturbed by the gay men's clannishness was bizarre, as I myself spent time at Fire Island segregated from the world.

It was weird that I wanted a union of everyone in Charleston. I seemed to be trying to bury my secret life, finally and without fanfare, as one-half of a same-sex couple. Frank and I had already made straight friends in West Virginia. Two of our best friends were the widow and her daughter next door, who we went out to dinner with once a week. We were friends with the musician across the street. Our attorney also was a friend.

Dear West Virginia gay guys at our party,

I've felt that West Virginia and Charleston seemed remote. No big cities are anywhere near Charleston. People sometimes pride themselves on never having left the state.

But when you isolated yourselves from the straight people at the party Frank and I gave, it really brought home the remoteness. Weren't you aware that most straight people now accept gays, that two-thirds favor same-sex marriage? Have you kept up with this news? We're all together now.

The need for us to segregate ourselves is over. The point of our party was togetherness, not that any observer could have guessed it.

I was disappointed that you stayed together by yourselves, crowded into the foyer, but I understood. The new world of acceptance is strange for me, too. I'm just now adjusting.

I forgive you for not going with the spirit of the party. I was you, just a short time ago.

Vince

Despite my criticism of others, even currently I often choose by preference a gay couple or a gay group. I find that logical. I was no longer working for an employer who might be opposed to a gay worker, nor teaming up with business colleagues who might object to my orientation. I no longer had to worry about any of that, and I could select who I wanted as a friend. I could have gay friends and I could have straight friends. I could mix them if I chose. Here in the Mountain State, I was having an extraordinary experience, with a new kind of people who didn't seem to care that I was gay. Back in Uniontown, they had been small-town people, too, but those were the days I had to be hidden. The same in Cleveland, and even often in New York, the world's capital of diversity. In France, where it was clear that Jack was my partner, the French seemed to ignore our situation, a good thing. But in Charleston, I didn't even have to come out. Frank told people I was his partner, and when your partner says you're his partner, you're out. How easy that was!

CHAPTER **20**

The Test. A friend failed.

I HAVE ALWAYS sort of wondered how many straight people would harbor an unspoken dislike of me if I were not incognito. Perhaps, because of Charleston liberals, I am overcoming my paranoia a bit, appreciating a new society, especially with the young, As a gay man, I have now come to expect to be tolerated, to be accepted, two words that in the past I abhorred in the context of gays in society. Rah! I am tolerated! Double rah! I am accepted! I have reached the point that I am not grateful to be accepted, but outraged if I'm not.

I have devised a little test to see whether a friendship with someone straight is worth pursuing, whether the "out" me will be accepted. It started with a woman classmate from St, John's High School, Gloria. Gloria was one of the two girls I was so friendly with during high school. The other was Caroline, a sweet person, who, unfortunately, died young. Gloria and I greeted each other warmly at class reunions, and often sat by ourselves to exchange data on each other's lives, and reminisce about our high school days. On my part, the information I gave was never total, because I never told Gloria about my sexual orientation, and that I lived with a male partner who I loved. There are many people with whom I cloaked myself in secrecy, and Gloria was just one.

After she was widowed some years ago now, we began contacting each other frequently by email. This went on for years until my worry about the words tolerated and accepted surfaced. I had still never indicated to Gloria that I am gay. I began to be a little wary of her tolerance and acceptance when I observed that she was closing her emails to me with "God bless."

It's curious that a person citing God can be a red flag to me. What, I wondered, would be her reaction if I dropped the phrase "my partner, Frank, and I," into one of my emails? Would she, reassuring me of acceptance, mention the names of a male couple who were her friends? I've had that happen. Would she advise conversion therapy or praying to God for forgiveness? Would she discuss my orientation openly and casually, and maybe even say she suspected it because I was friends with two girls, her and Caroline, in high school? Or would she ignore my self-outing as though she had not read my revealing phrase?

Gloria did none of those things. She stopped all contact with me. The emails that appeared in my inbox every few weeks have not arrived there for two years. To beat a dead horse, I emailed her a few months ago: "It's a while since we've been in contact." No response from that either. Face it, Vince, it's over. I have concluded that I am not tolerated, not accepted by this woman I have been friends with for 70 years. The God that Gloria in her emails asked to bless me, advised her to have nothing more to do with this lowly creature. How bizarre it is that religious people can be at the head of the line of those who hate. "Thou shalt love thy neighbour as thyself." Matthew 22:36-40, KJV, quoting Jesus.

Frank put the best possible spin on Gloria's ignoring me. Maybe when she was first widowed, Frank theorized, she saw in my friendship something that would build into more. "Now you've told her you already have someone," he concluded. I don't think so, Frank. There's no point denying that I am hated. Nice try to let me down easy.

Should I forgive Gloria and have no hard feelings? Should I, in the future, once again see if she's changed her mind about me? The latter question was just answered. I looked up Gloria's name on the internet, and found an obituary only a month old. So there will not be a chance for a sweet reunion. Another door closes.

Dear Gloria,

It's odd to be writing you after I've learned you died. But if you're right, and there is a heaven, maybe you'll be reading this.

You stopped all contact with me when I mentioned I had a male partner. Thus ended 70 years of intimate friendship. It was a blow to me that you thought so little of our relationship that you cut me off without a word. For many weeks, I kept checking my email first thing in the morning, hoping to see your name there. I missed having someone to write to about politics, about items in the newspaper, about my concerns of getting older. I missed hearing about your musician son, about your move to Pittsburgh, about what you did day to day. Fact is, I missed you, Gloria, and I hoped that you missed me and would break down and answer my emails.

Revealing that I was gay also revealed your intolerance. You were a fervent Catholic, so, possibly, your moral compass forbad you to have anything more to do with me. But even Pope Francis favors civil unions for homosexuals. I can accept your opinion, if you were following your conscience, although I ask what kind of conscience would separate you from a lifelong friend who only wished good things for you.

How I wish I could go back to one of our class re-

unions, where we sat together aside from the others, and laughed about silly little things in our high school days. I wish I could go back briefly to the time before I revealed to you that I'm gay.

For old times sake, I forgive you and your rejection of me, Gloria.

Your nearly lifelong friend,
Vinny

I think the test was worthwhile. It has shown me in no uncertain terms that this woman was not willing to accept me as I am, and that any time devoted to her in the past 70 years was a waste of time. What is the point of having a friend when you must hide your nature, when you must be undercover? I've decided I'm going to employ this test on anyone when it appears a friendship is imminent. I no longer will lead an incognito life. I'm going to search out prejudice. I will not tolerate nor accept a friend who is not a friend.

My being out to people, to people who may become friends, is new to me. Gloria must have been confused at my mention of a male partner. She thought I was a widower. At a class reunion many years ago, I was feeling quite out of place with most of my classmates having brought their spouses, and telling of their children. So, in the tradition of my old Priscilla fabrication, the make-believe girlfriend when I was living at my mother's house in Cleveland, I came up with another instant name: Francoise. The story went like this: Francoise was my French wife whom I had met at the French consulate in New York where she worked when I was taking French lessons. She wasn't with me at the reunion because she was in Paris, her job with the consulate, naturally, requiring her to travel frequently to France. And, years on, the story progressed. We had a son, Mark, eventually reaching the age of 20, who was in school in France. One year Francoise would have passed away, relieving me of any need to produce her. Mark would be in London as a young architect at the same period that I lived in Brighton with Jack. If there had been more reunions, Mark probably would have made me a proud grandfather. Maybe even of twins. My tale permitted me to be a member of the high school gang with spouse and child as all the others, but made my persona at reunions totally false.

To any classmate of mine who may be alive and reading this, I am sorry for my deceit. You know the truth now.

Some of Frank's and my entertainment in West Virginia was in taking short trips around the state of two or three nights. We saw some good towns: Morgantown, vibrant with the university. Some towns that once were prosperous, such as Wheeling, that fifty years ago had a thriving steel industry. There are some picturesque little towns too, such as Lewisburg, profiting from the White Sulphur Springs resort nearby, and Hinton, ideal because of its scenic setting among rivers and mountains. And, alas, we drove through — quickly — many decrepit little towns or villages, no longer fed by coal, where young people have vanished along with most everything else except a dollar store and a thrift shop.

A particularly fascinating stop was near Wheeling, for a tour of the former gothic West Virginia State Prison in Moundsville. It was a prison until 1995, its cellblocks holding up to 2000 men. Ninety-four men were executed here, most by hanging; in later years, some by the electric chair. For many years, the prison was listed by the US Justice Department as one of the ten most violent institutions of incarceration in the country. The tour includes the recreation room, where most of the 34 murders occurred, and walks you past the many 5x7-foot cells. The tour guide pointed out the crude holes in the solid walls between many cells, of about the size of a baseball and several feet above the floor. He identified these as "glory holes," but discretely avoided explaining their use. The tour included the library, chapel, the electric chair called

"Old Sparky," and a glimpse into a pitch-black below-ground solitary confinement cell. Ugh!

So we did our particular WV-FL two-state back and forth for ten years, with summers in West Virginia, then the thousand mile trip to Fort Lauderdale, with Nigel the cat, in the fall, and back again in the spring. Some years our relaxing Florida sojourn was interrupted by a restful cruise to the Caribbean. One year, we rented an apartment for a month or so in San Miguel de Allende, Mexico; another year, it was an apartment in Antigua, Guatemala. For Christmas, by this time in our relationship, I knew exactly the gift to get Frank: travel. We were in an apartment near the Piazza Navona in Rome one time, and another year in Sicily. Frank, Italian, easily adapted to the local routine when he was going to cook in. He would go to a small grocery nearby and buy what was needed for just that meal. It insured that the ingredients were fresh, and also, if you had a yen for a particular food that day, it was satisfied.

One of the winters in Fort Lauderdale, we did not travel. My sister had fallen on the floor going into her bedroom. She was unhurt, but the fact that there was no apparent reason for her to have fallen concerned me. Also, she had voluntarily given up driving, without any prodding. When passing a bus, she clipped the side view mirror of her car. She was losing her judgment of distances, she concluded. I was relieved at this decision of hers, and increased the visits of her home health care worker to a few hours five days a week, instead of just two days. The presence of this young woman would not prevent a fall when she was not there, but as she would be preparing meals and keeping the rooms neat, my sister would be called on less to do these things herself and, I told myself, be less exposed to a possible fall. I would continue going to her house on Saturdays and we would do the grocery shopping together.

Pat and I had been close since childhood. Perhaps this was fostered by the desertion of our father; that we were a tiny family of just three, now reduced to two with the death of our mother; the interest we always had in the other's education and career. Pat listened intently to stories I brought home during my reporting days, was there, of course, at my college graduation, and I at hers. She followed my life when I moved to New York, in our weekly phone calls.

In turn, I watched as she completed high school that she had dropped out of years before. I observed her move from a secretary to an executive assistant. Then I took more than a mere brother's pride in her graduation from her college summa cum laude, and advised her when she was writing the speech she would give. It was a dinner of celebration at a good restaurant when she became a compensation analyst for the Defense Department.

But it was a terrible turn, the year she was diagnosed with Lewy Bodies, a cousin of Parkinson's Disease. In fact, the disease is called Lewy Body Dementia, but I have always disliked that final word, so I don't usually include it. This particular scourge, and Parkinson's, is prevalent in our father's family. A patient can get tremors, as with Parkinson's, but my sister did not. Neither did she have memory loss, also a symptom. She did have a problem with balance. Not unusual with Lewy Bodies, my sister had begun sometimes interpreting an everyday object as something strange, not a fearful object, but odd. One time, for example, we were in the car when she marveled at the existence of a clown by the road. It was a stop sign. And a cognitive issue was starting.

I was becoming aware that what was needed was not a daily health care worker for a few hours, but 24-hour care. Frank and I began looking. We visited large and small assisted living facilities (ALFs) all over Broward County. We found what we were looking for just a couple of miles from Pat's house, in the same town. From the outside, and the inside, too, it appeared as an ordinary, upscale house. It was Mediterranean style, just one floor, with four bedrooms and three baths. Two health care workers were there all day, and there was one at night.

What we particularly liked about it was that it resembled Pat's own house, with a large kitchen-family room where the few occupants gathered to talk or watch TV. Outside this room through glass doors was a large, enclosed patio. In her own house, Pat spent all of her time in her kitchen-family room, and this would feel like home, I hoped.

It was owned by a remarkably attractive woman in her 30s of Indian heritage, the country, and her husband, who I never met. She managed two ALF houses the couple owned, and her husband the two others. Frank and I had a long conversation with the woman. She showed me the most recent Florida inspection report, which indicated just one minor issue, now corrected. The house could accept only six occupants, but my sister would make just four and she would have a large private room. I, in turn, told the owner-manager of my sister's need for close supervision, that she had now fallen twice, and that it was urgent I get her Into an ALF to prevent another fall and a possible injury. She assured me that Pat would be well supervised.

It wasn't a problem to get my sister to agree to go there. She was suffering with slight cognition problems. I know she realized this. She talked to me about her illusions, interpreting normal objects such as the stop sign as strange beings. She recognized that this was not normal. She also was aware, more than me, I'm sure, that her balance was poor, and another fall could cause a serious injury.

I also told Pat an untruth: that the move would be temporary. I don't want to use the word "lie," because I kind of convinced myself that this was so, although I had made no plans as to when she would return home and under what care. I had investigated the cost of 24-hour care in her home, and it seemed extraordinary. I assured Pat that I had made arrangements to have the lawn mowed, the bushes trimmed, and that her house would be well-maintained, which I made certain it would be. She received these assurances without comment. I also told her that Sandra, her health care worker, who she had become friendly with, would be visiting her at the new place three times a week, and that she could go out to a restaurant for lunch with her as she had been doing when she lived at home. Pat liked that idea. So I had her large-screen TV, a comfortable lounge chair, and a favorite painting moved from her house to her bedroom at the ALF.

The first two months went well. Pat spent her days in the kitchen-family room with the other inhabitants, all women. The two health care workers during the day prepared meals that everyone ate together at the large table. I visited twice a week, and Sandra, three times. Pat seemed always to be in good spirits, and seemed to be enjoying the social life. She asked about her house; I went into detail about the flowers, and one time brought her a bouquet of hibiscus from her yard. She asked about her investments. I told her that, although this was a year of the Great Recession, she had been wise to purchase annuities that could not drop in value no matter the market. She smiled at that, apparently understanding my explanation. She did not mention any desire to return home.

CHAPTER 21

The niches: one vacancy.

ONE MORNING I got a phone call from the owner of the ALF. Pat had fallen during the night and was in the hospital. Frank and I went to the hospital at once. She had suffered a fractured hip, and was already out of surgery, having had the hip replaced on her own approval. I was aghast that Pat had fallen. To avoid a fall, and an injury such as this, was precisely why she was in this ALF and what I had spoken about with the owner-manager prior to her admittance. My faith in her word that it would never happen is why I chose her ALF.

I met with the owner that day. She revealed a few things that stunned me. I was shocked to learn from her that the health care worker at night had the owner's approval to nap. To me, this meant that there was no supervision at all the night when Pat fell, probably en route to the bathroom. I told the owner that I would hire a health care worker for nights for my sister, someone who would sit in her bedroom, and whose assignment would be to see that a fall never occurred again. She then informed me, also for the first time, that there is a simple electrical device available that sounds an alarm when a patient begins to get out of bed. I could not believe what I was hearing. First, that the worker supervising my sister was likely asleep, and that the alarm that would have warned her of my sister's movements was not installed and never even considered.

Although aghast at what I was being told, I expressed to the owner only mild displeasure. The day had been a difficult one, and I was too exhausted to accuse or threaten. I did not remind her of her assurance, prior to Pat's admittance, that my sister would be well supervised and safe. What good would that do now? The harm was already done. It would be up to me to keep Pat safe. I could not trust anyone.

The next month is a blur to me, and maybe it's better that way. In the hospital, I was aware that the Lewy Bodies was beginning to cause a more serious decline in Pat's cognition. I have been told that a trauma such as Pat suffered can be responsible for the advance of symptoms. Pat was now about to be released from the hospital. I could not think of an immediate solution to her need for care other than to return her to the ALF responsible for her injury, temporarily, until I could find a more suitable placement. And I had instituted my own precautions. I envisioned at worst a couple of weeks before a move. My sister went back to the ALF, I ordered a private night health care worker, and there were no more falls. Pat, with Lewy Bodies progressing, and now physically weakened by surgery, was staying in bed and no longer joining the other women for the social life in the family room. The doctor had ordered her not to move her body suddenly and briskly for a time, so as not to displace the new hip until the surgery healed. But, lying in bed, Pat did move. The new hip was displaced, there was pain, and my sister was back in the hospital. By massaging the area externally, the doctor was able to force the hip back into place.

But two days later, the hip was displaced again and Pat was returned for the third time to the hospital. The hip could not be massaged into place, and would require another surgery. The doctor was of the opinion that, because of the growing cognitive impairment, Pat would be unable to follow instructions about minimal movement if another surgery was performed and the hip repositioned anew. He predicted that the hip would again be displaced, requiring still another surgery. The doctor said that with each surgery, Pat would become weaker. He strongly suggested that the prosthesis be removed surgically, with no replacement, and therefore no additional surgeries after this one.

This, he explained, would mean that my sister would walk with a limp, as one side of her body would be shorter than the other. Custom-made shoes could be ordered. The doctor saw no other possibility. My sister, perhaps because of pain or weakness, had suddenly become less cognizant, and was not consulted. I had to decide for her. I agonized over the decision, then sadly agreed. My assent to maim my sister for the rest of her life tore me apart. I could much easier have decided such a matter for myself, but this was hard. I did not see that I had a choice, but I felt I was betraying her, that I was injuring her, that I myself would be the cause of her being disabled.

Then it was back to the same ALF again. In the flurry of activity, I did not have the time—not even the mental sharpness—to conduct the search for another one. I trusted that my precautions would suffice: employing a night health care worker, having Sandra there three times a week during the day, and my being there two times to carefully monitor the quality of Pat's care. I also had confidence in the daytime health care workers, who, in the past, I had observed keeping a close eye on Pat.

I need not have worried about another fall. Pat did not attempt to get out of bed without help. She was too weak. I now changed my visiting schedule to every day, and Pat and I had conversations about our shared childhood, her college, her life in Cleveland and her time in Florida. She seemed to have almost totally recovered from her period of incognizance. She did say one thing that startled me. "If we hadn't been brother and sister," she said, "we could have been husband and wife." It was a strange thing to say, but I readily agreed. Pat smiled.

The next morning the phone rang a little after 8:00, and I got it.

It was one of the women at the ALF, who said that Pat was not doing well, and that it would be a good idea if I came there this morning. It didn't seem too urgent to me; Pat had seemed to be doing better when Frank and I left the prior evening. Nonetheless, Frank and I set out immediately. We had a brief stop to make on the way, but try as I might, I cannot remember what it was.

When we entered Pat's room, both of the health care workers were there. I went to go over to Pat's bed, but was stopped by

You see Pat's personality here.

one of the women, who touched my arm. "She's gone," she said. I was shocked and overwhelmed. Shedding any concern about proper composure, I broke into sobs. The two women and Frank rushed over to console me.

I never did go to Pat's bed, and I do not regret it. Better that my memory is of her smile the evening before. What does bother me is the few minutes the stop en route took. I keep wondering whether, if we had arrived just moments earlier, if I would have been with her at the end. Pat was 78, and I suppose that's not a short life. But our mother lived to almost 95. I had hoped to see Pat at least equal that, and I knew that the repeated surgeries and growing weakness were to blame.

We went straight to the funeral home, Frank and I, to the same one that had directed the funerals of my mother and of Jack, both just a few years earlier. On the way there, my mind wandered. I was three years old and had fallen from a neighbor's porch onto a cement sidewalk.

My big sister, arm over my shoulders, was leading me home, me bawling my head off. Then I was a teenager, and the roles were reversed. I was consoling Pat on the breakup of her brief marriage. Then I was in the auditorium of my sister's college, sitting next to our proud mother, watching my sister honored as the summa cum laude student. Then it was just a couple of months ago. We were in a restaurant nearby. Frank was with us, and we were all laughing and enjoying ourselves. Was it the Italian restaurant, the Mexican, Red Lobster? Little did it matter.

If I had just one single minute today with Pat, I would quickly tell her one thing: I loved having her as my sister.

Frank and I arrived at Our Lady, Queen of Heaven Cemetery on a beautiful sunny Florida morning. Pat's only good friend in Florida was at her house in Brooklyn. Frank and I called at the administration building. I carried the urn with Pat's ashes to the pavilion with long rows of niches, Frank right next to me, and placed the urn in the open niche. A priest said a short prayer, the door of the niche was closed, and Frank and I left.

Rest In Peace, my sister Pat, my much-loved sister.

I reflected on the passing of people I loved. Within just a few years, three of the four niches were occupied. The empty one awaits me. I met Frank after Pat and I had already gotten just four niches, so there is no place for him. Besides, he wants his ashes scattered in the great outdoors.

Frank and I had rented various vacation apartments in Italy, Paris and London through rental services on the Internet. I have always worried about the possibility that, when we arrive in Europe to take possession of our rental, we find a catastrophe. One generally ends up paying 100% of the rental when booking, or shortly thereafter, so your bargaining power in case of an uninhabitable rental is close to nil. Such a possibility is lessened by ratings of the rental agency, a number of photos of the rental, and reviews of past tenants. I'm always suspicious of the latter, figuring that many who put forth the effort to submit a review are employees, relatives, and friends.

The rental in Sicily, in the historic center of Palermo, was probably the least pleasant, but due to no fault of the rental agent. Looking on the internet, I was excited about the two-bedroom apartment with 20-foot ceilings, situated in a historic palazzo. There were many photos, and they showed the type of dwelling that an American would hope to find in Europe. We were warned up front that the entry courtyard was under renovation, but in fact that aspect presented no problem.

We found the apartment spacious, charming, with elaborate 18th-century architectural details. It was better than the photos.

But arriving in Palermo on the same flight as we did, was a cold wave the likes of which this subtropical paradise had not seen in 40 years. The temperature outside plummeted — and inside, too. As we talked, vapor appeared each time we opened our mouths. The landlady came to our aid, or so we at first thought. A gas company dropped off something called a bombola, a bomb-looking device filled with pro-pane that, when lighted, gives off a comforting heat in a circle big enough to enclose two chairs tightly pressed together. Certainly, after the bombola ran a while, the room would become snug and warm.

But remember the 20-foot ceilings in the photo of this palatial palazzo? We had forgotten them as we waited to enjoy our toasty prem-ises. It took us a while to figure out that all the heat was in the top six feet of the rooms, while we were in the bottom six feet. So we spent several days and evenings in our warm-weather shorts and t-shirts, and wrapped in heavy blankets and seated as close to the "bomb" as we could get. We moved forward our planned tour of the island and found hotel rooms with eight-foot ceilings, and warmth. By the time we returned to our grand palazzo, the cold had abated. The only other issue with this rental was an uninvited night time visitor, a mouse. The landlady was astonished that we would even mention the presence of such a small guest. This is, after all, the historic center, she exclaimed, apparently believing that history excused all. She did, however, introduce to the apartment her black cat who proved a welcome roommate. It was always a conflict in my mind. How do you get rid of a pest without harming it?

All of our vacations were taken during the winter when we were in Florida. That was except for short trips such as those for my class reunions, and a three-day visit to Cleveland so that I could retrace my life there as a reporter, as a student, and as a neophyte gay man. I have always relished immersing myself in nostalgia.

The six months each year we were in Charleston was with not a whole lot of friends. There was Maxine and her daughter, Paulette, next door, the widow and her daughter with whom we went to dinner every week or so; the artist, Nancy Louise, whose house Frank had bought when we first arrived, and the mostly older gay men of Prime Timers who seemed to show little interest in a friendship with us outsiders and, if truth be told, whose company we sometimes found excruciatingly dull. At a gathering, we would time and again sneak a peek at our watches to see if it was yet time for a polite exit. I don't know if there was a single time that we weren't the first to leave. By such hasty departures, we could have been giving off we're-better-than-you vibes. Looking back, many of them were nice enough chaps, just not for us.

Frank's sister, Joan, had a logical explanation for why we were making so few friends. A friend is someone you see regularly, she offered, not someone you see only half the year. I remember when we met two interesting women with whom we wanted to pursue a friendship. We had a pleasant dinner at a good restaurant with them—and told them that in two days we leave for Florida. They must have forgotten our plan, because a week after that, we received an emailed invitation to their house. We declined, of course, telling them it would be six months until our return. Not surprisingly, any spark of a friendship with them died with our email answer.

So we found ourselves spending months in our grand, large quarters in Charleston, but with little to do. Frank would occasionally do a painting, and he watched a lot of old movies on Turner Classic Movies, but you don't have to be in West Virginia for that. Oh, yes, he had his tomato garden, which he took great interest in: big tomatoes, little tomatoes, tiny tomatoes, red ones, a sort-of-orange tomatoes, sweet tomatoes, green tomatoes. The green ones were actually future red tomatoes, but Frank would pick them early, and fry them so that I could savor fried green tomato sandwiches. My mother had often made them when I was growing up, and I loved them.

I had less activity in West Virginia than Frank. I followed the news closely on TV. Obama was president, no thanks to this state. I downloaded the New York Times on my Kindle each Sunday, and reading it was a day-long activity. While Frank occupied himself with the task of growing tomatoes, I was in charge of flowers and the appearance of the front yard.

When we bought the big house, there was nothing but grass. Frank was opposed to each and every blade on environmental grounds: it takes energy and fuel to cut it. So we got a slew of plugs of English Ivy and, in no time at all, the lot was covered. Then it was my duty to remove a patch of Ivy here and there and put in flowers for color. I put in a lot of daisies, the white Shasta daisies and the yellow Black Eyed Susans, and also some blue hydrangea bushes. Forming a border along the public sidewalk and our yard, we put in a row of red knockout roses that bloom prolifically all summer, without much effort by us. Then two purple-leaf plum trees. And a winding brick walk through the whole thing that I laid myself, foot by foot, day by day, over a summer, as we collected old bricks from a building here and there that was being torn down. When we were in Uniontown one time for me to attend my class reunion, we saw a pile of bricks abandoned next to a creek. Two hundred of those Pennsylvania bricks are in our West Virginia walk.

On one of my birthdays, Frank walked me along the brick walk. Hanging from one of the plum trees, overhanging the walk, was a sign that Frank had had made: "Vincent's Walk." Does the reader see why I am so fond of this guy?

CHAPTER **22**

The Hunt. Rockefeller property rejected.

BACK TO THE discussion of six months a year in Charleston. We had not made any intimate friends. We had tried. Either we didn't like them, or overwhelmingly it seemed, they didn't take to us. We had cards printed with out phone number, and had given them out at every opportunity. The cards could have been blank: no calls. We had serious discussions between us, looking for an idea of why no one ever called. Are we talking too much about New York or Florida? We hardly mentioned them, but even one time might be too much for people who pride themselves on never leaving the state. Let's make sure we talk about nothing but them. So we eliminated the "I" word and just talked about you, you, you. No calls. Reluctantly, we had to conclude that West Virginians just did not like us.

Then we had to come up with the reason. It couldn't be us, of course. It had to be them. Maybe it's because we go to Florida six months a year. Maybe our house is too big. We zeroed in on envy as the reason. Ah, yes, the green-eyed monster. Jealousy! That left our personality off the hook. We did wonder that maybe we're not scintillating company. No, that just couldn't be! We concluded we must leave.

There were other reasons to consider leaving the beautiful Mountain State. Day in and day out we weren't doing very much with ourselves. We had exhausted all the towns in the state that we had wanted to visit. I liked the condo in Fort Lauderdale; Frank yearned for a large wooded property like he had in Berkeley Springs. Actually, he now had such a property that he bought the first thing when we came to Charleston. It was nearby, 75 acres along the Big Sandy, a fast-running stream. Part of the property was a hill, or mountain. But there was no house. From time to time, we talked about building something small on it, but had never gone further with that idea. Frank did need a property where he could roam about, carving out trails on his own land. With our growing talk about relocating, it didn't seem that Frank's little jungle would be in West Virginia.

One of the most important considerations for leaving, I mention last. Frank is very close to his sister, Joan. She was living with her husband in Williamsburg, Virginia, and two nieces also were in Virginia, in Charlottesville and Alexandria. It would be good to be near Frank's relatives. With my sister gone, I had no immediate family.

For those reasons, we were about to embark on a three-year quest for the perfect—what? House in the middle of a city that I'd like, and close to Frank's relatives, or a house on a lot of land in the country for Frank, or a big house in the city and little place in the country? That was our whole problem. We couldn't make a decision on what we wanted. Any house, and any location, was fair game at one time or another. It would be great to be in Virginia where Frank had relatives and where trains took you right into Washington.

So, we set out and found a large kind of unattractive house—on a beautifully landscaped five acres—just outside Waynesboro, Virginia, with four bedrooms, four baths, a two-story family room. Best of all, it had a really nice pond on a stream down a slope from the house, with a little white bridge over it, and a small waterfall. We signed a contract.

It was going to be about 45 days until the closing, and that gave us plenty of time to think about the things we didn't like about it. I went first: I didn't like the town much. It was Frank's turn: the five acres weren't wooded. My turn: it was too remote, an hour from Charlottesville, and only three trains a week into Washington. Frank: but the inside of the house is wonderful, and it has that great pond. Me: Yes, but...

Mother Nature came to our aid during a storm, by releasing a torrent of water that overflowed (overflew?) the pond, rushed down the stream to the property next door, and turned that neighbor's pond into an overflowing mud hole. I might qualify the description of that neighbor as "that litigious neighbor." He somehow blamed our future pond's original construction for his washout.

Frank and I would face at the moment we closed on the purchase the excitement of being new homeowners and new defendants as well. The sellers kindly offered to release us from the contract, and we accepted. With some regrets. It was a wonderful big house with five handsome, albeit landscaped, acres, and a magnificent pond.

Back to square one.

We then read with interest articles on the 10 best university towns, the 10 best economical towns, the 10 best towns for retirees. One morning, the real estate broker who lived nearby called to tell us that she had a wonderful property on 30 acres, almost in town, that we had to see. In West Virginia, but what the heck! It was a house high on a mountaintop, overlooking the city, with a view of the airport on another mountaintop nearby. So the entertainment for an owner could be to sit on the front patio and watch and hear planes take off and rise up over his house and disappear behind his woods.

Another property the broker insisted that we see was owned by now ex-Senator Jay Rockefeller, who retired from the Senate at the end of his term, and had put his small (for him) Charleston estate on the market. It was a few acres, seven if I remember right, probably the biggest residential tract of any right in the city. The house was large, with many bedrooms and baths, and had character and charm. But the acreage of this little estate was nothing but steep wooded hills, the house situated, barely, on the only level land. There was no view; the land was thick with tall trees. We concluded that the property of a Rockefeller was not good enough for us. Mr. Rockefeller was slumming when he visited this house. He also had a 21,000 square-foot mansion in Washington's Rock Creek Park that he bought for $6.5 million.

Time marched on and life continued sans new house. Frank has always liked to make a big celebration out of holidays, like Christmas and birthdays. Jack and I had never done this. Frank would give many gifts, maybe ten items, all things he observed that I like: my favorite candy, dental sticks that I use, and so on. Then there would be a bigger gift, such as an IPad Pro one year.

The first few years with Frank, it was a problem for me at holidays to equal his creativity. As I got to know him better, I became attached to his idea of many small gifts, and at Christmas enjoyed opening them: first Frank, then me, then Frank, then me. For the big gift, I often relied on something that I knew Frank would receive enthusiastically, scheduling a trip. For someone who claims he loves his home, he's quick to leave it. I always arranged an extended stay through one of the sites that offer apartments and houses. One year it was London. On the day we left, Frank was eager.

On our arrival, the driver took us through Sloan Square in upscale Chelsea. A few blocks later, we stopped outside the classic, red-brick townhouse containing our rental. There was a low stoop with a wrought-iron railing on three or four steps. But inside, we were confronted by 43 steps before us, by later count, in order to ascend to our Internet-found vacation flat on the third level. I was relieved that the driver the Internet apartment rental company sent to meet us at Heathrow insisted on mounting the steps with my largest and heaviest bag. Neither of us is young, and I was about to find that after I've climbed about 20 of the steps with my light bag, I'd already be huffing and puffing. How out of shape I am! Frank does much better.

Later, I was further reminded of my age when young Brits on the Underground kept offering me their seats. It was quite annoying, those bloody Brits. It was a consideration for age that I don't believe you'd find in the United States.

This was the third time in a few years that I had searched the Internet for a vacation apartment, rather than to go to a hotel. We were attracted by the ability to live like residents, to shop at the supermarket, opt to have dinner at home, relax in a comfortable living room.

As we entered the building, into a small vestibule with traditional molding on walls and doors, no doubt once the elegant entry to a private house, our noses were assailed by the acrid smell of paint. Indeed, several young men were on the stairwell spreading a new coat of ghostly white over everything. They had laid a plastic runner down the flight of carpeted steps as protection.

"Don't touch the handrail!" one shouted at us. "We just painted it. Not the wall, either!" This warning did not sit well with me, as I am not the steadiest person on two feet, but I had no choice but to keep my body squarely in the center of each step as I went up, and to make certain I held my bag away from everything.

Caroline, a smart-looking middle-aged Scottish lady from "A Place Like Home," the Internet rental firm, greeted us at the door of the flat, gave us her personal mobile phone number, and showed us around. There was a lounge, or sitting room, what we call the living room in the US, with a three-window bay overlooking the common rear garden behind the block of houses. A huge tree, leafless at this time of year, dominated.

Matching sofas faced each other on either side of the fireplace, with the TV inserted in the hearth. Cut into the lounge and open to it was a small modern kitchen. There was wall-to-wall carpeting.

In the rear, fronting on the street, were two bedrooms sharing what was once a three-window bay. One bedroom now had two of these windows and had a king-sized bed. The other bedroom, narrow, had a single. The beds had plush white down comforters. There was an ample bathroom off a hall.

All linens, towels, kitchen needs, were included. A more adequate supply of soap and bathroom tissue would have been nice.

All appeared pretty much like the photos on the web. I had paid the rental agency for 10 nights occupancy, the equivalent of about $250 per night, the rate of a mid-priced hotel. The security deposit on rentals is £400 to £800, depending on the price and length of stay, refunded within a week after the end of the rental if there are no damages. The total bill must be paid in advance, by credit card, when reserving. So if you would find your rental completely unsuitable upon arriving and seeing it, you would have no bargaining power at all to get your money back.

Asked about the situation where an arriving guest finds an accommodation unacceptable, Nick, of A Place Like Home, explained what is done. "In an instance where a guest arrives and has the viewpoint that the flat doesn't meet their standards, we generally ascertain why and attempt to place them in accommodations they deem acceptable." He continued, "In the event we can't do that, and on the acceptance that their concerns are valid, we will refund them the rental cost and they find their own accommodation." Nick stressed that the utmost effort is made to find them a suitable place, upgraded if necessary, and that in the nine years he has been with the firm, only a handful of cases arose where a guest found an accommodation unsuitable. Those instances are usually down to a guest mistake as to which floor the flat is on, or something as such, he added.

To locate apartments, I had entered in Google "vacation rentals London." Perhaps a dozen companies came up, each offering 20 to 50 flats and houses at various prices, in different areas. The difficulty I found was that the choice was almost too large to make a decision easily. Each entry had many photos and complete details.

I had also checked out several five-star hotels offered by airlines at a special rate, slightly more than we were paying for the two-bedroom flat. The two I noted were Le Meredian right on Piccadilly, and the Royal Horseguards Hotel near Parliament Square. Both were certainly convenient, but not in a neighborhood where you could tell yourself that you were a local. And no kitchen, no sitting room...

The apartment we had rented for five weeks in Rome really had no problem to speak of. It was a fine location, near the Piazza Navona, just one flight up, nice-sized living room, dining room, equipped kitchen, two bedrooms, two baths. As every apartment we rented, it had a washing machine. No drier, but a drying rack. The only issue in Rome, not serious, was that when we arrived at the flat after a flight from the US, there was no one to meet us and unlock the door. After I fumbled a while to make a phone call in Italy, the rental agent did show up promptly.

The Rome apartment went by the general rule: the mid to upper $200 to $300 per night, with a small discount for a long term, such as a month. Including everything. Prices are always shown clearly on the internet with the details of the rental. As you would expect, two or more bedrooms are more expensive than smaller flats.

So, despite a few little bumps in the road, we no doubt will continue booking vacation rentals through photos and descriptions we find online. That is, until the day we arrive in a foreign city after a long flight and find a habitation not fit for human occupancy, or discover that the rental company we paid in advance is nowhere to be found. That could happen.

CHAPTER 23

The Legacy. A surprise outcome.

AT THE SAME time as our property hunting was going on, we were discussing the tragedy of my sister's premature death. It distressed me when I thought that she should have lived 17 years longer, to reach the age of our mother. I went over in my mind and with Frank my conversation with the owner before Pat entered the ALF. I told the owner that Pat had fallen twice in her house, and, fortunately, wasn't seriously hurt. I told her that this good luck couldn't last, and that I needed a place where Pat would be safe.

I remembered her assurances about the care at her ALF, her guarantees that her employees would watch my sister scrupulously, and that no accident would happen there. The woman was so charming, but I realized she would, of course, be nice to a potential client. In all her amiability, she never broke into it to tell me that her worker at night is permitted to nap, nor that no one would be "scrupulously" watching Pat at night. Nor did she inform me that there was a simple, inexpensive alarm available that would sound should Pat start to get out of bed. But even an alarm may not have gotten a napping health care worker to my sister's side in time, I realized. I weighed all of this in my mind.

Sometimes I woke in the middle of the night pondering my sister's premature death. I began demonizing the attractive owner of the ALF as a mythical temptress who lured me into conspiring in my sister's death. I felt guilty for selecting this ALF, and I yearned to redeem myself. I wanted justice for Pat. Or was it revenge? I dwelled on my conviction that this woman and her husband should not be operating ALFs where people's lives were at risk, with fragile clients under their care. Notwithstanding their state license and state inspections, they were dangerous. Would some other dependent woman die as Pat had? Would her family members be racked with guilt for having placed their loved one there, as I now was? Would they, too, wake up in the middle of the night, thinking?

Frank and I talked about all the issues that were bothering me. Justice for Pat. Closely related: punishment. Neglect that could carry over to other patients. After several months of back-and-forth and indecision, I decided to speak to an attorney. I met with a lawyer in Miami who specializes in nursing home neglect, and told him the details of Pat's death, and that I thought that the owners of the ALF should not be in the assisted living business. I told him I believed they were a danger to their clients.

I filed suit.

The attorney recommended a claim for a total of $1,500,000, which included reimbursement to Pat's estate for medical costs, pain and suffering, and for neglect leading to death. That amount seems large as I type it here, but when the attorney suggested that figure, it was painful to hear that my sister's life, on which I could put no price, would come to only that. No amount can be placed on the life of a loved one, but this seemed so inadequate. Nonetheless, I accepted the attorney's advice without discussion.

An answer to our complaint was not forthcoming, and we were granted a default judgment, the precise amount to be set by a jury.

Before a hearing to assess damages was scheduled, a lawyer representing the two defendants, the husband and wife owners, notified my attorney that the complaint had not been served properly, and that they would move to open the default. That didn't happen. Then the ALF attorney revealed that the defendants, some months before Pat's death, had let their liability insurance lapse. Later, we were informed that the defendants no longer owned any ALFs and were considering filing for bankruptcy. Then again, their attorney said they would move to open the default.

They didn't try to open the default, nor file for bankruptcy, but several years passed with threats to do either. Finally, the date for the hearing to set damages was here. Frank, who would be a witness, and I were in a courtroom of Broward County, watching the rapid selection of five jurors. The only dismissal was of a man who said he could not award anything when the defendants had defaulted, and were not present.

I testified that I had emphasized to one of the defendants before Pat entered the ALF the need for special care to avoid another fall, and that I was assured that my sister would be safe. I told the jury of my special relationship with Pat, that our father had abandoned us, that we had been a closely-knit family of just three, that twice a year I went to Cleveland to be with my mother and sister, that they had moved to Florida to be near to me, that I felt a responsibility for my sister's welfare and that I felt now, because of the defendants' neglect, that I had failed her. Admitting this brought a quiver to my voice, but I recovered quickly.

I told about my sister's life: that in her 40s she went to college and graduated summa cum laude; that she had been a compensation analyst for the Defense Department in charge of three states; that she had two black cats, Monty and Mitzi, that she was crazy about; that she had a brand new house she talked about all the time; that we often spent a Saturday morning at a nursery selecting a plant for her yard; that every

Saturday or Sunday afternoon was our time at a restaurant together. Frank, who had been present at every pertinent time, supported my testimony.

The jury's verdict exceeded our claim of $1,500,000. It awarded Pat's estate $1,750,000. I remember today the sympathetic middle-aged African-American woman on the jury who smiled at me as the award was read.

I felt quite good that day. For Pat, it was a jury verdict giving her a measure of justice. Nothing could restore Pat to life, but it was more than we had sued for, telling my sister that she was valuable.

I was the sole heir to Pat's estate and the representative/executor. The award would come to me, well over a million dollars after attorney's fees. I couldn't help feeling good about this coming bonanza, and that thought made me feel guilty. I analyzed my feelings. I would gladly give up the million dollars plus to have Pat back. No amount of money would compensate me for the loss of my sister. I also was confident that Pat would be happy that her death, futile as it was, at least brought a million dollars to her brother. So I convinced myself not to beat myself up about feeling good about the money.

Year after year passed with my attorney unable to collect a cent on this judgment. These were years when my mind kept going to the defendants, aware of the difficulties they could be having with such a large judgment against them on the record. I remembered the stress Jack and I had felt when we had to turn our complex of renovated cottages in Southampton over to the bank. They must be going through the same thing, or worse, I kept thinking. Their credit rating must be as low as they go. It's because of me, because I had gotten this big judgment against them. I would try to shake that thought and think of the neglect of Pat, that my sister was gone, never to live out a full life, never again to feel the joy she experienced upon walking through her yard each morning to see the latest flowers to bloom.

Five years after the verdict, after our failed efforts at collection, we settled for the defendants' offer of $50,000. Some of the money went to attorney's fees, some went to Medicare under a statute I had never heard of, whereby Medicare puts a lien on awards in order to recoup monies paid out. Pat's estate got very little compensation for her loss of life. I certainly didn't get a million dollars, and I felt let down.

As I thought about the case, my mood began to improve until it reached "quite happy." I began thinking about what we did collect. It was a glorious award that was nowhere to be found in our judgment. The defendants no longer had an assisted living facility. My attorney had confirmed it. They were out of the business. I was certain that it was Pat's lawsuit that brought it about.

This was Pat's legacy. No harm could come to a future client. Justice had prevailed.

Dear Defendants Found Negligent In Caring For My Sister:

Even though you defaulted and did not appear at trial, the jury has in essence convicted you in the death of my sister. The jury awarded more than the requested damages. You, too, admitted guilt by leaving the Assisted Living business. You realized —too late for my sister — your inadequacy. At least, by your your own withdrawal, you will no longer be a danger.

Now it is left to me to consider forgiveness. I can forgive you for the suffering you caused me. That's mostly over now. Of course I still miss Pat. But I have adjusted to her absence, to the lack of phone calls, to no longer hearing her infectious laugh, not to be looking forward to joining her every weekend. I repeat: on my behalf, I forgive you, because you certainly did not intend to cause me hurt.

Concerning forgiveness for my sister: if it weren't for your neglect, she may have lived another 17 years, to the

age of our mother. She'd still be here enjoying the life that she found fulfilling. She's not here for the house she loved, her flowers she tended, her cats she babied, her friends, her restaurants, her interest in the world. You deprived her of everything.

It's not my place to intervene and forgive you in her name, and she's not here to do it.

**Sincerely,
The Brother**

Although the ALF was found at fault, I am left with questions of myself that I can't get out of my mind. Should I have taken the word of the owner concerning supervision? Should I have asked, specifically, if the night care worker naps? Should I have insisted on speaking to the staff, especially the night worker, myself? Should it have occurred to me that there may be a bed alarm on the market to alert staff if Pat got out of bed? Was I neglectful in my investigation, and am I partly to blame for my sister's death? I go around and around with questions, and I don't come up with an answer.

I must address my frequent feeling of guilt because of something I did or did not do. I feel guilty because I lied to my mother about a non-existent girlfriend. I feel guilty because I left my last agency in a childish pout. I feel guilty because I did not visit my mother the day before the night she died. I feel guilty because, with my sister, I may not have investigated deeply enough the ALF where she died.

These are all things that I do think about occasionally, but these feelings of guilt are not, and should not be, ruining my life. I am happy most of the time, and I wonder how that is possible with such weighty issues, even occasionally, on my mind. I conclude that it's because, in truth, I realize that most of my guilt is manufactured in my busy head. Lying to my mother about a non-existent girlfriend? Back then most gay men were living an undercover life of lies—brought on by society's condemnation.

So I didn't see my mother on her last day. I was a loving son, and she knew it. Next: choosing an ALF that didn't supervise my sister properly? I certainly did more in groundwork than most would-be clients, before selecting the ALF: interviewing the owner, examining the premises, checking the state inspection reports. It is the ALF that is the guilty party.

I'm hardly the only human being to experience guilt. Feelings of guilt, apparently, afflict a good part of mankind. The internet is loaded with self-help for those poor souls: 12 ways to overcome guilt, 15 methods, etc. I must convince myself that my guilt feelings are creations within me, maybe a part of my grief over lost loved ones, and are not for what I have done.

CHAPTER 24

Ditto The Hunt.
Hunt expanded to 3 states.

I WOULD NOW miss not being able to phone Pat, to go to a restaurant with her, and not being able to invite her to visit us, maybe for a holiday, and to stay a while. However, I recognize that life goes on.

It was time to get back to house-hunting. We had struck out in Waynesboro, rejected the Rockefeller mini estate, did not find a town under "The Ten Best Towns..." By this time, we realized that we definitely wanted to be within an easy train to DC. For that reason alone, staying in Charleston was out. We wanted to be close to Frank's relatives, too.

We got out a map. North Carolina? Too far from DC. Pennsylvania? Not great train service to DC. Virginia we had already tried with Waynesboro. Ah, Maryland! Wasn't the District of Colombia cut out of Maryland? We even liked the politics. So off we went. In Hagerstown, we saw three houses.

Then to Frederick, another possible place. It's a nice, neat town with a park and little lake in the center. There is a train station with direct service into DC several days a week. We looked at city houses, each of which would have satisfied a buyer who, at an older age, was not intent on upsizing. We just could not get the idea of "big" out of our minds.

Than we saw "the house." It was a three-story red brick Federal classic on a tree-lined street smack in the center, maybe a thousand feet from a street with restaurants, coffee shops, and people. And it was right next to a pocket park about a hundred feet wide and as deep as the rear fenced-in yard of the house. Somewhere, I don't remember where, we got a price of $350,000. Finally, a town where large houses aren't so expensive! So, we were really excited and wasted no time in calling the realtor whose name was on the sign. She deflated our balloon at once. The $350,000 bought just one floor of this house, a two-bedroom apartment.

Back home to West Virginia, a state that's looking better and better.

CHAPTER 25

Supreme Court Plaza. Are you looking, Justice Roberts?

I'M NOT THE type to marry someone of the same sex, or the opposite sex for that matter, unless I would be given a really good reason to do so. Being fond of the person, love, wouldn't cut it. Frank one day gave me that reason.

The merits of same-sex marriage is much debated among gay people, with some valuing the ability, finally, to access society's foremost rite, and others claiming we lose our identity as a community with such obsequiousness. The latter group argues that, heretofore, gays have arranged our lifelong unions just fine, with gay attorneys having created documents that protect us legally, although admittedly not being able to provide the benefits the government reserves for married couples.

But Frank's idea intrigued me. It was still two years before the Supreme Court's 5-4 decision on same-sex marriage, but it had been legalized in the District of Columbia back in 2009. Frank suggested that we marry on the front terrace of the United States Supreme Court

itself. This would express in clear fashion our right to marry, and our contempt for the mere questioning of our equality. How could I resist?

With two friends, Joe and Don, taking photos, the 16 Corinthian columns of the United States Supreme Court as a backdrop, on a sunny

May morning in 2013, we recited the respected verse before an official of the District of Columbia. During the ceremony, I completely forgot that one of my reasons for our union was to proclaim our right to marry. My only thought that morning was being united to Frank. I do not call Frank my "husband." A husband, to me, is as it's always been, someone with a wife, not another husband. I'm more comfortable with gender-free "spouse." Half the time I just say partner.

In Charleston, we still went to Prime Timers events. We did meet one interesting fellow, a black man. At our invitation, he stopped by the house for a wine and then we went to a restaurant for dinner.

When entering, I thought to myself: two white men and a black man for dinner. Then I thought: Why did I think that? Am I a racist?

I'm for everyone's rights. I proclaim it! Equal rights for African-Americans, of course. And for: transgendered, rednecks, Latinos, Indians and Muslims, women and men, the disabled and the athlete, gay people and straight people, evangelicals and atheists, Hillary's "deplorables" and the elites. I believe in the Constitution, that we're all equal.

I am a proud liberal, maybe even a progressive. I favor social welfare programs, because I believe the fortunate have a duty to take care of the luckless.

But I worry about thoughts I have. I worry that I am a closet racist.

The dictionary definition of a racist is a person who feels discrimination or prejudice against people of other races, or who believes that a particular race is superior to another. I do not think I fit either of those descriptions, but yet I wonder about myself.

When I share the elevator in my condo building in Washington with an attractive woman who is black, I think "attractive black woman," not just attractive woman. Is this prejudice, or just an observation? It's a fact that I never think "attractive white woman."

I've never had a black friend, and with a black acquaintance, I've never forgotten that he is black. I don't think of blacks as inferior, but

I question whether I don't consider myself socially superior. It's a fine line.

When a black family bought a house next to my sister, I waited to see their lifestyle, half expecting a problem of some sort. Would there be loud rap music? I had remembered driving in poor black neighborhoods and seeing trash strewn about, and groups of men on street corners conversing in shouts. Did I expect this of middle-class black people? Was this prejudice?

Here's a cliché. I would be fearful on a dark street with several black man walking behind me, whereas white men would disturb me less. With black men I might think of crime and Chicago's South Side. Prejudice.

I eagerly voted for Barack Obama, but then I realized an entire black family was occupying the White House. It took me a while to accept it. Certainly prejudice. These thoughts, I am afraid, do follow the definition of a racist.

But I have always held racists in contempt. I side with blacks when there is a police shooting. I applaud "Black Lives Matter." I feel empathy when blacks want Confederate monuments removed. I blame black poverty and black crime on the lack of opportunity. I shake my head in disgust when I hear a report of a racist act.

Do my racist prejudices negate any contrary sympathies I feel? Or do they expose me as a hypocrite?

I was raised in Uniontown, that, I believe, had less than a dozen black families at the time. As far as I know, there was no racism; there was virtually just one race. I don't recall even seeing a black person, in person, until I went to Cleveland after high school. My total lack of exposure to black people did not prevent me from being prejudiced.

In Cleveland, I remember driving through a large park where all the people I saw were black. Although I had no reason to dislike black people, I felt annoyed that they dominated this park. When I was a reporter in Cleveland, I became aware that a story of a white person may run on page one with a photo, whereas the same story concerning a black person merited merely a paragraph on a back page. I didn't give this prejudicial treatment by the editors a second thought.

When a black man was elected mayor of Cleveland, I resented it. It was as though the opposing team had won. Where did I get such an idea?

My father of course wasn't around, and my mother was liberal. I never heard her speak against blacks, or even mention them. She had no occasion to, living as we did in our white town.

Don't they say that racism is the result of childhood brainwashing? There was certainly no such indoctrination in my family. However, I was exposed to the conspicuous bigotry of virtually all white society prior to this century. Media, and especially film, joined in. Black people were always shown as subservient to whites. They were the maids and the gardeners serving whites. Or they simply were portrayed as inferior, lacking in intelligence. This was brainwashing, and I see the effect of it in myself today. Maturity, education, and life have brought welcome change in me. But, still, there are moments of bias remaining. When that happens, I make an effort to confront any negative feeling and subject it to logic. That always works.

I wonder if, beyond indoctrination in youth, there is also a yet-to-be-discovered gene that predisposes humans to bigotry toward anyone different from ourselves. That would explain why so many of us have been willing to accept racism.

I would hate that gene. I would want to fight my own nature.

Frank and I were getting impatient now at not having found a house or even a town. Our impatience was with ourselves. Almost on a whim, we would try Charlottesville, Virginia again, where Frank has a niece, and where we had looked for a house ten years earlier, before our move to West Virginia. It's easy to Washington by train. We knew Charlottesville was a good town since it voted 80% for Hillary Clinton. It's in a weird political situation, not being in any county whatsoever. It's completely surrounded by Albermarle County, which went Republican. In fact, Donald Trump has a winery in the county.

Charlottesville is a prosperous, pleasant university town that nearly everyone likes. In the center is what is called the Mall, a wide outdoor pedestrian area of many blocks, with numerous outdoor restaurants and cafes and tables shaded by huge old trees. It's the place where townspeople saunter up and down hoping to run into a friend and go together for a cafe au lait. Charlottesville is home to Thomas Jefferson's handsome University of Virginia with its beautiful classic buildings, and his nearby Monticello home.

Off to Charlottesville we went.

The realtor, Tom, that we had contacted, had seven houses to show us. We diligently tagged along. Nice unusual house, but too small. A big formerly elegant house near the Mall — but it would take several hundred thousand dollars and several hundred years to get into shape. One house had a wide but steep and long staircase up to the front porch. Hey, we're not young!

It was after 5:00 when we got to the seventh and last property on the realtor's list. I was tired after all this looking, and I was sure Frank was. I was hungry because I had just a light lunch, and I was certain Frank was, because he always was. Frank asked Tom, that if he were buying, what house of those we were seeing would he buy, and he had said it would be this last one. His opinion, and our long day, may have colored somewhat our reception of the house.

It sat there, mostly brilliant white in its Key West design, with a wide porch across the front of both the ground floor and second floor. It dazzled against the green hill behind it, and the foliage around it protected it from the view of any neighbor. What's more, its three floors were bright and sunny, with glass everywhere, four bedrooms and four baths. And it was built recently; no renovation needed; no risking thousands of dollars. Move in the day of the closing. And it was in an HOA that had 16 wooded acres along the nearby river. Perhaps Frank wouldn't need his own wooded place in the country after all, we thought.

We were enthusiastic about this house that needed nothing, and relieved that there exists a house in the US that we would consider buying, and a town we liked. So, in the car going back to the realtor's office, we made an offer, which was accepted a few days later. We were off to the races!

The Charlottesville house. We never moved in.

I'm going to make the final outcome of this purchase brief because it shows our indecisiveness, but it also shows our creativity. We closed on the house, signed a rent-back agreement of a few months with the sellers, and never occupied the house we bought. We decided we just did not want to move there. Then, to support our change of heart, we created a number of reasons the house was not suitable. It wasn't sitting in the middle of acres of our own land; it didn't have a pond, as Frank did in Berkeley Springs; the steps down to the river in the HOA's 16 acres were long and steep and didn't have a handrail; at 3000 square feet, the house wasn't big enough; we didn't like the street leading up to it; it was too far from downtown and too hilly to try to walk; the supermarket was too far away; Charlottesville was too complicated to drive around in, not like the grid of Manhattan.

So, eventually we sold after paying some months of taxes, insurance and HOA fees, and a broker's commission. We lost, but by then something had come up that made us forget our loss. But before that, after deciding not to move into the ready-to-move-into Charlottesville house, we went to the condo in Fort Lauderdale for the winter.

CHAPTER **26**

Paradise Lost.
DNA catastrophe

IN PUBLICATIONS AND on the internet, we were seeing advertisements for DNA testing from companies like Heritage and Ancestry. Frank's nephew had his report, and found some surprises. We were intrigued, so we both ordered the kits, returned the requested samples of saliva, and waited for the results. I was confident of what a report would say in my case: Italian, from my mother's father, Massimo Filippi, who emigrated to America from Trento, Italy, and Irish, since both of my paternal grandparents were Irish. Somehow I was ignoring the influence of my maternal grandmother who came here from Hungary. I expected my report to be simple: 50% Italian, 50% Irish. Frank's of course would call him 100% Italian, since all of his grandparents were Italian.

After a few weeks, I got an email from Ancestry: my DNA report was ready for viewing on the internet. I eagerly followed the link. I was curious but I'm not sure why. I already knew the result. 50% Italian, 50% Irish. Suddenly I remembered my Hungarian maternal grandmother. Oh, I suppose there would be a little Hungarian. Why had I even bothered with this DNA thing? I knew who I was.

Sure I liked the Irish part. Some years ago I even got Irish citizenship. Actually that's misleading. If a grandparent was born in Ireland, you were born an Irish citizen. You don't become a citizen; you've always been a citizen. So I became acknowledged as a foreign-born citizen and I take every opportunity to boast about my Irish passport.

The Hungarian would be, well, ok. No, better than ok. I hear Budapest is a wonderful city, and the Hungarians, fun-loving people. A bistro with a violinist? That would be the life.

But what I valued the most is the Italian part. I've been proud of it all of my life, bragged about it. Between talking about my Irish passport and my Italian heritage, I am an interesting person at parties, the few I'm invited to.

Oh, the blessings of being Italian! The Roman Empire, gladiators and legends like Ben Hur and Spartacus. I am of that illustrious race. Leonardo and Michelangelo. Verdi. The eternal city, where we rented an apartment for five weeks to live among my people. Pasta and vino. La Dolce Vita.

I followed the Ancestry link and stared, blinking my eyes, at the report. There must be some horrible mistake! I was shocked. Not one iota of Italian in this so-called DNA report. Not a single mention of the words Italy or Italian. What goes here? I check the name at the top; yes, it's my name.

It stated figures that were a blur to me at first: 35% Irish; they had gotten it down to County Mayo; 32% English or Welsh, that's logical, the English were always imposing themselves on the Irish; 13% Germanic and 12% Eastern European, that's my maternal grandmother, who I had ignored, no doubt.

And 2% each for France, Sweden, Norway, the Balkan states. What a mongrel they're saying I am. I quickly added up the percentages: 100%. So it couldn't be that they accidentally left out my 50%, or at least 25%, Italian. This was willful! Could they not give even 2% to Italy?

Where, I ask, is the DNA passed to me from my grandfather Massimo Filippi, born in Trento? That's Trento, ITALY, and there can't be a more Italian name then Massimo Filippi. He sure wasn't Irish.

With hesitation, I revealed the catastrophe of my report to Frank, reluctant to let him know that I may not be of his acclaimed race after all, He had just gotten his report, too. Can you believe it? He's 92% Italian. I wondered. Is our relationship based on his belief that I share at least a big part of his ethnicity? Was it a scam when I represented myself as being part Italian?

I couldn't dial Ancestry fast enough. I told the agent that I wanted to appeal. She had never heard of such a thing, and instead would email me a publication explaining unexpected results. And I searched the Internet. I didn't like what I read.

Every source pretty much agreed that you inherit specific blocks, but perhaps no particular gene from a parent, although each supplies half of your DNA. They in turn do the same from their parents, and so on. I suppose, in an individual, an unfortunate soul such as me, an ancestral ethnicity can be lost, My first thought had been to possible hanky panky, that my mother's father may not have been her father, But this explanation, if nothing else, gets my grandfather off the hook.

To all this science, I say hogwash! In my heart, I know I'm Italian, maybe more than 1/4. Hardly anyone eats as much pasta as I do, and pizza. I'm always thinking about a trip to Italy. I'm even going to learn Italian.

Sono Italiano! Sono Italiano!

Our winter in Florida was interrupted by an internet ad among those being sent us by a realtor. It was for a large house — 6200 square feet, all kinds of bedrooms, 6 1/2 baths —on seven acres with a pond, just outside Culpeper, Virginia. Just what two older people need.

We flew right up to Culpeper, or, rather, Charlottesville, the closest airport, 40 miles away, and learned that the house was two weeks away from its sale at a foreclosure. Some of the 6200 square feet was in a walkout basement with a large living room, two bedrooms and two baths, but the main floor and second floor were quite huge. The imminent foreclosure caused the seller to adjust the price to where we could pay it. The good price compensated for the loss we suffered in the sale of Charlottesville. We are finally happy, with the little town of Culpeper, with our big house on nice land, and with our pond. Who said we could not be satisfied? Well, we're not satisfied that there are snapping turtles in the pond, and we hope they're not being unpleasant to the fish. We have met a few gay men in town, but Culpeper is not Greenwich Village in the old days. We do know a lot of people who share our politics and values, even though the town favors the other party by about 60-40. Frank's sister, Joan, was provided an assigned bedroom and is visiting frequently We are making use of Amtrak for the hour and a half into DC.

We are going against the rule for our age, and upsizing. We just recently got yard help. Frank went to a gathering of Culpeper Persisters (The name comes from Senator Elizabeth Warren's persistence in speaking when the Republican Senate Majority Leader tried to silence her.) and at the event Frank wore a large sign over his chest announcing our desire for yard help. Just the kind of thing Frank does.

The Amtrak trip into Washington invites a comparison to the 15

Finally a house we're satisfied with.

hours it took to get to the condo in Fort Lauderdale. I had liked so much living in New York, and Washington, in many areas, such as around DuPont Circle, has a similar vibrancy. It also seems that winters in Florida are getting warmer, often too

The pond from the house.

warm for Frank's liking, and humid, too. So we began looking for a condo in Washington. After seeing about 20, we chose one off upper Connecticut Avenue held by the Estate of Bernice Sandler. We looked up her obituary, and learned that she was famous. Her efforts brought about Title IX, which banned discrimination against women in education. She's in the Women's Hall of Fame.

We sold Florida, and will be spending summers in Culpeper, and winters, except maybe for trips to a milder climate, in Washington. We must be the only people who have chosen Washington, D.C. over Florida for the winter.

CHAPTER 27

Subject Verboten.

WE STILL PLAN to travel, although I am getting older, or in fact have already gotten old, vintage, as I said earlier. It's something I try not to acknowledge. I believe that your health may conform to your attitude. I must think young. I must be interested in and select subjects of conversation like someone 20 years younger. Or someone 50 years younger. That will help to keep me young. I have learned, for example, that if you bring the subject of dying up at a dinner party, you may never be invited back. It is practically verboten to speak of it, even though it will be the most important event of everyone's life.

But at age 87, although I am in good health, I can't help thinking that dying can't be far away. I've found that the best thing when the thought occurs is to keep it to myself because no one wants to talk about it. It's too depressing.

It never occurred to me to even give dying a thought through my 50s, 60s, even 70s. I've read that you're old when the actuarial tables of life expectancy give you 15 years or less to live. I object to this standard because it doesn't consider physical and mental fitness. My arrival at the point where I could actually die of "old age" hit me one day like a flash of lightning and a clap of thunder, when I was already 80. It was a shock, even though I had been noting that about half of my classmates from my 1952 high school class of 38 students had already died.

How could I be of dying age? I'm too young! How could this have happened? Why, I feel a commonality with teens, with 20s and 30s and 40s and 50s... People I see in their 80s are old! They are old people! Why, I'm not an old person! Can't I at least claim to be...late middle-age? A while ago, I took one of those tests on the Internet where you provide answers about your health and ancestry to determine your true physical age. I came in 12 years younger, a big boost to my ego. Does that make me late middle-age? Not quite. I need to take more tests.

I wonder to myself how long it is before I see the pearly gates, or whatever. My mother died at just under 95. Perhaps, with luck... At our new building in Washington, Frank and I talked to a woman 105 years old. She was with a care worker, but was in surprisingly good condition. I can do that. When I do go, I hope my leaving is not a gruesome event. A quick heart attack maybe.

When I hear of the death of a friend, I Google to get the obituary. Somehow, there seems to be a satisfaction in reading the details. Strange. In my psyche I may be congratulating myself that once again it is not me. I worry that getting relief from my friends' passing would make me out to be—repugnant.

I can still picture in my mind Jack, my mother, and Pat, without photos. However, my memories of their personalities are fading. I remember that Jack and I always found things the other said funny, but I can't recall one thing. My mother and sister always fussed around the kitchen preparing a holiday meal, but what did we talk about at the table? I want to hold onto precious moments, but they're leaving.

I'm not at all ready to go, nor may ever be. Frank and I seldom have a day that we do not enjoy. I want to be here to know how our political turmoil is settled. I want to see the highways streaming with autonomous cars set up as little living rooms. I want to know how climate change finally comes out in the year 2050 or 2100. I want to know what the world will be like, if there is one, 200 or 500 years from now. And I shudder to think of a time when I will have been dead a million years.

I wonder about after-I'm-gone. Will Frank be sometimes painfully startled on seeing someone in a crowd that looks like me, as I occasionally am with my mother, sister, and Jack? Will I return to inhabit my partner's dreams, as my loved ones do mine?

In my life I was a reporter, and a Madison Avenue advertising man. I lived 10 years in France and five in the UK, so it is not that I haven't experienced life. But I want more. Nonetheless, I have prepared for the big departure. I did all the usual documents. I wrote detailed instructions on financial accounts for Frank. I want things to go smoothly for him. He's six years younger than I am, so I assume–really hope–that I will exit first.

What neither of us has done is follow the advice of an old friend given Frank years ago. "Have very young friends," he suggested. "They'll take care of you."

I get mixed reactions from friends my age about their thoughts on death. One said he never thinks of it. "My mental picture of me is the same it has been for 50 years," he said. In opposition, another man referred to the "death cloud" hovering over us. A woman in an assisted living facility says most people there are "jolly," though it's their final residence. Frank, on this subject, says he's ok with it. A woman friend, 85, seemed overwhelmed with concern about the future home of her rice cooker she brought back from California years ago. These are called the golden years?

I read recently that in Sweden, at age 80, you are expected to clear out all the items of your life that would be of little value to heirs, and thus to relieve them of the burden. It's called dostadning, or "death cleaning."

After many years, I am finally about to sell/give away/throw away personal items of my mother and sister that were precious to them. What about my sister's college yearbook, her cap and gown that she saved? It seems that you can sell anything on EBay.

I have tried death cleaning keepsakes of mine such as the embroidered child's bedspread, with the rabbits and chicks, that my mother made for my kindergarten naps. To date, still no takers, still trying.

So here I am, waiting in line for my turn to enter eternity, yet somehow enjoying life and enthusiastically making plans for Washington, despite the Grim Reaper I can see standing on the horizon. My intention is to reach 100 and get the usual birthday card from the president. I just hope it's the one I voted for; I would hate to turn out the light with the other party in power.

Am I in crisis over dying? The definition of crisis is, "a time of intense difficulty, trouble or danger." The danger is certainly there. Is this a time of intense difficulty for me, with the thought of dying probably within the next ten years? I wouldn't say "intense," but, rather, I am "concerned." Concern, and some acceptance. I might as well accept it, because it's unavoidable. Also, I have a certain satisfaction, a sense of fulfillment with a life I'm happy to have lived. Maybe that is the problem: I'm happy with my life. Therefore, I have no desire to leave. If I were miserable in this world, I'm sure I wouldn't mind exiting. So in the next years I'll have to pay the penalty for having enjoyed life, and that's dying when I don't want to. I won't have regrets about wasting it. So, am I in crisis about dying? I don't know. I'm not sure. Really, though, I'm no different from just about everyone my age. All my peers ponder the day it all ends. You've seen friends go, but you're not eager to join them. But Frank, always singular, isn't concerned. He wanted merely to reach 80, and he did, in October, 2020.

While I'm waiting, I might as well be having a good time. For my 85th birthday, Frank arranged a week in a rental apartment in New York, the city where I lived for 25 years, the longest of any place. I still consider myself a New Yorker, although it was my first return since Jack and I left for France in 1988, 31 years before. The rental was in Hell's Kitchen, an area of Manhattan that suited its name when I last saw it, but now was filled with new buildings and construction.

I couldn't wait to go by our old 15-apartment building at 107 East 63rd Street that we had owned. I saw that the present owners removed the awning out to the street that Jack and I had installed. Why would they do that? The coffee shop on the corner of Lexington looked the same from the exterior. There was still the floor-to-ceiling glass where Jack and I sat every morning gazing at people rushing to work. But the counter, stools, tables and chairs were white now. Everything looked plastic, 21st century

The building that Jack and I sold first, at 246-248 East 51st Street, is now a condo that had a 2-bedroom apartment on the market at $600,000. We bought the whole 23 apartments in the building in 1976 for $212,000, and sold it a few years later in a rising market for $750,000. It appeared that only a minimum of improvements was made: new windows, and a rococo entry. To me, a tenement yet. The stores, I imagine, would help lower the monthly maintenance charges. The building has an advantage in that there's a beautiful pocket park with a giant waterfall in the same block.

We went by Jack's old ground-floor apartment in the Village, where his bathtub was in the kitchen. I was surprised the building was still there after 57 years when Jack lived there. As I stood across Charles Street, I could visualize Jack and me in 1962 entering the front door that first night that we met. I could see the daily routine of Jack's grey cat, named Cat, sitting in one of the two front living room windows waiting for Jack to return home from work. Coincidentally, there was a cat asleep in one of the windows as I looked. On viewing the apartment, I admit to a strong pathos at the loss of youth, at the death of Jack, at the unstoppable march of time.

While my return to New York, and the nostalgia it brought, was overall a joy to me, it had its eerie mode. It was as though I had been asleep for 31 years, and that I was awakened to a city, my city, that had undergone a mutation. Everything was familiar but everything was changed. The crowds held few people my age. Everyone was a millennial. New buildings marked each block that I once knew so well.

St. Patrick's Cathedral looked sparkling new and brilliant, like the day it was completed in 1878. But I wondered if it lost some of its character in no longer looking its age. It was said that the restoration was critical, or the building would soon be beyond repair. The cost was $175 million. Can you imagine the annual income a fund of that amount would produce? Even if just the urgent repairs had been done, maybe a fund could have

Nostalgia on my return to New York. This is the building where Jack lived when we met so long ago. Nothing has changed. The two windows on the main floor were in Jack's living room.

ended with a balance of $100 million, enough to provide income for charitable works such as helping poor people or the homeless. But who am I to suggest the way religion spends its income? It's not my money. In addition, any argument about the funds being used for charity is specious. The $175 million was from donations specifically for the cathedral restoration. If the purpose were for a fund whose income would aid the poor, I doubt if it would raise 10 percent of that.

Rockefeller Center, across Fifth Avenue from St. Patrick's, seemed crowded, with several outdoor restaurants taking space on the terrace in front of the RCA building. En route back to our rental accommodation, every other block sported a new building since I was last there, or one under construction.

But I was reassured that it was still my New York when we entered Washington Square Park on a sunny Sunday morning. In the middle of the wide walkway in the center of the park stood an ebony grand piano, full size, shaded by tall trees. I noticed that the legs were on wheels. A young man sat at the keyboard enthusiastically playing classical selections from an iPad mounted on the music rack. An appreciative audience, filling benches nearby, applauded each piece.

I was gratified at the sight: the unexpected, the illogical, the astounding. My city hadn't changed after all.

A Steinway in Washington Square Park. Is there another city like New York?

I learned through the internet that the pianist is Colin Huggins, 41, from Decatur, Georgia. He moved to New York City in 2003, purchased an upright piano, and played it in Union Square. He conducted campaigns for funds to upgrade, first acquiring a baby grand, then a Yamaha full-size grand, and finally a world-class Steinway grand. He is generally found in Washington Square three times a week, and plays 12 hours a day in order to support his writing ambitions. He rents a storage area on Spring Street, about a half mile away, and pushes his piano, on its wheels, up Sixth Avenue and back again, on the days he plays.

It bothered me so much in early 2020 when New York City became the epicenter of the Coronavirus. It's painful to see such misery there, and anywhere. Problems in Italy affected me particularly. I contacted a relative in Trento, and everyone was okay. I wondered, with tens of thousands of American citizens dead, why the flag across America was not lowered to half mast. Then the White House finally ordered it, after pressure. It takes the death of a single politician to lower the flag to half mast. For regular Americans, it took thousands of deaths. There would be hundreds of thousands more.

CHAPTER 28

The Final Exam.
My life rated 1 to 10.

NOW TO RATE my life. I can put it off no longer. I have gone through all those years, and it is time to bite the bullet and come up with a number, 1 to 10. What should play a role in ranking someone's life? Is it whether you've been happy in your life, or is it whether you've made others happy? Is it that you have made a contribution to society, or is it that you are prosperous yourself and live well? To what extent has my sexual orientation defined my life, and for good or bad? Maybe it's all of those things that put the number on a life.

How should an extraordinary life, rather than an ordinary one, be rated? Even if a little of the extraordinary is extraordinarily bad.

Unfortunately, my life has centered around myself and my loved ones, with very little concern about contributing to the larger world out there. But, I point out, I have made an effort to be kind. When someone is relating a misfortune that is befalling them, I try to be optimistic and devise possible solutions. I empathize when a tragedy occurs, and I feel the hurt of others inside me. I try to be there when someone needs a friend. As just one example: a vet was going to give a prognosis on a friend's sick and beloved dog on a particular day. I made certain to phone him on that day in case he would need someone to talk to. A small thing, I admit.

I was a loving son to my mother, a good partner to Jack to the final moments, and I tried the best I could to take care of my sister, although that didn't end up well. With Frank, I take an interest in everything he does, or try to, and I am there for him as a partner and spouse. The mere fact that I have the joy of living these years with Frank should boost my life rating several notches. Before Frank, there was Jack, 40 more years of wonderful. How many people had the good fortune of two perfect partners?

I've tried to go by medicine's Hippocratic Oath: "First, do no harm." But isn't that the very minimum that can be expected—to do no harm? Where is my contribution to the human race?

I see Frank tutoring immigrants, serving food to a line of the homeless, writing and calling congressmen to support good causes, giving talks at a senior citizen center. I do nothing of the sort. Oh, I have joined the NAACP and the Democratic Committee in my town. It's not that I do not have strong feelings on today's issues. It's that I'm a joiner but not much of an activist.

I almost forgot: sometimes I give $5, rather than just a dollar, to a homeless man, to make his day. But is the reason more that it makes my day? In a thrift shop, I gave $20 to two women who couldn't pay for the clothes they selected. And I felt great, but things like that aren't every day.

Let's say it. I'm no different from 90% of everyone. Not many people volunteer for good causes. Most people pass their lives worrying about themselves and people they love, not about the whole of mankind. I take the attitude that's sort of like telling a cop that everyone speeds, so why shouldn't I?

Maybe I'll redeem myself in the future. Frank and I have a plan on what to do with whatever money's left when the last one exits. I'm obsessed with security and can't bear to give away a large sum when we may yet need it. Maybe that's because I was poor as a child. Frank proposes funding several college scholarships for needy students. That would have a long-term effect.

I would like to give a pack of money now and then, after we're dead of course, to several mothers with two children whose husbands have abandoned them. I'm thinking back to my own mother and her house cleaning job, her humiliation at being on relief, her worry about the expense of Christmas. In the afterlife, I would find great pleasure in knowing that we saved a few women from what my mother went through. However, I question whether it would improve my life's rating to hold onto my money until after my life.

Frank surprised me. He says I do contribute, by taking care of my mother, my sister, my first partner, and by trying to be kind. He says I don't have to write a Declaration of Independence or Magna Carta. What a relief to hear him talk. Maybe I'm not all that bad.

Now, I want to talk about politics, because maybe I'll get a point or two. It seems that when I see a Democrat speaking on TV, I agree with every word, but with a Republican, I abhor every word. To me, the Republican party totally lacks compassion. I'm hardly one to reference the Bible, but I point out to Christians that each of the four Evangelists, Matthew, Mark, Luke and John, quotes Christ and his directives to care for the poor. You'll find similar mandates in every religion. The point of a government is so that citizens, poor people perhaps above all, can have a better life. I don't see that Republicans agree with that. I favor capitalism, believing that a government can never approach the efficiency of an industry with a profit motive. However, the drive for profits cannot take top billing. Let's think of the unfortunate. The Karl Marx maxim, "From each according to his abilities, to each according to his needs," on its face sounds ideal, although either party would find anything by Marx anathema. But doesn't the progressive income tax of our own democracy aim to fulfill that maxim? Certainly,

Democrats are way closer to the rich helping the poor than the Grand Old Party. My feelings are so strong on politics that I am a member in good standing of the partisan divide we talk about. I go so far as to choose only friends who share my views. I don't like people who don't agree with me. Gosh, did I just write that?

What perplexes me is how anyone gay can be a Republican. There's a gay organization, small, I'm guessing, called Log Cabin Republicans. The name comes from Abraham Lincoln, and his boyhood in a log cabin. The group promotes limited government and conservatism, as most Republicans, and aims to change attitudes towards gays from within the party. The Log Cabin fellows have their work cut out for them. Don't they know that Republicans often hate us? They don't want us in the military. They don't want to bake a cake for our weddings. And sure enough, they're going one day to try to throw out same-sex marriage, because they can't stand gay people being equal in anything. Whereas, Democrats welcome us. We're part of the diversity they boast about.

Then the rate given my life has to consider children, and the lack thereof. For some time, I have missed not having children. I'm at the age I'd have grandchildren and maybe great grandchildren. How fantastic it would be to have big family get-togethers. I missed all of that because, being gay, I never married.

Some gay people who were unsure of their orientation when they were young, or fighting it, did marry and have children. These marriages sometimes ended disastrously for the man, the woman, and the children, but not infrequently the separation was amicable and the family relationship intact.

Not having married, I brought no children into the world. Because of my nature, several people were not given life; I deprived them of life itself, a heavy burden. But isn't it comparable to a heterosexual couple that opts not to have children? Their sexual orientation doesn't prevent it. Does anyone else think about the people who might have lived but were never given the chance, who were deprived of life? I do. I wonder about my children never born, what kind of people they would have been, the lives they would have led, and their children. To console myself, I should think about overpopulation.

Which brings me to abortion. I am pro-choice because I believe a woman must have control over her own body. However, I can understand those opposed to abortion. They believe a fetus is already a human life. I do not, but if I did, I'd be right there with them. One would think that this devotion to life of anti-abortionists would carry over to opposition to capital punishment and war. Not so.

Certain people will rank my life low for no reason other than that I am gay. They'd be annoyed that I'm a happy gay man. I had no choice in the matter, to be straight or gay. Way back when I was five, with Judy and Burnell, playmates across Lemon Street, I made my choice in sexual orientation: I preferred Burnell. My nature has selected males ever since puberty, and I've been content. True, it wasn't always pleasant having an undercover life separate from my surface life. Pete Buttigieg, in his 2020 campaign for president of the US, speaking of Vice President Mike Pence's anti-gay record, commented: "...the thing that I wish the Mike Pences of the world would understand, that if you have a problem with who I am, your problem is not with me. Your quarrel, sir, is with my Creator."

But how much does happiness in life count in the rating of a life? I would be rated extraordinarily high in that classification because, although I've had troubles, and some tragedies, all in all it's been a good trip. I'm happy gay—and I was happy in my other life, my surface life, with straight people, although anti-gay bias didn't help. I'm happy as I write this.

Happiness in an older person is quite different than when you're young, or even middle-aged. I no longer have the periods of sustained ecstasy that I did in my youth. Example: Frank and I recently bought the apartment in Washington that we wanted, and I did not feel overjoyed about a new apartment and a welcome change in lifestyle, as I would have in earlier years. I felt content. What does make me happy—but let me use instead the word "content"—is the condition of my health. I'm also content that my financial situation is secure, that I have a good partner, and that I've survived to this age. Things that would have made me happy in the past, such as going on a glorious trip, or even an evening with friends at a nice restaurant, don't make me really happy anymore, just content. I think that by the time you get to my age, you've had so many good experiences in life that you become blasé. I do miss the strong emotion that younger people can feel, but console myself by the knowledge that the reason I am immune to intense happiness is that I've experienced so much of it. I am happy as the word applies to someone my age: content. I'm happy, or, rather, content, to have that.

Some would lower my rating because in my early life I was sexually active. Many young gay men are. Gay life when I was young was much like non-gay life is today. Sex was available. You participated, as young people generally do now. Soldiers in a foreign country during a war behave in the same fashion when sex is available. That's what men usually, or, at least, often do. If I'm rated badly, then most males should be rated badly. Today, society has moved to the point that sexual intimacy is recognized as a natural thing, and its denial in the long term can be harmful.

In truth, I don't like revealing my sexual exploits in this book, as I have. There are people that I don't want to know absolutely everything about me. I would rather they read just about my "pebble pal" that I would kick home from school, or the chateau, and not some of the things I'm not so proud of. However, I'm writing about my life, so I grit my teeth and include all. Well, mostly all.

What about my love of animals? Nigel, my Siamese cat, benefits. He gets an expensive cat food, and a new dishfull if he's tired of a certain flavor. I value the life of an insect. Bees, they merit respect. It's far better to remove the screen from a window to let a bee go free than let him languor inside and die.

Don't get me started on the engineering feats of spiders. It's the use of the marvels they create that bothers me: to trap flies and other living beings, and end their lives by eating them. In my opinion, the whole idea that living creatures must eat other living beings to survive is contrary to mankind's expressed belief in the value of life. The oceans are at war, with big fish devouring little fish by the giant mouthful. An eagle swoops down and grabs a terrified squirrel. Even my loving cat will kill a mouse. This perversion existing in nature alone would make me deny the existence of a supreme being. Intelligence would never produce a world designed around predator and prey. Is this any way to have ordered the world? And here I am, criticizing predatory animals when rational man does the same thing. Worse, I am guilty of sometimes falling off the wagon and eating meat myself, the body of a formerly living being. Oh, what a hypocrite am I!

On the upside, I count all the experiences I've had. Not one in a thousand high school students gets chosen as editor of a teenagers' section in the local paper. My partner and I were lucky to buy two Manhattan apartment buildings at rock-bottom prices, and watch them soar in value. How many other people have cruised down the Hudson River in a small boat, out into New York Harbor and the Atlantic Ocean with skyscrapers towering over them, and the Statue of Liberty herself looking on? I escaped from police pursuing me on Fire Island. I got a court to render justice in my sister's death. I lived in glamorous places that provided me with a cornucopia of memories. It's a life I will hate to leave someday, someday far, far away.

Some will say, perhaps good Christians, that I should lower my life rating because I am an atheist. I'm innocent on this point also. One day, I merely no longer believed. I had nothing to do with it at all. I do believe, however, that my non-belief is the true belief.

There is a factor that will help the rating of my life, and is also a strong influence on me to forgive past bias. That is the remarkable people I have encountered in life, straight, gay, bi, trans, etc. I could use any complementary adjective, and it would fit: generous, unselfish, kind-hearted. Who could ever forget Mrs. Paulo and Mrs. Maruca who created a pretext to care for my sister and me when my father disappeared? Who cares if they might have been anti-gay? Not me! Who couldn't forgive our landlord even if he was biased? He lowered my mother's rent when my father disappeared. And the nun who bent her rules so I could take that good job, and the priest who ordered uniforms for all girl students...and the...and the...

I have continued to see kindnesses, perhaps not quite as soul-stirring as those of Lemon Street, everywhere in the US, in France, in the UK. I mentioned briefly the occurrence at the airport in Paris. Jack and I collected our car that we had parked in the garage for several months while in the US. The cashier at the exit, a young man, was so alarmed at the amount he would have to charge us that he went to his supervisor and got a 50% reduction. We were total strangers to him, but nonetheless he was putting into practice the golden rule.

A recent incident involved a young man in front of me checking out at the dollar store, who insisted on paying for my $5 worth of items. I urged him to find someone needy for his generosity. "You're there," he said. "It's meant to be." A charity in our neighborhood in Washington asked for a few beds for kids under its care, and was overwhelmed. "Please. We don't need any more beds. Thank you." The people I met all over the world could have been from kind Lemon Street! Even drivers who invite you to pull out in front of them, someone who holds the door open, a person with a smile for you, are good people.

Unlike me, some in this world have a bad opinion of their fellow human beings. Historians agree that Presidents Lyndon Johnson and Richard Nixon were both untrusting and paranoid. President Donald Trump, speaking to a motivational seminar in 2000, said: "Be paranoid. Now that sounds terrible. But you have to realize that people, sadly, sadly, are very vicious. You think we're so different from the lions in the jungle? I don't know."

I disagree. I've read of vicious people, but never met one personally, that I know of. In my life, I have met many everyday people who glow from an inner beauty. As you've seen, I am not religious, but I borrow a word to say that we have saints among us. These people make me proud to be in the human race. There are the others, of course: the greedy, the power-grabbers, the war-mongers, who take from the world and give only harm back. Our earth can be a terrible place. But the hate mongers have not affected my life. The saints have. Their presence pushes my life's rating up. Should I forgive them if long ago by chance they had the same anti-gay prejudices as the whole of society? No need to ask.

However, before I get carried away with praise, I do remember some incidents, and annoying people. Not many, maybe a few dozen. The unpleasantness was fleeting, but, nonetheless, I must write a letter to those thankfully rare people.

To the few dozen irksome people in my life:
You people came close to spoiling everything. I'd be having a good day, and one of you killjoys would appear.

You who asked me when I was getting married? Actually, what you were doing was reminding me of my outlier standing in society. You weren't intentionally trying to put me on the spot, but I was never sure what to answer.

You, young man, who gave me the middle finger when I was, improperly, blocking your way in a turning lane. Not a nice gesture. That finger has become America's most used digit. Too bad.

Occasionally, one of you sports fans, on a Big Game day, would expose my oddity by asking me "What's the score?" The score of what? The score of "My Fair Lady?"

I could go on, but to what point? You're all forgiven

because, for one thing, my self-interest requires it. Tolstoy's advice to forgive, that "only then will we live in peace," is on my mind. So, carry on with your lives and pay no mind to me.

—Yours truly,
Someone from the past

Giving a rating to my life is complex. Considerations like having hidden being gay from many people, careers I didn't like, debatable contribution to society. On the other hand, caring for loved ones, a lifetime of two perfect partners, lifelong friends. happiness (or contentment) most of the time. And now, my effort to forgive.

But do you know what? Maybe rating my life need not be that difficult after all. When you get to my age, I'm thinking it's simply how you feel that your life was, and is. Sad times, I am apt to suppress; happy times, I remember in detail.

I remember my life as sensational. Never a dull day, or hardly ever. I'd do it all over again, given the chance. I could even consider my life a 10 out of 10, if I weren't afraid I would look boastful. So here goes, the official rating of my life. Drum roll please...

I rate my life a 9!

Wow! And that's conservative.

Thank you for following my life. I wish you a life rating as high as mine, and may you secure the rewards of forgiveness.

Me, now. The Forgiving Fellow.

I'd be happy, or content,
if you chose to post a review on Amazon.
Good, or even not so good.